The Basic Bible

The Basic Bible

*160 key readings with notes
edited by John Rogers*

Hutchinson of London

Hutchinson & Co (Publishers) Ltd
3 Fitzroy Square, London W1P 63D
London Melbourne Sydney Auckland
Wellington Johannesburg and agencies
throughout the world

First published privately under the title
Biblos: A Silhouette of the Bible 1976
This edition first published 1977

The editor and publishers gratefully acknowledge permission to use the
following copyright material: New English Bible, Second Edition ©1970 by
permission of Oxford and Cambridge University Presses; passages from the
Jerusalem Bible published and ©1966, 1967 and 1968 by Darton, Longman
& Todd Ltd and Doubleday & Co. Inc. by permission of the publishers;
passages from Letters to Young Churches, revised edition, by J.B. Phillips
by permission of Collins Publishers; extracts from the Authorized Version of
the Bible, Crown Copyright, by permission.

ISBN 0 09 131710 X (cased)
      0 09 131711 8 (paper)

Printed in Great Britain by The Anchor Press Ltd
and bound by Wm Brendon & Son Ltd,
both of Tiptree, Essex

with all my love
to Josephine, Lucinda and Hannah,
and many excellent friends

to Andrzej and Camilla
in memory of an enchanted
visit after Christmas 1985
and in honour of
all our trees

John

The past is the parent of our present.

All progressive branches of study must be rooted in a modest but well-informed knowledge of the past, even if only to ensure that the thought-forms which have been received may be discarded intelligently!

Many who would value a basic knowledge of the Bible have complained that their teachers and text books always seemed to have a religious axe to grind. They would like to have received the central thought-forms so that they could draw their own conclusions.

The Basic Bible is a careful selection of key readings mainly in modern translations. The readings, though shortened, are not paraphrased so that they may retain the authority of original texts — in so far as that is possible.

The notes are largely factual, gathered from about seventy sources ranging from the works of Bishop Charles Gore to those of Sir James Frazer. The notes do not conspire to put across any particular sectarian slant but to explore some of the first layers of meaning in the Bible.

The Basic Bible is designed for every sort of reader as an introduction, to be abandoned later — possibly in favour of fuller texts and more scholarly commentaries if the appetite persists.

Routes through The Basic Bible

The three-star readings
For a first look at the main text, ignore the notes and select the 60 readings marked with ***. These are the most central ones in the Bible. This first selection represents about two per cent of the total Bible wordage and will take you about two hours to read slowly.

The two-star readings
If you have more time, combine these *** readings with the 50 ** ones.

The one-star readings
When the 50 * readings are included, all 160 readings represent about five per cent of the total Bible wordage.

The Index
The key words printed down the margin of each right-hand page are all to be found in the comprehensive index at the back of the book.

Alternative routes
Teachers or students who are interested in using *The Basic Bible* for study in a thematic or a seasonal pattern may obtain a free copy of these suggested frameworks by writing to the publishers.

Maps

at the end of the book after the Index

Readings

Readings

Readings

1 Creation

***

from Genesis 1 and 2 : Authorized Version

In the beginning God created the heaven and the earth. And the earth was without form, and void; and darkness was upon the face of the deep.

And the first day, the Spirit of God moved upon the face of the waters, and God said, 'Let there be light' and there was light. And God saw that it was good.

The second day, God divided the waters which were under the firmament from the waters which were above, and God called the firmament Heaven, and saw that it was good.

And the third day, God said, 'Let the dry land appear,' and it was so. God called the dry land Earth, and the waters he called Seas. And God said, 'Let the earth bring forth grass, the herb and the fruit tree:' and it was so. And God saw that it was good.

The fourth day, God said, 'Let there be lights in heaven to divide the day from the night, and let them be signs upon the earth for days, seasons and years.' And it was so. And God made two great lights; the greater light to rule the day, and the lesser light to rule the night. He made the stars also and set them in heaven. And God saw that it was good.

The fifth day, God said, 'Let the waters bring forth abundantly the moving creature that hath life.' And God created every creature that moveth, and great whales and every winged fowl that may fly above the earth in the open firmament of heaven. And God blessed them saying, 'Be fruitful, multiply and fill the seas and the earth.' And God saw that it was good.

The sixth day, God made the beast of the earth, the cattle and everything that creepeth upon the earth (and it was good).

And God said, 'Let us make man after our likeness.' So God created man in his own image, male and female created he them. And God blessed them, and saw everything that he had made and, behold, it was very good.

Thus the heavens and the earth were finished. And on the seventh day God rested and blessed the seventh day because in it he had rested from all his work.

Thought until recently to have happened about 4000 BC
Written down about 500 BC

Of course, this story is poetry rather than history. It emerged from a   *poetry*
people who lived in tents, taking their flocks wherever they could
find water and fodder and peace. In the dark they lay for long hours
looking up into the sky, dozing and dreaming and telling each other
stories.

The first pen was the human tongue, and the first book was the
brain's memory cells. Primitive peoples like these have astonishing
memories. Memories proved essential to the writings of the
Bible — see the dates at the tops of the notes that follow.   *Bible*

Modern theories of evolution are remarkably similar, at least in their
sequence of events, to the Bible's first story about 'Creation'. The   *Creation*
big difference today is the omission of the divine dimension. The
story opposite shows clearly how its ancient authors believed there
was a super-human 'presence' behind the universe, that it was   *God*
essentially 'good', and that they themselves were a reflection, or an   *good*
'image', of that presence.   *image*

As for the technical age of this universe, it is anyone's guess. The
age of our small solar system is probably getting on for about 5000
million years and has on Earth resulted in a total of about $1\frac{1}{2}$ million   *history*
known species of animals, plants, viruses and so on.

The species 'Man' has been on the planet 'Earth' for only about 2   *Man*
million years. And for almost all that time he made only the most
primitive of tools. By about 10,000 years ago he was in some places
taming animals and cultivating plants; it was not long before skills
like weaving were learnt and wheels being used. The first villages
were in the basins of the great rivers: Nile, Euphrates-cum-Tigris,
Indus, Hwang-Ho.

2 Adam and Eve

**

from Genesis 2 and 3 : Authorized Version

And the Lord God planted a garden eastward in Eden, and there he put Adam (the man he had formed out of the dust of the ground) and breathed into his nostrils the breath of life; and man became a living soul.

And the Lord God commanded Adam saying, 'Thou mayest eat freely of every tree of the garden, but thou shalt not eat of the Tree of Life in the midst of the garden.'

And the Lord God brought unto Adam a woman. Adam called the woman Eve because she was the mother of all living. They were both naked, the man and his wife, and were not ashamed.

Now the serpent said unto the woman, 'In the day ye eat of the tree which is in the midst of the garden, your eyes shall be opened and ye shall be as gods, knowing good and evil.' And when the woman saw that the tree was good for food, she took of the fruit thereof and did eat, and gave also unto her husband, and he did eat. And they hid themselves from the presence of the Lord God amongst the trees of the garden.

And the Lord God called unto Adam, 'Hast thou eaten of the tree whereof I commanded thee that thou shouldest not eat?' And the man said, 'The woman gave me of the tree and I did eat.' And the woman said, 'The serpent beguiled me and I did eat.' And the Lord God said unto Adam, 'Dust thou art, and unto dust shalt thou return.'

So the Lord God sent him forth from the garden of Eden to till the ground from whence he was taken. And God did make coats of skins, and clothed Adam and his wife Eve.

The story was being told in Babylon in 2000 BC
This version was written down in about 900 BC

In the Hebrew language *adam* meant 'the first man' and *adamah*   *adam*
meant 'the soil'. 'Life', in the Hebrew mind, was identified with   *life*
'breathing' and 'the wind', and its quality was 'spiritual' or non-
physical, and it came from the unseen 'Source of Life'. But it could
not be defined.

'Life' today cannot yet be defined. Biologists identify 'life' when
they see an object breathe, feed, excrete, grow, respond to outside
changes, move and reproduce itself. Broadly speaking these
characteristics are found in plants as well as animals, but there
comes a point, with viruses for example, when it is very difficult
indeed to say where 'inanimate' becomes 'animate'.

The problem of the 'origin of life' is also still unsolved. It is only
possible to say that the first forms of life on this planet must have
appeared between 3000 million and 500 million years ago.

'Eve' meant 'life' or 'mother of life'.   *eve*

For another story about the serpent see reading 158.

The human mind has always been unwilling to feed on plain   *understand*
facts — it has always laced and spiced them with fanciful stories.
Mental digestion involves a whole spectrum of processes reflected
in the essential meanings of words: plain 'science' means plain   *science*
knowledge, and to 'analyse' means to split up and release; plain
'history' means visiting, questioning and also recording, and   *history*
'legends' are like reading between the lines; 'fables' follow,   *legend*
'fabulous' ideas and then 'myths' with only a shadow of historical   *myth*
fact; finally 'poetry' has always contained the essential idea of   *poetry*
'creating and workmanship'.

3 Cain and Abel

from Genesis 4 and 8 : Authorized Version

Abel was a keeper of sheep, but his brother Cain was a tiller of the ground. And it came to pass that Abel brought an offering unto the Lord of the first-lings of his flock. The Lord smelled a sweet savour and had respect unto Abel and to his offering.

And Cain brought of the fruit of the ground, but unto Cain and his offering the Lord had not respect. And Cain was very wroth and his countenance fell. And it came to pass, when they were in the field, that Cain rose up against Abel his brother, and slew him. And the Lord said unto Cain, 'Where is Abel thy brother?' And he said, 'I know not: am I my brother's keeper?'

And the Lord said, 'What has thou done? The voice of thy brother's blood crieth unto me from the ground. Now thou art cursed from the earth: when thou tillest the ground it shall not yield strength unto thee: thou shalt be a fugitive in the earth.'

And Cain said unto the Lord, 'Behold, thou hast driven me out this day and I shall be a fugitive in the earth; and from thy face shall I be hid. My punishment is greater than I can bear.'

And Cain went out from the presence of the Lord, and dwelt in the land of Nod, on the east of Eden.

Thought to have happened before about 2000 BC
Written down about 900 BC

These people thought of themselves as 'imitations' of their maker: they said he had created them 'in his own image'. Yet in stories like the one opposite they spoke as if *they* had made *him* in *their* own likeness. Furthermore, the writers of this story were clearly on the side of the nomadic herdsmen and against the vegetarian farmers whom they had invaded.

anthropo-morphism

The worst punishment for man is to be removed from all that he knows and loves — it is utter hell. See the definition of 'hell' in notes to 68.

punish

'Eden' possibly had a geographical locality in the mind of writers but it cannot be identified today.

Eden

4 The great flood

**

from Genesis 6 to 9 : Authorized Version

God saw that the wickedness of man was great in the earth, and it grieved his heart. He said unto Noah, 'Behold, I do bring a flood of waters upon the earth to destroy everything that is in the earth. But, make thee an ark of gopher wood; the length of the ark shall be three hundred cubits, the breadth fifty cubits, and the height thirty cubits. Rooms shalt thou make in the ark, with lower, second and third stories. Pitch it within and without with pitch, and set the door of the ark in the side thereof.'

And Noah did according unto all that the Lord commanded him. Noah and his wife went into the ark, and his sons (Shem, Ham and Japheth), and his sons' wives entered into the ark in the selfsame day; they and every beast, all the cattle and every creeping thing that creepeth upon the earth, and every bird of every sort. They went into the ark, two and two, male and female, as God had commanded.

And it came to pass, the windows of heaven were opened, and the rain and the waters of the flood were upon the earth. The mountains were covered and every living substance was destroyed; Noah only remained alive, and they that were with him in the ark.

And the ark went upon the face of the waters.

And it came to pass at the end of forty days that Noah sent forth a dove (to see if the waters were abated), and she returned to him in the evening; and, lo, in her mouth was an olive leaf.

And God spake unto Noah saying, 'Go forth, thou and thy wife, and thy sons and thy sons' wives with thee; bring forth with thee every living thing that is with thee. Be fruitful, and multiply and replenish the earth. And, behold, I do set my bow in the cloud, and I will look upon it, that I may remember the covenant between God and every living creature upon the earth.'

There must have been at least one major flood in the memories of these people. Here is an extract from a Babylonian story of a flood: 'On the mountain of Nisir the boat held fast . . . when the seventh day dawned I loosed a dove . . . she flew away, but finding no resting place she returned. Then I loosed a swallow, and . . . she returned. I loosed a raven. She saw that the water had retreated, she ate, she flew around, she cawed, and she did not come back.'   *flood*

This flood was between the rivers Tigris and Euphrates. However, the Bible's Mount Ararat, at nearly 5200 metres (17 000 feet) seems a little far-fetched.   *Ararat*

When Noah reached dry land his first act was to step ashore and offer a great thanksgiving sacrifice, and the Babylonian story said that it was of such a sweet savour that 'the gods crowded like flies'. And this may have been the distant origin of a Jewish name for the Devil: 'Beelzebub', meaning 'Lord of the Flies'.   *Devil*

Between two or more people, a 'covenant' was a sort of peace agreement. It was a coming together, a fitting together of wishes, planning a common course of action. It involved promises on both sides. The people who produced the legend opposite believed in this sort of relationship with their maker. The rainbow was to them a token of their covenant with him.   *covenant*

'Covenant' is a central theme throughout the Bible.

A promise spoken or written was a vital and precious thing to these people. The worst crime in the book was to break it: 'breach of promise', trust spilt, relationship lost, anathema. In ancient Mesopotamia everyone of importance had his own signet which he solemnly pressed into the wax sealing his letters. Tens of thousands of these have been unearthed. It was his signature and witnessed the authority of his name.   *sincere*

name

The word 'testament' also contains the idea of 'witness'. The Christian religion divides its Bible into two: the writings of witnesses BC are the 'Old Testament', and of witnesses AD are the 'New Testament'.   *Bible*
testament

In the Jewish religion the first five books of the Bible were their 'Torah' (in *The Basic Bible* Readings 1 to 18) — the word meant 'Will of God'; the names of the books are Genesis, Exodus, Leviticus, Numbers and Deuteronomy.   *Torah*

5 Babel

from Genesis 11 : Authorized Version

The whole earth was of one language. And it came to pass, as they journeyed from the east, that they found a plain, and they dwelt there.

And they said one to another, 'Let us build a city and a tower whose top may reach unto heaven; and let us make us a name, lest we be scattered abroad upon the face of the whole earth.' And they had brick for stone, and slime had they for mortar.

And the Lord came down to see the city and the tower which the men builded, and the Lord said, 'Behold, nothing will be restrained from them now which they have imagined to do: the people is one, and they have all one language, and this they begin to do. Let us go down and confound their language, that they may not understand one another's speech.'

So the Lord scattered them abroad from thence upon the face of all the earth: and they left off to build the city.

And, because the Lord did there confound the language of all the earth and did scatter them abroad, therefore is the name of it called Babel.

Ziggurats in Mesopotamia were massive temple-towers. The one at Ur covers 0.6 hectares (1½ acres). This one at Babel was a fraction of the size. Its purpose was to get them closer to their gods and also to offer their gods a ladder down to earth. (See note to 33 on 'gods'.) Ziggurats were in some respects similar to Egyptian pyramids (note to 12). And they were also startlingly similar to the temples of the Mayas found in Mexico and of the Incas found in Peru and beyond. (Thor Heyerdahl's *Ra* expedition sought to explain the link.)

ziggurat
building

'Slime' — probably bitumen. Fired bricks survive to this day but, unfortunately for archaeologists, many mounds of shapeless clay are all that remain of the more common sunbaked bricks in this area.

ceramics

'Babel' in Hebrew was connected with their word for 'confusion'. These people who produced the legend opposite lived in the mountainous country of Canaan and seem to have disapproved of these 'pseudo-mountains' in the plains of Babylon. So this legend was their cartoon and 'The Lord God', as in most stories, had the upper hand.

Babel
mountains

anthropo-morphism

They also had to explain how it was that, if all peoples were descended from Adam and Eve, there existed so many different languages. As they believed that all things came from 'The Lord God', they had to conclude that he had deliberately divided the nations to stop them getting above themselves!

language

6 'Father of nations'

***

from Genesis 12 to 22 : Jerusalem Bible

Yahweh said to Abram, 'Leave your country and your father's house, and make for the land I will show you; for your name will be so famous that it will be used as a blessing.' So Abram took his wife and all the people and possessions they had acquired in Haran, and they set off for the land of Canaan.

He went to settle at Hebron, and there he built an altar to Yahweh at the Oak of Mamre.

Now it happened some time later, as the sun was setting, that Abram fell into a deep sleep and the word of Yahweh was spoken to him in a vision: 'Have no fear, Abram; I am Yahweh who brought you to this land. Here now is my covenant with you: YOU SHALL BECOME THE FATHER OF A MULTITUDE OF NATIONS. You shall no longer be called Abram; your name shall be ABRAHAM. I will give you and your descendants after you the whole of the land of Canaan—and I will be your God.'

Now Abraham and Sarah his wife were old, well on in years, and Sarah had ceased to have her monthly periods. So Sarah laughed to herself, thinking, 'Now that I am past the age of child-bearing and my husband is an old man, am I really going to have a child?'

But Yahweh asked, 'Why did Sarah laugh? Is anything too wonderful for Yahweh?'

Abraham was a hundred years old when his son was born. He named him Isaac. The child grew and was weaned, and Abraham gave a great banquet.

(It happened some time later that God put Abraham to the test.)

Happened some time between 2000 and 1700 BC
Written down about 900, enlarged in 800 and again in 500 BC

This is the official beginning of the tribe's history. Haran lay on the main trading route between Babylon and Egypt. So did the district called Canaan. News and information were carried by traders.

history

Abram may in fact have been the name of a man or it may have been the name of a tribe. But the point of the story, like the point of most of these old stories, is not to lay down an exact history; it is to show a *grand plan* behind the history.

Abraham

Names were tremendously meaningful to these people. 'Abram' meant simply 'Praise be to God'. When, in his old age, his life took up a new course, he was given a new name to go with it: 'Abraham' meant 'Father of Nations'. Anything could become a name: 'Isaac' meant 'Laughter'. Village life in England has produced other names. Butcher, Baker, Cooper, Archer, Priest, Smith, Squire, or for another set of reasons, Brook, Bridge, Field, Heath, Marsh and so on.

names

'Yahweh', the name of their god, was probably pronounced *yar-way*, but this is not certain. It was considered disrespectful to write his name in full. Instead they put only the four consonants J H V H. In the Middle Ages, when the Bible was first translated into English, the vowels e, o and a were wrongly put in to produce the invented word 'Jehovah'. This mistake has only recently come to light.

Yahweh

'Yahweh' probably meant something like 'He who is *present* and *active*' or, broadly speaking, 'Creator'. It is sometimes spelt 'Jahweh', because in Hebrew transliteration, J and Y are interchangeable, and so are V and W.

Creation

7 Abraham's trust

from Genesis 22 : Jerusalem Bible

Now it happened that God put Abraham to the test. 'Abraham,' he called, 'take your son, your only child Isaac, whom you love, and offer him as a burnt offering—I will point out to you a mountain for the burnt offering.'

Rising early next morning Abraham saddled his ass and took with him his son Isaac. He chopped wood for the burnt offering and loaded it on Isaac, and in his own hands he carried the fire and the knife. Then the two of them set out together.

On the third day Abraham looked up and saw in the distance the place God had pointed out to him. When they arrived at the place Abraham built an altar and arranged the wood. And Isaac spoke: 'Father,' he said. 'Yes, my son?' 'Look,' he said, 'here are the fire and the wood, but where is the lamb for the burnt offering?'

Abraham answered, 'My son, God will provide for the burnt offering.' Then he bound his son Isaac and put him on top of the wood on the altar. He seized the knife and stretched out his hand to kill his son. But Yahweh called to him from heaven, 'Abraham! Do not harm the boy! For now I know you have not refused me your son, your only son.'

Looking up, Abraham saw a ram caught by its horns in a bush. He took the ram and offered it as a burnt offering in place of his son.

Later he called this mountain 'GOD WILL PROVIDE'—and hence the saying today.

'Sacrifice' meant 'to make something sacred or holy', or 'to put aside for a special use'. These primitive people wished to please their god in heaven above with nothing but the best: offerings of the highest quality, fire, mountain-tops, clouds, rising pillars of smoke; the spilling of blood, powerful feelings of union with each other and with their god, all these signified to them his presence.

sacrifice

communion

An 'altar' was simply a high place made formal by the construction of a table of stones. A sacrifice forged a fusion of the people with their god: they became 'one', they achieved 'union' or 'communion'.

altar

To 'offer up' the most precious thing was not strange to them. In their primitive minds it was logical. If their god was 'the maker and giver of all things', he must be offered the best of his gifts. It was the only way to recognize adequately his 'worth' his 'worth-ship', the only way to 'worship' him.

worship

So it was with all gifts: on the one hand, to gain the approval of the receiver, to harness and control his emotions; on the other hand to recognize his true worth, to admire and congratulate him. These are the mixed motives of the giver. (See the beginning of notes to 33.)

give

The point of this legend was to demonstrate the absolute obedience of Abraham. 'Obedience' and 'obeisance' mean in effect to be silent and hear the wishes of another and to submit one's own wishes to his or hers, regardless of the consequences. It was a tall order, a formidable test. People in love experience the same sort of challenge.

obey

8 Jacob becomes 'ISRAEL'

***

from Genesis 25 to 33: Jerusalem Bible

Jacob was a quiet man staying at home among the tents. His brother Esau, on the other hand, was a hairy man of the open country—he had a taste for wild game. When the boys grew up, Esau hated Jacob and thought to himself, 'I will kill my brother Jacob.' So Jacob set out for Haran.

When he reached a certain place, since the sun had set, he lay down where he was and passed the night there. He had a dream: there was a ladder standing on the ground with its top reaching to heaven, and there were angels of God going up and coming down. And Yahweh was there saying, 'I am Yahweh, the God of Abraham and of Isaac. I will give you and your descendants the land on which you are lying. Wherever you go I will keep you safe and bring you back to this land.'

Jacob awoke from his sleep early in the morning. He was afraid and said, 'This is nothing less than the gate of Heaven!' He took the stone he had used for his pillow and set it up as a monument; he named the place Bethel.

Moving on, Jacob went to 'the Land of the Sons of the East'. He stayed with his uncle Laban for twenty years and he grew extremely rich, and became the owner of large flocks, with men and women slaves, camels and donkeys, and with two wives and eleven children. (And Jacob had fallen in love with Rachel and she had given birth to a son named Joseph.)

Then, in time it happened that Jacob saw from Laban's face that things were not as they had been. So he put his children and his wives on camels and he fled with all he had and went away crossing the River Euphrates making for his father Isaac in the land of Canaan.

The night he crossed the Jabbok, he sent them across the ford and was left alone. And there was a man that wrestled with him until daybreak. And Jacob's hip was dislocated as he wrestled with him. Then as day was breaking the man said, 'Your name shall no longer be Jacob, but ISRAEL.'

The sun rose and Jacob resumed his journey limping because of his hip. And so he arrived safely in Canaanite territory.

Happened some time between 2000 and 1700 BC
Written down partly in 900 and partly in 800 and slightly enlarged in about 500 BC

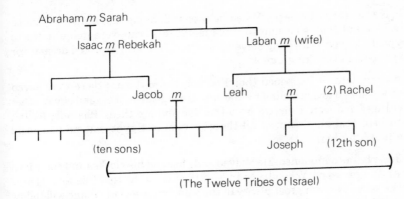

Abraham *m* Sarah

Isaac *m* Rebekah — Laban *m* (wife)

Jacob *m* — Leah *m* (2) Rachel

(ten sons) — Joseph (12th son)

(The Twelve Tribes of Israel)

Esau and Jacob were twins. Esau had been born first and there was *Esau* a legend that Jacob had emerged clutching his elder brother's *Jacob* heel — hence the name 'Jacob' which meant 'heel catcher'. Jacob was in fact a cunning child and delighted in making a fool of Esau, who was more athletic than he. But his character improved in time: he changed from being a selfish power-seeker to a true servant of Yahweh his god — hence his change of name to 'ISRAEL', meaning 'God's Assistant'. And, according to tradition, his twelve sons were *Tribes of* the fathers of the Twelve Tribes of Israel. *Israel*

There was a long story about Jacob's two marriages, worth reading *Jacob* in the original. He loved Rachel dearly, but certain local customs prevented him from marrying her for seven years. But the seven years 'seemed to him like a few days because he loved her so much'.

Angels were an idea learnt from the Persians. Yahweh, the maker *angels* and keeper of the universe, was so high and excellent, they said, that heavenly servants were needed to carry messages to his lowly creatures on Earth. Artists have traditionally given them wings and made them look rather clean, or even shining. But in the Bible these 'heavenly messengers' were quite often ordinary people saying just the right things at just the right time. They were often strangers but their identity was unimportant because they were only acting as mediums or mouthpieces.

9   Joseph in Egypt

**
From Genesis 37 to 47 : Jerusalem Bible

This is the story of Joseph. When he was still young his brothers came to hate him and they sold him to some merchants who were going down to Egypt. In Egypt as a young slave he was popular; he interpreted dreams for the prisoners in the king's gaol.

Two years later it happened that Pharaoh had a dream: there were seven cows, sleek and fat, standing by the Nile among the rushes; and seven other cows, ugly and lean, came up from the Nile and ate them. Pharaoh, feeling disturbed, told his dream to all the wise men in Egypt, but no one could interpret it for him.

So Joseph was summoned. He shaved and changed his clothes and came into Pharaoh's presence. When he had heard the dream, he told Pharaoh, 'There will be seven years of great plenty in the land, but a severe famine will follow them. Pharaoh should now choose a man to govern Egypt, to impose a tax and to store food during the good years, as a reserve for the famine.'

Then Pharaoh and his ministers asked, 'Can we find any other man like this possessing the Spirit of God?' So Pharaoh said to Joseph, 'You shall be my chancellor, and all my people shall respect your orders.'

Now Joseph was thirty years old when he was made governor of Egypt. He went and stored the corn like the sand of the seas, so much that it was beyond all reckoning. When the famine began, people from all over the world came to Egypt to buy grain.

And Pharaoh told Joseph to fetch his father and his brothers from the land of Canaan for, he said, 'The best that Egypt offers is yours.'

So, father Jacob, taking his sons and daughters and their families and all that they had acquired in Canaan (in a word, all 'The Children of Israel'), came to Egypt and settled in Goshen. And Pharaoh was pleased.

Happened between about 1700 and 1600 BC
Mainly written down in 800 and slightly enlarged in 500BC

Roughly along the present line of the Suez canal, the Egyptians had built a chain of forts to protect their land against multitudes of famished nomads from Canaan and beyond, who were attracted by the fertility of the Nile delta. But in about 1700 BC the forts proved too weak to repel invasion. This is the plain history behind the story opposite.

The human mind is like an iceberg in that only a fraction of it projects into 'consciousness'. Dreams, however, offer glimpses into deeper regions. These people regarded dreams as seriously as modern psychiatrists do. They considered that anyone who could interpret them accurately was a wise man with divine knowledge 'possessing the Spirit of God'.

dreams

Spirit of God

There is nothing magical about these things. Pharaoh knew what the economic state was, though he may not have wished to think about it. He was worried and the pressure of his anxieties was released in the natural way of dreams. Joseph had probably heard plenty of inside information in the royal jail and by then had learnt about the irrigation problems of the Nile — which incidentally are exactly the same today. Add to these things the cunning inherited from his father and the courage which comes when there is little to lose, and the story is made. It is worth reading in the full version.

Joseph (BC)

'Pharaoh' was simply the Egyptian word for 'Ruler'.

pharaoh

10 Israel enslaved—Moses born

***

from Exodus 1 and 2, and Acts 7 : Jerusalem Bible

The sons of Israel grew in numbers greatly, and they grew powerful. Then there came to power in Egypt a king who knew nothing of Joseph. 'Look,' he said to his subjects, 'these people, the sons of Israel, have become so numerous and strong that they are a threat to us. We must be prudent and take steps against their increasing any further: if war should break out they might take arms against us and add to the number of our enemies.'

Accordingly, the Egyptians forced the sons of Israel into slavery, and made their lives unbearable with hard labour. The king of Egypt then spoke to the Hebrew midwives: 'When you midwives attend Hebrew women, watch carefully. If it is a boy, kill him; if it is a girl, let her live.'

There was a man of the tribe of Levi who had taken a woman of Levi as his wife. She conceived and gave birth to a son and, seeing what a fine child he was, she kept him hidden. When she could hide him no longer, she got a basket for him; coating it with bitumen and pitch, she put the child inside and laid it among the reeds at the river's edge. His sister stood some distance away to see what would happen to him.

Now Pharaoh's daughter went down to bathe in the river, and among the reeds she noticed the basket, and she sent her maid to fetch it. She opened it and saw a baby boy, crying; and she was sorry for him. 'This is a child of one of the Hebrews,' she said.

Then the child's sister said to Pharaoh's daughter, 'Shall I go and find a nurse among the Hebrew women to suckle the child for you?' 'Yes, go,' said Pharaoh's daughter; and the girl went off to find the baby's own mother! To her the daughter of Pharaoh said, 'Take this child away and suckle it for me. I will see you are paid.'

So the woman took the child and suckled it. When the child grew up she brought him to Pharaoh's daughter who treated him like a son; Pharaoh's daughter named him Moses because, she said, 'I drew him out of the water.' So Moses was taught all the wisdom of the Egyptians and became a man with power.

Happened about 1300 BC
Mainly written down in 800 BC, *slightly enlarged about 500* BC
(One verse from the Acts of the Apostles written about AD *85)*

A gap of about 400 years since the flourishing times of Joseph. By now all the descendants of Jacob are known as 'Sons of Israel' or simply 'Israelites'.   *Israel*

The Egyptians had an immigrant problem. Foolishly they treated the Israelites as inferior. Joseph had been a brilliant chancellor during hard times, but he had soon been forgotten. The Israelites were not allowed to have any really responsible jobs, and most of them had been reduced to slavery: for Rameses II, king of Egypt, had a big building programme.   *immigration*

The Egyptians had expelled the Israelites from Thebes in the south, and now they inhabited the fertile land of Goshen. The Egyptians feared and despised them. They called them 'Hebrews' meaning something like 'wretched foreigners', or worse. When these Sons of Israel later escaped from Egypt, they were proud of this rude name because it reminded them of the slavery they had been rescued from.   *Hebrews*

Being treated as under-dogs, the Israelites had to depend upon cunning for their survival. This is a charming story of cunning. Moses' mother must have been the first woman in the world to be paid for looking after her own baby!

Levi was the third son of Jacob, and his descendants had traditionally tended the Ark of the Covenant and seen to its safe transportation (see reading 19). Much later they became assistant priests to the descendants of Aaron, the Levite who was made the first high priest (see notes to 11). This at least was the rough history of Jewish priesthood.   *Levites*   *priests*

11 Moses is called to lead

from Exodus 2 to 4, and Acts 7 : Jerusalem Bible

Moses, a man by now, set out at this time to visit his countrymen, and he saw what a hard life they were having; he saw an Egyptian strike a Hebrew, one of his countrymen. Looking round he could see no one in sight, so he killed the Egyptian and hid him in the sand.

On the following day he came back, and there were two Hebrews, fighting. He said to the man who was in the wrong, 'What do you mean by hitting your fellow countryman?' The man retorted, 'And who appointed you to be judge over us? Do you intend to kill me as you killed the Egyptian?' Moses was frightened. 'Clearly that business has come to light,' he thought.

When Pharaoh heard of the matter he would have killed Moses, but Moses fled from Pharaoh and made for the land of Midian. So Moses settled with the priest of Midian who gave him his daughter in marriage. He became the father of two sons.

During this long period the king of Egypt died. The sons of Israel, groaning from the depths of their slavery, cried out for help and their cry came up to God. God looked down upon the sons of Israel and he knew Moses was looking after the flock of his father-in-law in the land of Midian.

Moses led his flock to the far side of the wilderness and came to the mountain of God. There he was amazed by what he saw: a bush was blazing but it was not being burnt up. 'I must go and look at this strange sight,' Moses said, 'and see why the bush is not burnt.' As he went nearer to look at it, the voice of Yahweh was heard: 'Moses, Moses!' he said. 'Here I am,' he answered. 'I am the God of your ancestors.' Moses trembled and did not dare to look any more. 'Take off your shoes,' said the voice, 'for the place on which you stand is holy ground.'

And Yahweh said, 'I have seen the miserable state of my people in Egypt. I mean to deliver them out of the hands of the Egyptians and bring them up to a land rich and broad, a land where milk and honey flow. So come, I send you to Pharaoh to bring my people out of Egypt.' Moses said to Yahweh, 'Who am I to go to Pharaoh?' 'I shall be with you,' was the answer. 'Now go and I shall tell you what to say. There is your brother Aaron is there not? I know he is a good speaker. He will be your mouthpiece.'

So Moses started back for the land of Egypt.

Happened about 1300 BC
Mainly written down about 800 BC, *slightly enlarged about 500* BC
(One verse from the Acts of the Apostles written about AD *85)*

'Wilderness' meant open countryside, fairly barren and uninhabited, sometimes plain desert. It was the ideal place to which to escape from the madding crowd and think things over. *desert*

The 'mountain of God' here was Sinai (see reading 17).

'Moses', to this day, is the greatest of human names in the ears of a Jew. To a Mohammedan it is equal with 'Jesus'. To a Christian it signifies a vital ingredient in that culture which mothered his own religion. To anyone else 'Moses' was, at least, a very great leader. *Moses* *leader*

The Burning Bush: was there a sunset behind the bush, or was it a mirage or the hallucinations of a lonely man? It does not matter: the name 'Moses' became the embodiment of many of the important ideas in the Old Testament, and this weird theophany was the turning point in his career. *fire*

Fire was the earliest chemical discovery for mankind. It brought both life (heat and light) and death (transforming physical things to 'spiritual'). In all sun-worshipping religions, it represented the presence of the god on earth. It was 'divine' stuff, that is 'of god-like quality'. *divine*

Moses was both attracted and repelled: see note to 92 on 'awe'. He took off his shoes: see notes to 107. Their word for 'to be' was related to the name of their god—see note to 31 on 'Yahweh'—so 'I am the God of your ancestors . . . . I shall be with you' was a use of words which is lost in English. *'I am'*

Moses was afraid of making public speeches because he had a stutter. *leader*

The land of milk and honey was Canaan, see reading 19.

Aaron became the first high priest of the nation. Priests had a two-way function: to lead the worship of the people to their god and to interpret his will to them. The priestly blessing which Aaron and his sons used to give is still heard today: *Aaron* *priests* *bless*

'May Yahweh bless you and keep you.
May Yahweh let his face shine on you and be gracious to you.
May Yahweh uncover his face to you and bring you peace.'

12 Moses approaches Pharaoh

from Exodus 4 and 5 : Jerusalem Bible

Then Moses returned to his relatives in Egypt and Aaron met him and kissed him. Moses then told Aaron all that Yahweh had said when he set him his task. They then went and gathered all the elders of the sons of Israel together. The people were convinced that Yahweh had seen their misery, and they bowed down and worshipped.

After this Moses and Aaron went to Pharaoh and said to him, 'This is what Yahweh, the God of Israel, has said: "LET MY PEOPLE GO!" ' 'Who is Yahweh,' Pharaoh replied, 'that I should listen to him and let Israel go? I know nothing of Yahweh, and I will not let Israel go.' They replied, 'Give us leave to make a three days' journey into the wilderness to offer sacrifice to Yahweh our God.'

The king of Egypt said to them, 'Moses and Aaron, I will not let Israel go. What do you mean by taking the people away from their work? Get back to your labouring.'

That same day, Pharaoh gave this command to the people's slave-drivers and to the overseers: 'Make these men work harder than ever, so that they do not have time to stop and listen to glib speeches. Now that these common folk have grown to such numbers, they are lazy, and that is why their cry is, "Let us go and offer sacrifice to our God." '

And Pharaoh said, 'Up to the present you have provided these people with straw for brickmaking. Do so no longer; let them go and gather straw for themselves. All the same, you are to get from them the same number of bricks as before.'

The slave-drivers went out with the overseers to speak to the people. The slave-drivers harassed them and flogged the foremen who had been appointed for the people.

After this the foremen went to Pharaoh and complained: 'Why do you treat your servants so?' they said. 'No straw is provided and still the cry is "Make bricks!" And now your servants have been flogged!' 'You are lazy, lazy,' he answered. 'That is why you say, "Let us go and offer sacrifice to Yahweh." Get back to your work at once.'

As the foremen left Pharaoh's presence, they met Moses and Aaron who were waiting for them. 'May Yahweh punish you as you deserve!' they said to them. 'You have made us hated by Pharaoh and his court.'

Happened about 1300 BC
Written down mainly about 900 and slightly enlarged in about 500 BC

The kiss was given as a sign either of love and affection (as in this *kiss*
reading), or of respect for a superior (as in reading 23), or of super-
stitious hope for good luck from an idol (like touching wood).

'Elders' were simply senior members of the community whose *elders*
experience and wisdom were generally respected.

The pyramids of Egypt were constructed about a thousand years *pyramids*
before this date. The Great Pyramid is taller than Salisbury
cathedral. It was built of over 2 million shaped stone blocks of $2\frac{1}{2}$ *building*
tonnes average weight. These would have required about 100 000
slaves working for 30 years to manoeuvre into position. This
indicates the scale of the building tradition in Egypt.

Domestic buildings were made of sun-baked clay bricks. Mud was
brought from the environs of the Nile. Straw was usually carted in
from the fields by the farmers – until this story anyway. It was finely
chopped and mixed with the mud to bind it together, and also
sprinkled in the wooden moulds to prevent the wet bricks from
sticking. Drying and sun-baking took a couple of weeks. The bricks
were laid out in rows – the paw-prints of stray dogs can still be seen
on them today.

A proportion of these bricks were kiln-fired and used for more *ceramics*
permanent and decorated buildings. The Egyptians had discovered
the first glaze in about 5000 BC – long before the Chinese were
making china. They found that, when sand was mixed with the clay,
the soda compounds migrated to the surface during drying so that
firing produced the famous turquoise glaze known as 'Egyptian
Paste', though this glaze was used more frequently on small objects
and sculpture than on buildings.

A brickmaker and his mate could produce over 2000 bricks a day. *slaves*
The Hebrew slave gangs had their own foremen. All were
supervised by Egyptian slave-drivers. Egyptian overseers inspected
the work, recorded it in writing, made estimates and arranged
distribution: they were the white-collar workers.

13 Plagues in Egypt

**

from Exodus 5 to 10: Jerusalem Bible

Once more Moses turned to Yahweh. 'Lord,' he said to him, 'why do you treat the sons of Israel so harshly? Ever since I spoke to Pharaoh in your name, he has ill-treated your people.'

Then Yahweh said to Moses, 'You will see how he will be forced to let them go out of this land. I make you as a god for Pharaoh, and Aaron your brother is to be your prophet. You must tell Pharaoh all I command. In the morning wait for him by the bank of the river. Say to him, "Here is Yahweh's message: YOU SHALL LEARN THAT I AM YAHWEH BY THIS—THE WATER OF THE RIVER SHALL BE CHANGED INTO BLOOD." '

Moses and Aaron did as Yahweh commanded, and all the water of the river changed to blood. The fish died and the river smelt so foul that the frogs came up and covered the land of Egypt.

Pharaoh summoned Moses and said, 'Entreat Yahweh to rid me and my subjects of the frogs, and I promise to let the people go.' When Moses had gone from Pharaoh's presence he pleaded with Yahweh about the frogs, and the frogs died. But as soon as Pharaoh saw that relief had been granted, he became adamant again and refused to listen to Moses and Aaron.

Then throughout the land of Egypt the dust on the ground turned into mosquitoes, and the mosquitoes attacked men and beasts. And great swarms of gadflies found their way into Pharaoh's palace and ruined all the land of Egypt. All the Egyptians' livestock died, but none owned by the sons of Israel died. Next day Pharaoh made inquiries but did not let the people go.

Then soot from the kiln in the air brought out boils breaking into sores on man and beast. Yahweh thundered and rained down hail. Lightning struck the earth. Throughout the land of Egypt the hail struck down everything in the fields, man and beast, all the crops and every tree. (Only in the land of Goshen where the Hebrews lived was there no hail.)

Then the east wind brought the locusts and for three days there was deep darkness over the whole land of Egypt.

Pharaoh summoned Moses: 'Out of my sight! Never appear before me again, for on the day you do, you die!'

Moses replied, 'You have said it! Never again shall I appear before you.'

This is such a good story that it seems a pity to unravel the myth-maker's embroidery. However the plain history may contain some of the following theories.

If Moses had been brought up in the royal court, he could easily have had access to the ear of the pharaoh, and he would know enough about the tricks of Egyptian wizards to outwit them.

Moses

None of the plagues is incredible to anyone who has visited Egypt — and the interpretations are only strange to those who know nothing of these people's superstitions about the elements and other natural phenomena. The plagues may all have been the effects of volcanic action located in the great geological split which extends from the Jordan valley through the Red Sea to the upper reaches of the Nile. Volcanic mud could have coloured and contaminated the water and volcanic ash could have filled the air, and all else would have followed. Or the coloured water may have been caused by the population explosion of a microscopic dinoflagellate (known today as a 'red tide') which leads to the sort of biological imbalance described in the reading.

plagues

superstition
elements

At all events, Moses showed the cunning of his mother and his ancestors by seizing a heaven-sent chance to lead his people out of slavery.

14   The Passover night

***

from Exodus 12 to 14 : Jerusalem Bible

Moses summoned all the elders of Israel and said to them, 'You are to hold a sacred gathering. For seven days you will eat unleavened bread. On those days no work is to be done; you are allowed only to prepare your food. And on the seventh day there is to be a feast in honour of Yahweh. On that day each man must take an animal from the flock (either sheep or goats), one animal for each household, and slaughter it.

'Some of the blood must be taken and put on the two doorposts and the lintel of the houses where it is eaten. That night, the flesh is to be roasted over the fire; it must be eaten with unleavened bread and bitter herbs. You shall eat it hastily with a girdle round your waist, sandals on your feet, a staff in your hand. Whatever is left, you are to burn. Let none of you venture out of the house till morning. Then, when Yahweh goes through Egypt to strike it, and sees the blood on the doorposts, he will pass over the door and not allow the destroyer to enter your homes and strike.

'You must keep these rules and, each year at its appointed time, you must keep the sacrifice of the Passover. And, when your children ask you, "What does this mean?" you will tell them, "It is the sacrifice of the Passover: it is in honour of Yahweh who struck Egypt but passed over our houses!" '

The sons of Israel then departed, and they obeyed Moses.

And, at midnight, there was a great cry in Egypt; Pharaoh and all his courtiers and all the Egyptians got up in the night, for there was not a house without its dead. And the Egyptians urged the Israelites to hurry up and leave the land because, they said, 'Otherwise we shall all be dead.'

So the Israelites did this.

Happened in about 1300 BC
Written down about 900 BC, enlarged about 500 BC

It looks a neat story. But in fact it is probably a combination of several events and customs. Firstly, two primitive customs. Farmers in Canaan always celebrated a spring festival at which they ate barley loaves baked with unleavened bread (made without yeast) and prayed to the Lord of the Harvest to give them a summer of fat crops. Nomadic tribes in that part of the world customarily killed the first lamb of the new season as a thank-offering to the Lord of Life; they used to sprinkle the blood around on their tents and on themselves to give them good luck and to frighten away evil spirits. These two customs make the background to this story.

bread

meat
blood
evil spirits

Secondly, the main event which seems to have made the escape possible was a disastrous epidemic in Egypt. The Israelites took advantage and ran for their lives! In fact there is evidence that there were several escapes over some years. But this does not affect the point of the story because, for the Israelites, the Egyptians' bad luck and their own good luck were all part of a great plan. They literallly believed that their god had arranged the whole thing for them. They have been celebrating 'Passover' each year ever since and, looking back over their history, they see that they have been saved on many other occasions and in many different ways.

Passover
history

This is the original story which demonstrates the importance of the word 'salvation' to the Jews. It meant being saved from awful slavery or disaster, usually in the nick of time. It also implied that someone outside was doing the saving.

salvation

15 Exodus

***

from Exodus and 14 and 15 : Jerusalem Bible

When Pharaoh, king of Egypt, was told that the people had made their escape, he and his courtiers changed their minds about the people. 'What have we done,' they said, 'allowing Israel to leave our service?' So Pharaoh had his chariot harnessed and gathered his troops about him, taking six hundred of the best chariots in Egypt, each manned by a picked team, and he gave chase to the sons of Israel as they made their triumphant escape.

And, as Pharaoh approached, the Israelites looked round—and there were the Egyptians in pursuit of them! They were terrified and cried out to Yahweh. To Moses they said, 'What good have you done us bringing us out of Egypt? We would rather work for the Egyptians than die in the wilderness!'

Moses answered the people, 'Have no fear! Yahweh will do the fighting for you: you have only to keep still.' Then the angel of Yahweh drove back the sea with a strong easterly wind all night, and he made dry land of the sea. The waters parted and the sons of Israel went on dry ground right into the sea. The Egyptians gave chase: after them they went, right into the sea, all Pharaoh's horses, his chariots and his horsemen.

In the morning watch, Yahweh looked down on the army of the Egyptians, and threw the army into confusion. He so clogged their chariot wheels that they could scarcely make headway. "Let us flee from the Israelites,' the Egyptians cried, 'Yahweh is fighting for them.' And, as the day broke, the sea returned to its bed. The fleeing Egyptians marched right into it. The returning waters overwhelmed the chariots and the horsemen of Pharaoh's whole army; not a single one of them was left.

But the sons of Israel had marched through the sea on dry ground, with water to right and to left of them. That day the people put their faith in Yahweh, and in Moses his servant.

It was then that Moses and the sons of Israel sang this song in honour of Yahweh:

> 'Yahweh is my strength, my song,
> He is my salvation.
> Yahweh is a warrior;
> Yahweh will be king for ever and ever.'

And all the women followed Aaron's sister with timbrels, dancing.

'Exodus' means 'departure'. The sea was the north-western tip of   *Exodus*
the Red Sea. A combination of spring tides and a strong wind could
have caused this phenomenon — ask anyone who lives along the
East Anglian coast. There is also some remote geological evidence
of a minor earthquake. But perhaps it is simpler to imagine that the
Hebrew slaves of Goshen knew their way about the marshes better
than the Egyptian charioteers. It doesn't really matter what actually
happened. What does matter is that these Hebrews, like their
descendants to this day, on looking back, regard the 'Exodus' as the
greatest event in their history.

A 'timbrel' was like a tambourine but smaller and without the   *timbrel*
jingling discs. Women played them while dancing, to help the
rhythm.

The view of their god, Yahweh, was primitive at this stage: a great   *theology*
warrior-king pushing people about like puppets, unseen, operating   *warrior-god*
from the heavens above. But this view changed in time.

16 Survival in the desert

from Exodus 15 to 18 : Jerusalem Bible

Moses made Israel move from their camp at the Sea of Reeds, and they made for the wilderness of Shur where they travelled for three days without finding water. They reached Marah but the water there was so bitter they could not drink it. The people grumbled at Moses. 'What are we to drink?' they said. So Moses appealed to Yahweh, and he pointed out some wood to him; this Moses threw into the water, and the water was sweetened.

From Marah they set out again and reached the wilderness of Sin. And the whole community of the sons of Israel began to complain against Moses and Aaron in the wilderness and said to them, 'In the land of Egypt we could eat meat and bread to our heart's content! As it is, you have brought us to this wilderness to starve to death!'

Moses and Aaron said to the whole community, 'You shall learn that it was Yahweh who brought you out of Egypt. Your complaining is not against us, but against Yahweh.'

And so it came about: in the morning there was a coating of dew all round the camp. When the dew lifted, there on the surface of the desert was a powdery thing, delicate, as fine as hoarfrost on the ground. When they saw this, they said to one another, 'What is it?'

'That,' said Moses to them, 'is the bread Yahweh gives you to eat. Gather enough of it for those who share your tent.' The sons of Israel did this; each found he had gathered what he needed.

On the following day Moses took his seat to administer justice for the people, and from morning till evening they stood round him. Observing what labours he took on himself for the people's sake, the father-in-law of Moses said to him, 'It is not right to take this on yourself. You will tire yourself out, you and the people with you. Take my advice: choose from the people some capable and incorruptible men, and appoint them to administer justice at all times—so sharing the burden with you.'

Moses took his father-in-law's advice and chose capable men from the ranks of the Israelites and set them over the people. Then he said, 'Listen carefully to the voice of Yahweh your God, and do what is right in his eyes.'

Happened after about 1290 BC
Written down about 900 BC *and enlarged in 800 and 500* BC

Above all his considerations, Moses had to establish his authority. It was, he said, Yahweh who had rescued them — he himself merely gave the orders in the name of Yahweh. It was a powerful arrangement. And also in practical terms, he organized the people into family groups and delegated judicial authority to deputies in each group. *authority Moses organiza- tion*

'Marah' in Hebrew meant 'bitter'. Perhaps Moses had learnt to use the sweetening herb when he was a shepherd among the Midianites.

The words, 'What is that?' were in Hebrew something like 'Manna'. It may have been a desert fungus unknown to them — but, as it appeared in the nick of time, they took it to be 'the bread of heaven'. Dew, they believed, was the creative fluid of the maker himself: it brought about the germination and growth of things, they thought. 'Bread' and 'meat' in the Bible often means food in general. *manna bread meat*

Furthermore, laws which were clearly laid down and fairly administered, were the bones and muscles of the community. Law protects the cell-like independence of each individual on the one hand, and on the other it establishes the bridges of obligation between him and his peopled environment. 'Corrupt' lawyers rupture these walls and bridges. So do unjust laws. *law*

'Justice' means 'rightness'. The words 'right' and 'righteous' come from a Latin word meaning 'straight' or 'upright'. It was used primarily in an architectural sense, (right angles, rectangles, rectify, direct) and was therefore measured alongside the natural law of gravity. In society, these people measured right and wrong alongside what they believed were the natural laws of the creator. (See reading 17.) *righteous right and wrong*

For 'administer' see note to 107 on 'minister'.

'Sea of Reeds' was the Red Sea.

'The wilderness of Sin' is the name of a place in the Sinai peninsular and has nothing to do with 'sin'. *desert*

17 Moses on Mount Sinai

***

from Exodus 19 and 20 : Jerusalem Bible

Three months after they came out of the land of Egypt, the sons of Israel reached the wilderness of Sinai. There, facing the mountain, Israel pitched camp. Moses went up the mountain.

Now at daybreak on the third day there were peals of thunder on the mountain and lightning flashes, a dense cloud and a loud trumpet blast. And inside the camp all the people trembled. Like smoke from a furnace the smoke went up, and the whole mountain shook violently.

Louder and louder grew the sound of the trumpet. With peals of thunder Yahweh came and called Moses to the top of the mountain; and Moses went up. All the people shook with fear and they kept their distance.

Then God spoke all these words. He said, 'I am Yahweh your God who brought you out of the Land of Egypt, out of the house of slavery.

'You shall have no gods except me.
You shall not make yourself a carved image.
You shall not misuse the name of your God.
Remember the sabbath day and keep it holy.

'Honour your father and your mother.
You shall not kill.
You shall not commit adultery.
You shall not steal.
You shall not bear false witness.
You shall not covet anything that is your neighbour's.'

Yahweh was thought to come down to Earth sometimes, but he seldom came in person lower than the mountains and the lonely places. His language was that of natural phenomena — earthquakes wind, and fire, and so on. His voice, the thunder, was very frightening to these people, and they believed that he was very powerful and, if annoyed, very fierce.

Yahweh
mountains

elements

It is not surprising that these people, wishing to keep on the right side of Yahweh, gradually acquired lists of his laws. This is the most famous list: 'the Ten Commandments', also called 'The Law of Moses', and elsewhere in these notes 'Moses-law'.

law

Moses-law

The first four concerned their attitude to Yahweh: ignore all minor gods in Canaan and Egypt (monotheism); make no substitutes for Yahweh (no idolatory); breathe his very name with respect (no blasphemy); and set aside one day in seven for his his sabbath, his day of rest. 'Holy' meant 'set aside for a special use'.

mono-
  theism
idols
blasphemy
sabbath
holy

The other six laws concerned their treatment of each other. 'Honour' meant 'show respect for' or 'recognize the true value of'; the authority of parents was most highly respected. Life was sacred and even the killing of animals had to be done with circumspection. 'Adultery' was neglecting a marriage partner and going off with someone else as if they instead were the marriage partner. Stealing undermined another man's livelihood or even his safety. 'False witness' meant telling lies and its worst form was telling lies in a law court, that is 'perjury'. 'To covet' something meant to long to own it. 'Neighbour' meant generally 'other people'.

honour
parents
kill
murder
adultery
steal
perjury
covet
neighbour

These ten rules formed the core of Moses-law. Others were added. The Moses-law was the backbone of authority in this society.

authority

18 The golden calf

from Exodus 32 and 34, and Deuteronomy 5 : Jerusalem Bible

When the people saw that Moses was a long time before coming down the mountain, they gathered around Aaron and said to him, 'Come, make us a god to go at the head of us; as for this Moses, the man who brought us up from Egypt, we do not know what has become of him.' So they all took the golden rings from their ears and brought them to Aaron. He melted the metal down and cast an effigy of a calf. 'Tomorrow,' he said, 'will be a feast in honour of Yahweh!'

And so, early the next day, they offered communion sacrifices before the effigy. 'Here is your God, Israel,' they cried, 'who brought you out of the land of Egypt!' Then all the people sat down to eat and drink, and afterwards got up to amuse themselves.

Then Moses made his way back down the mountain with Yahweh's words inscribed on two tablets in his hands. As he approached the camp and saw the calf and the groups dancing, Moses' anger blazed. He threw down the tablets he was holding and broke them at the foot of the mountain. He seized the calf they had made and burnt it, grinding it into powder which he scattered on the water.

Aaron said, 'Let not my lord's anger blaze like this. You know how prone this people is to evil. They said to me, "We do not know what has become of this Moses," and they brought gold to me, so I threw it onto the fire and out came this calf.'

When Moses saw the people so out of hand, he called the whole of Israel together on the following day and said to them, 'Listen! You have committed a grave sin. But now I shall go up to Yahweh: perhaps I can make atonement for your sin.' And Moses returned to Yahweh. 'I am grieved,' he cried. 'This people has committed a grave sin, making themselves a god of gold.' Yahweh said to Moses, 'Cut two tablets of stone like the first ones which you broke and I will inscribe on them the words that were on the first tablets.' And so he inscribed on the tablets the Ten Words of the Covenant.

When Moses came down from the mountain of Sinai, the skin on his face shone so much that Aaron and the sons of Israel would not venture near him. But Moses called to them and said to them, 'Listen to the laws that I proclaim in your hearing today. Learn them and take care to observe them.'

Happened sometime after about 1290 BC
Written down between about 900 and 500 BC

They had broken Rule 2 of the Moses-law (reading 17) — no substitutes. Yahweh was invisible — it was an insult to try to make him visible, just as following Rule 3 it became an insult to say his name carelessly or even aloud. This is why Jewish painting and sculpture is almost non-existent.

idols

gods
art

Idols, psychologically speaking, interrupted a face-to-face relationship with the living god which they were supposed to represent. It was easier to get on with an idol just as it is easier for a shy child to talk to its toys, or for a shy person to talk to a pet rather than the pet's owner!

Worse still, man-made substitutes for their god meant that he was being made 'in the image of man' and that was opposed to the truth of the matter, they thought (see notes to 3).

Gold, the metal of the sun, symbol of life, fertility and growth: this concept had been learnt in Egypt.

gold

The word for 'sin' had its roots in the idea of 'seed running to waste', 'failing in one's object' and 'making ineffective'. It contains the same idea to this day as a technical term in archery: to 'sin' is to 'miss the target'.

sin

To those people the whole concept of sin and faith was of fundamental importance. In the primitive mind, the red sun at sunset penetrated the dark womb of mother earth and in the morning came 'out of his pavilion like a bridegroom' (Psalm 19) leaving her fertile and able to support the life of her creatures and, they believed, when they imitated this process of reproduction they could survive and flourish.

sun

copulation

The word for 'faith' was rooted in the idea of 'making fruitful' taking part in the life-giving process of the maker. By the time of the reading opposite, however, faithfulness was not a simple matter of copulation! By trial and error, generations of emerging society had produced a few refinements! The Moses-law was a crystallization of these refinements. To ignore it was 'to sin', they said.

faith

'Atonement' or 'at-one-ment' was 'becoming one again'. It was the central link between being miserably adrift and being blissfully restored. It was a very important factor in the Bible — see notes to 73 and also note to 7 on 'communion'.

atonement

19 Joshua at Jericho

from Joshua 1 to 3 and 6 : Jerusalem Bible

When Moses the servant of Yahweh was dead, Joshua gave the people this order: 'Get provisions ready for in three days you will cross the Jordan and go to take possession of the land which Yahweh is giving you.'

Then Joshua sent out two spies secretly. They went and entered the house of a harlot called Rahab. The woman took the two men up to the roof and hid them under flax she had heaped up there. She said to them, 'All who live in this territory have been seized with terror at your approach, for we have heard how Yahweh dried up the Sea of Reeds before you when you came out of Egypt. Now then, show kindness to the people of my house, and preserve us from death.' The men answered, 'When we enter your land, we will deal with you kindly and faithfully. You must tie this scarlet cord to the window and you must gather all your family with you in your house.'

Then Rahab let them down from the window by a rope, for her house was inside the wall itself. They left her and crossed the river to Joshua, and told him: 'Yahweh has delivered the whole country into our hands, and its inhabitants tremble at the thought of us.' Early in the morning Joshua set out with all the Israelites. The priests took up the Ark and moved to the front of the people to cross the Jordan.

Now Jericho had been carefully barricaded against the Israelites. Joshua had given the people the order, 'Do not utter a word till I say, "Raise the war cry." Then you are to shout.' They marched round the town for six days. On the seventh day they rose at dawn and marched seven times round the town in the same manner. At the seventh time Joshua said to the people, 'Raise the war cry.' Then the people shouted, the trumpets sounded, and the wall collapsed then and there. At once the people stormed the town, every man going straight ahead, massacring all men and women, young and old. The young men who had been spies went in and brought out Rahab in safety and all who belonged to her.

Then they burned the town and all within it except the things of silver and gold; these they put into the treasury. And Joshua's fame spread all through the country.

Happened between about 1250 and 1200 BC
Written down mainly in about 600 BC

Nomadic stock-breeders invade settled arable farmers: carnivores versus vegetarians. Active touches passive. Sun to Earth. Gold to green, and red to blue: warrior god to virgin mother. Male mates female. Distant rhythms reverberated behind the mind of these writers.

'Joshua', the Hebrew name, came from a Sūmerian word meaning 'juice of life which saves, restores, heals'; and 'Canaan' from another word meaning 'marriage couch of heaven'. In this reading 'the Land which Yahweh is giving you' was in fact Canaan.

Joshua
Canaan

The Ark of the Covenant: a handled box, possibly shaped like a seat or throne, portable, containing the two stones of the Moses-law carried like a standard or a mascot into battle. The laws of the maker, 'the Words of Yahweh' were to them, in effect, Yahweh himself. The priests who carried it were, by tradition, descendants of Levi.

Ark

word

Levite

Roofs were flat, made of rafters and branches and plastered with mud. They were reached by steps up an outside wall, and they were used for drying vegetables, for ripening fruit, for sleeping in hot weather and saying one's prayers. In rustic areas they are the same today.

houses

prayer

A 'harlot' or a 'whore' or a 'prostitute' was someone who was in the habit of copulating with anybody either for religious reasons or later for cash. Canaanites still had religious orgies to encourage the germination of their crops. These involved eating and drinking, singing, dancing, and random copulation. 'Copulation' simply means 'fastening together' and should not be confused with 'the art of making love'. It is a purely technical word whereas 'fornication' (coming from the Roman word for 'brothel') has moral overtones and refers to the copulation of an unmarried couple; and so also has 'adultery', being the copulation of a husband or his wife outside their marriage.

harlot

copulation

adultery

Societies choose their own customs and encourage all members to conform. These customs are called 'morals'. Modern societies have not, broadly speaking, made any great innovations. Random copulation whether public (as in the religious orgies of primitive societies) or private (as in brothels for example) is discouraged by modern societies because of the danger of spreading venereal diseases. Unfortunately less attention is paid to the spreading of social neuroses like boredom, cynicism and blunt insensitivity. Yet these are just as destructive as VD.

morals

VD

But 'morals' are concerned with many things besides plain 'sex'. The moral code of a society is simply all its accepted 'customs'.

20   Gideon versus Baal

from Judges 6 to 8 : Jerusalem Bible

Whenever Israel sowed seed, Midian would march up and destroy the produce of the country. They came up with their cattle and their tents, and their camels were past counting. They left Israel nothing to live on, and the Israelites cried to Yahweh.

The angel of Yahweh came and sat under the terebinth at Ophrah. Gideon was threshing wheat inside the wine press to keep it hidden from Midian when the angel appeared to him and said, 'Yahweh is with you, valiant warrior!' Gideon answered, 'Forgive me, my lord, but if Yahweh is with us why is it that all this is happening to us now? He has abandoned us.' At this Yahweh turned to him and said, 'You will rescue Israel from the power of Midian. Go and pull down the altar of Baal.' Gideon did as Yahweh had ordered.

Then all Midian and the sons of the East joined forces, crossed the Jordan and encamped in the plain of Jezreel. And the spirit of Yahweh came to Gideon. He sent messengers throughout the land and they marched out to meet him. He took only three hundred of them with him and sent away all the rest.

Gideon then divided his three hundred men into companies. To each man he gave a horn and an empty pitcher, with a torch inside each pitcher. He said to them, 'Watch me, and do as I do.'

The camp of Midian was below his in the valley. They reached the edge of the camp at the beginning of the middle watch when the new sentries had just been posted. They sounded their horns and smashed the pitchers in their hands, and they shouted, 'For Yahweh and for Gideon!' And they stood still, spaced out all round the camp. Then the whole camp woke, and Yahweh made every man in the camp turn his sword against his comrade. They all fled and the men of Israel pursued.

Thus Midian was humbled. They did not lift up their heads again as long as Gideon lived.

Happened between about 1200 and 1000 BC
Mainly written down about 600 BC

The background of the reading opposite was the worship of Baal. It had a profound effect on the Israelites at this time.

Baal, the male god of Canaan and Syria, derived his name from a *Baal*
Sūmerian root meaning 'bore' or 'drill'. The word 'phallus' came via Latin from the same root. More generally it meant 'lord and husband'. There was a similar version of Baal in the Phoenician world (and later Greece): he was Adonis, god of corn and bread, the *Adonis* beautiful youth loved by Aphrodite and killed among the mountains of Lebanon by a wild pig; thereafter he was allowed to return to the *pigs* earth each year in the spring for the six months of summer time.

Phoenicians celebrated the rites of Adonis elaborately at Byblos, *Phoenicians* their most ancient city (said by the Romans to have been founded *Byblos* by Saturn) in the sanctuary of Aphrodite (Venus to the Romans and Astarte to Hebrews). Aphrodite was the ubiquitous goddess of love and fecundity. The return of Adonis after his death was brought about by her love and lamentation. Today any artificial stimulation which brings on a desire for erotic love is called an 'aphrodisiac'.

Though Byblos became the holy city of the Phoenicians, the original cult of Aphrodite seems to have been founded at Paphos in Cyprus. And all over the Phoenician world groves of trees sacred to the cults of Adonis and Aphrodite have been recorded—one was down in Bethlehem. *Bethlehem*

Most villages had sacred trees under which wise old men sat recalling the past and foretelling the future. Trees were symbolic of *trees* immortality (see reading 2) and, by listening to the spirits chattering in the leaves as the wind moved them, local prophets could divine a *wind* certain 'knowledge of good and evil'.

Terebinths or 'turpentine-trees' produced oil of turpentine. *oil*

Fire was kindled by boring a drill-shaped stick into resinous wood. *fire* Lamps with wicks of flax or hemp burned oil of olives or fat from *lamps* animals. Bitumen or pitch may have been used on this occasion. *torches*

'Angels' were often strangers whose remarks were later remem- *angels* bered as events unfolded and their words came true.

Psychological warfare is not a new thing (see also reading 19). Trumpets were the hollow horns of animals used to give signals, like *trumpets* a large hunting horn. They lacked tone, but they had great volume. The later metal trumpets were played musically and often in pairs.

21 Samson

from Judges 13 to 16 : Jerusalem Bible

As Samson went down to Timnah he saw a young lion come roaring towards him. Though he had no weapon in his hand he tore the lion in pieces.

At Timnah he talked to one of the daughters of the Philistines and he liked her. Not long after this he came back to marry her. He went to look at the carcase of the lion, and there was a swarm of bees in the lion's body, and honey. He took some honey and ate it as he went along. Then he went down to the woman and they made a feast, for such is the custom.

Then Samson said to them, 'Let me ask you a riddle. If you find the answer within seven days of the feast, I will give you thirty fine robes. But if you cannot, you must give me thirty fine robes.' 'Ask your riddle,' they replied, 'we are listening.' So he said to them:

'Out of the eater came what is eaten,
and out of the strong came what is sweet.'

But they could not solve the riddle. Then Samson's wife fell on his neck in tears and said, 'You do not love me. You have asked my fellow countrymen a riddle and not even told me the answer.' She was so persistent that he told her, and she in turn told her fellow countrymen. So on the seventh day the men in the town said to Samson:

'What is sweeter than honey,
and what stronger than a lion?'

Then, burning with rage, he went down to Ashkelon, killed thirty Philistines, and gave what they wore to those who had answered the riddle.

Not long after this, the Philistines came up and encamped in Judah. They seized Samson, put out his eyes and took him down to Gaza. The chiefs assembled to offer a great sacrifice to Dagon their god, and they shouted, 'Send Samson to amuse us.' So Samson was brought out of prison. But he said to the boy who was leading him, 'Lead me where I can touch the pillars so that I can lean against them.' And Samson put his arms round the two middle pillars supporting the building and thrust with all his might. The building fell on all the chiefs and on all the people. Those he killed in his death outnumbered those he had killed in his life.

Happened between about 1200 and 1000 BC
Mainly written down in about 600 BC

One of the most insignificant stories in the Bible yet one of the most popular, especially to modern myth-makers like Hollywood! Samson was fundamentally a Tarzan with a fatal weakness for women.

Samson strength

The delightful story of Ruth which follows this one in the Bible is not included in this selection. Ruth is infinitely preferable to this oaf! But, unfortunately, her story is too long.

Ruth

References to the Philistines in the Samson saga are historically important. They were Phoenician in origin, aggressive sailors who invaded from Crete during this period bringing with them the use of iron, beer drinking and the name 'Palestine' (after the Egyptian word 'Peleset' meaning 'sea peoples'). Phoenicians also invaded Egypt and North Africa to establish trade links, and they came as far as Britain for the tin: legends name Porthcurno and St Michael's Mount among tin-marketing centres.

Philistines Phoenicians

The Israelites, who had invaded Canaan under Joshua, finally conquered the hill country at the Battle of Megiddo (traditional scene of Armageddon a thousand years later). The Philistines now covered the lowlands and, from the story of Samson onwards, were a serious threat to the Israelites. All that remained of the original Canaanites was now to be found in the culture of their conquerors.

Canaan Megiddo

The wedding was at the house of the bride's father and the party lasted for a week. This reading omits the detail that the Philistine guests were so eager not to lose face over the riddle that they threatened to burn the bride's house down with her in it if she failed to find the answer!

weddings

Dagon was the Philistines' fertility god. It was their version of Baal (notes to 20).

Dagon

22 'The empire of Yahweh'—a Jewish song

from Psalm 103 : Jerusalem Bible

Bless Yahweh, my soul,
bless his holy name, all that is in me!
Bless Yahweh, my soul,
and remember all his kindnesses:

in curing all your diseases,
in crowning you with love and tenderness,
in filling your years with prosperity,
in renewing your youth like an eagle's.

Yahweh who does what is right,
is always on the side of the oppressed;
he revealed his intentions to Moses,
his prowess to the sons of Israel.

Yahweh is tender and compassionate,
slow to anger, most loving;
his indignation does not last for ever,
his resentment exists a short time only.

No less than the height of heaven over earth
is the greatness of his love for those who fear him;
he takes our sins farther away
than the east is from the west.

As tenderly as a father treats his children,
so Yahweh treats those who fear him;
he knows what we are made of,
he remembers we are dust.

Man lasts no longer than grass,
no longer than a wild flower he lives,
one gust of wind, and he is gone,
never to be seen there again.

Yahweh has fixed his throne in the heavens,
his empire is over all.
Bless Yahweh, all his angels!
Bless Yahweh, all his creatures in every part of his empire!

Bless Yahweh, my soul!

Psalms were sung from about 1000 BC
They were mainly written down between about 500 and 200 BC

It was at this stage of thinking that angels began to need wings, for *angels* how else could they carry messages from the consecrated emperor on his heavenly throne right down to weedy little people in the dirt?

This vision of the maker is more sophisticated than earlier versions *anthropo-* (see readings 2 to 9 and notes to 3 and 5). God was still anthropo- *morphism* morphic, that is 'like the shape of a man', but the shape was more clearly defined: he was tender, loving and kind, showed patience and compassion, exercised healing-forgiveness.

Other religions had similar scriptures about the maker. A Hindu of India wrote that he was 'the one God, hidden in all beings, the self *Hindu* within all beings, watching over all works, the witness, the knower, the time of time, the master of nature and of man, the liberation of the world'. A Confucianist of China wrote, 'How vast is God, the ruler of men below! I, the little child, day and night will be reverent. *Confucian* Solitary am I and full of distress.' The reading opposite however grew from religions in Egypt and Persia.

23   Samuel and King Saul

***

from 1 Samuel 3, and 8 to 11 : Jerusalem Bible

Now the boy Samuel grew up, and Yahweh let no word of his fall to the ground. All Israel came to know that Samuel was a prophet of Yahweh.

When Samuel grew old, he appointed his sons as judges over Israel. But his sons did not follow his ways: they wanted money, taking bribes and perverting justice. Then all the elders of Israel gathered together and came to Samuel. 'Look,' they said to him, 'you are old and your sons do not follow your ways. So give us a king to rule over us, like the other nations.'

It displeased Samuel so he prayed to Yahweh. But Yahweh said to him, 'Obey the voice of the people. They have rejected me from ruling over them. From the day I brought them out of Egypt, they have served other gods. Obey their voice; only, you must warn them solemnly.'

Samuel repeated to the people all that Yahweh had said. They said, 'Our king shall rule us and fight our battles.' Samuel listened to all that the people had to say. He then said, 'Go back, each to your own town. When that day comes, you will cry out on account of the king you have chosen for yourselves. He will take the best of your manservants and your maidservants, of your cattle and your donkeys, and make them work for him, and you yourselves will become his slaves.'

Among the men of Benjamin there was a man named Kish. He had a son named Saul, a handsome man in the prime of life; he stood head and shoulders taller than the rest of the people. At the break of day Samuel called Saul. They walked as far as the end of the town and Samuel took a phial of oil and poured it on Saul's head; then he kissed him saying, 'You are the man who must rule Yahweh's people, and who must save them from the power of the enemies surrounding them.'

So all the people went to Gilgal and there they proclaimed Saul king before Yahweh. They offered communion sacrifices there before Yahweh; and Saul and all the men of Israel rejoiced greatly.

Happened about 1000 BC
Written down between about 600 and 500 BC

The Israelites had been in Canaan now for about 200 years. They had fought hard against neighbouring tribes to establish themselves. Shiloh was one of their hill forts. Samuel lived there. He was their chief 'prophet', a sort of 'holy man' who spent most of his time alone worshipping Yahweh, a sort of priest. Also housed at Shiloh was the Ark of the Covenant. This was said to contain the two stones of the Moses law (reading 17). *Samuel prophet priest Ark*

Gilgal was a hill fort about four miles from Shiloh. Communion sacrifices were merely burnt offerings intended by the people to make contact with their god — and to put him in a good mood, in this case to gain his approval of their new king. *sacrifices*

Anointing was the vital act of consecration. Priests and kings were deliberately raised up by the people to be pourers of divine blessing among them. Vegetable oil symbolized the very life-juice of the maker and, they hoped, would render their leader more virile and ensure fecundity all round. *anoint kings*

24 David's youth

***
from 1 Samuel 16 to 19 : Jerusalem Bible

Now the spirit of Yahweh had left Saul and an evil spirit from Yahweh filled him with terror. And whenever the spirit troubled Saul, David the son of Jesse played the harp; then Saul grew calm, and recovered, and the evil spirit left him. Saul loved him greatly.

The Philistines mustered their troops for war. The Israelites also mustered to meet the Philistines with the valley between them. One of the Philistine shock-troopers stepped out from the ranks; his name was Goliath, from Gath; he was six cubits and one span tall. He shouted, 'I challenge the ranks of Israel today. Give me a man and we will fight in single combat.'

When Saul and all Israel heard these words they were terrified. David said to Saul, 'Let no one lose heart on his account. Your servant has killed both lion and bear, and this Philistine shall be like one of them.' Then Saul said to David, 'Go, and Yahweh be with you!'

So he took his staff in his hand, picked five smooth stones from the river bed, put them in his shepherd's bag and, with his sling, he went to meet the Philistine. And the Philistine cursed David by his gods, and said, 'Come over here and I will give your flesh to the birds of the air and the beasts of the field.'

David ran to meet the Philistine. He took out a stone and slung it and struck the Philistine; the stone penetrated his forehead and he fell on his face to the ground. Then David ran and, standing over the Philistine, seized his sword and drew it from the scabbard, and with this he killed him, cutting off his head. The Philistines saw that their champion was dead and took flight. The men of Israel, shouting their war cry, pursued. David took the Philistine's head and brought it to Jerusalem.

On their way back, the women came out dancing and singing:

'Saul has killed his thousands,
and David his tens of thousands.'

Saul was very angry and jealous. On the following day he fell into a fit of frenzy in his house, and tried to pin David to the wall with his spear. But David fled and made good his escape.

They believed about Yahweh that he controlled all spirits, good and evil, that he was the 'cause' of all things. What actually happened to poor Saul was that, having been an unwilling king in the first place, he had made his mistakes and the prophet Samuel had condemned him in the name of God so that he sank into a heavy depression. And sometimes he flew without warning into a wild temper. Madness in all its forms was put down to the work of evil spirits. The modern technical expression for Saul's condition is 'manic depression'.

Samuel

mad
evil spirits

'David' meant 'commander' or 'leader'. He was handsome, as the tortured Saul had been in his youth, and he was athletic, poetic and musical — what more could he wish for? So, when King Saul heard the top most popular song putting this shepherd-boy higher than himself, he could not contain his jealousy.

David

pop

The harp was possibly an instrument of about ten strings, portable, about the size of a violin, with a modest sound box at the top. But none of this is certain.

harp

A cubit measured about 45 cm (18 inches), that is the length of an average man's forearm, a useful gauge in building. And a span was half a cubit.

cubit

25 The death of Saul and Jonathan

***
from 1 Samuel 31, and 2 Samuel 1 : Jerusalem Bible and Authorized Version

The Philistines made war on Israel and the men of Israel fled and were slaughtered on Mount Giboa. The Philistines pressed Saul and his sons hard and killed Jonathan, Abinadab and Malchishua, the sons of Saul. The fighting grew heavy about Saul; the bowmen took him off his guard, so that he fell wounded. Then Saul said to his armour-bearer, 'Draw your sword and run me through with it; I do not want these men to come and gloat over me.' But his armour-bearer was afraid and would not do it. So Saul took his own sword and fell on it. His armour-bearer, seeing that Saul was dead, fell on his sword too and died with him. And so Saul and his three sons and his armour-bearer died together that day. When the Israelites who were on the other side of the valley saw that the men of Israel had taken flight and that Saul and his sons were dead, they abandoned their towns and fled. The Philistines then came and occuped them.

A man came from where Saul had been, his garments torn and earth on his head. When he came to David he fell to the ground and he said, 'The people have fled from the battlefield and many have fallen. Saul and his son Jonathan are dead too.' Then David mourned and wept and fasted until the evening for Saul and Jonathan and for the House of Israel. Then David made his lament:

'How are the mighty fallen!
The beauty of Israel is slain upon thy high places: ye mountains of Gilboa, let there be no dew, neither let there be rain upon you. Tell it not in Gath, publish it not in the streets of Askelon lest the daughters of the Philistines rejoice.
Saul and Jonathan were lovely and pleasant in their lives, and in their deaths they were not divided. They were swifter than eagles, they were stronger than lions.
How are the mighty fallen.
and the weapons of war perished!'

David's closest friend was Jonathan, the son of Saul. They were like *David* brothers. David had married Saul's daughter, Michel. Both she and Jonathan had had to protect David from Saul's mad hatred as it increased. David however longed for peace. He had the chance to kill Saul on one famous occasion, but he was not vindictive enough. He was sympathetic and loyal. *loyal*

An armour-bearer was chosen for his trustworthiness and bravery. *armour-* The Romans later had a similar appointment — 'shield-bearer' in *bearer* Latin was *scutarius* and the medieval English words 'Esquire' and 'Squire' came from that.

A 'lament' is a passionate and dramatic expression of grief. It is a *lament* very old phenomenon among civilizing peoples — see note to 26 on 'Tammuz'. It was believed in some way to revive a dead or suffering god, and in primitive times women were considered to be better at it than men; they had a greater capacity for pain and grief *women* (see readings 122 and 128), and they also had, of course, an apparently magical ability to arouse a man's emotions against his will. This ability seemed important to the primitive mind for in an agricultural setting it was considered necessary to rejuvenate the sleeping god of fertility at certain seasons.

But, whatever is believed about the god, lamenting and mourning have always had a profound effect upon the participants. By sympathetically acting out the tragedy of the smitten hero, whether in poetry or music or drama, the mourner himself is purged and revived. He passes through a valley of misery and finds well water to refresh and wash him clean. This formula was also understood by the Victorians when a loved one died. People who try to get by without it today often suffer harmful reactions later: the whole metabolism, not only the mind or spirit, seems to be in need of it.

26 King David

from 2 Samuel 5, 8, 11 and 12 : Jerusalem Bible

All the tribes of Israel then came to David at Hebron. They said, 'You are the man who shall be shepherd of Israel.' So all the elders in the presence of Yahweh anointed David king of Israel. He was thirty years old when he became king.

David and his men marched on Jerusalem against the Jebusites living there and captured the fortress of Zion. He went to live in the fortress and built a wall round it. David grew greater and greater, and Yahweh was with him.

At the turn of the year, the time when kings go campaigning, David remained in Jerusalem. It happened towards evening when David was strolling on the palace roof, that he saw from the roof a woman bathing; the woman was very beautiful. David made inquiries about this woman and was told, 'Why, that is Bathsheba, the wife of Uriah the Hittite.' Then David sent messengers and had her brought. She came to him, and he slept with her. She then went home again.

The woman conceived and sent word to David, 'I am with child.' Next morning David wrote a letter to Joab. (Joab was in command of the army.) He wrote, 'Station Uriah in the thick of the fight so that he may be struck down and die.' Joab, then besieging the town Rabbah, posted Uriah in a place where he knew there were fierce fighters. The men of the town sallied out and engaged Joab; the army suffered casualties, and Uriah the Hittite was killed.

When Uriah's wife heard that her husband was dead, she mourned for her husband. When the period of morning was over, David sent to have her brought to his house; she became his wife and bore him a son. But what David had done displeased Yahweh.

Yahweh sent Nathan the prophet to David. He came to him and said, 'Yahweh the God of Israel says this, "I anointed you king over Israel; I delivered you from the hands of Saul; I gave your master's house to you, his wives into your arms; and if this were not enough, I would add as much again for you. Why have you shown contempt for Yahweh, doing what displeases him?" '

David said to Nathan, 'I have sinned against Yahweh.' Then Nathan went home and David pleaded with Yahweh; he spent the night on the bare ground covered with sacking and refused to take food. On the seventh day, the child died.

Happened about 1000 BC
Written down between about 600 and 500 BC

The subtle point about Rule 7 in the Moses law (reading 17) was that the person who copulated with another was treating an absent marriage partner as if he or she did not exist. Because words and promises meant so much to these people, to break the terms of any agreement was, in effect, to put someone to death. The destructive web of deceit which often surrounded adultery made their dark secret love second-rate. *adultery*

The majestic power of the Bible as a book is that it does not leave out the faults of its heroes. There is no deceit in its tongue. Unfortunately there is not room in the reading opposite to include Nathan's story at the beginning of 2 Samuel 12, one of the great passages of the Bible. The genuine repentance of this young king is also echoed in Psalm 51. *Bible* *repent*

Between the great rivers of Mesopotamia where the life of early man depended upon the timely irrigation of his 'vegetables', belief in the 'Lord of Life' called Tammuz can be traced back to 3000 BC: there was a beautiful youth slain by the harvesters and his bones ground in the mill and scattered like fertilizer upon the fields. That was the myth. Parallel rituals involving human victims have been traced in Mexico, Africa and India. In Egypt, the worship of Osiris involved the slaying of a ruddy youth at harvest whose hair was the colour of ripe corn. See also the top of notes to 20 concerning Canaanites, Phoenicians and Greeks. This primordial formula which was dramatized in so many cultures—life with rejoicing, and death with lamenting and sacrifice, resulting in some sort of revival—has its distant echoes to this day. There is in Devon and Cornwall memory of the strange harvest ceremony called 'crying the neck'. The art of making corn dollies is probably not simply the rural art of making corn dollies! And such echoes exist in many undisturbed communities all over the world. *Tammuz* *life-formula*

The Hebrews inherited the Sumerian belief that the Father in Heaven needed to be stirred up and encouraged to perform his might act of procreation, and that a potent way of doing this was to raise up virile kings and priests who could imitate his power in battle and in bed. Such a leader was King David, anointed by Yahweh, endowed with his power and grace, strong and loving, mighty in combat and merciful too. David also fulfilled the Sumerian version of the ideal shepherd: he was clearly an honest and first-rate person by nature, a brave, sensitive and capable figure intimately connected with the vital processes of reproduction and birth. *leader* *David* *shepherd*

27 Absalom

from 2 Samuel 14, 15, 18 and 19 : Jerusalem Bible

In the whole of Israel there was no man who could be praised for his beauty as much as Absalom; from the sole of his foot to the crown of his head there was not a blemish on him. Absalom lived in Jerusalem. He would rise early and stand beside the road leading to the gate; and whenever a man with some lawsuit had to come before the king's court, Absalom would call out to him and say, 'Look, your case is sound and just, but there is not one deputy of the king's who will listen to you.' And so Absalom seduced the hearts of the men of Israel.

At the end of four years Absalom sent to Hebron. He sent couriers throughout the tribes of Israel saying, 'When you hear the trumpet sound you are to say, "Absalom is king at Hebron:" ' The conspiracy grew in strength and Absalom's supporters grew in number.

A messenger came to tell David, 'The hearts of the men of Israel are now with Absalom.' So David left on foot with all his household. David reviewed the troops that were were him, and appointed commanders and he stood by the gate as the troops marched out. He gave orders to Joab, 'For my sake, treat young Absalom gently.' And all the troops heard that the king had given these orders about Absalom.

So the troops marched out and battle was joined in the forest of Ephraim. There, Absalom's army was beaten by David's followers; it was a great defeat that day. The fighting spread throughout the region and, of the troops, the forest claimed more victims than the sword.

Absalom happened to run into some of David's followers. Absalom was riding a mule and the mule passed under the thick branches of a great oak. Absalom's head caught fast in the oak and he was left hanging between heaven and earth, while the mule he was riding went on. Someone saw this and cut Absalom down and finished him off. Then Joab had the trumpet sounded and the troops stopped pursuing, and the son of Zadok said, 'I must run and tell the good news to the king.'

David was sitting between the two gates. The lookout had gone up to the ramparts; he looked up and saw a man running all by himself. The man approached the king and said, 'Blessed be Yahweh your God, who has handed over the men who rebelled against my lord the king!' The king asked, 'Is all well with young Absalom?' The man answered, 'May all the enemies of my lord the king share the lot of that young man.'

The king shuddered. He went up to the room over the gate, and weeping said, 'My son Absalom! My son! My son Absalom! Would I had died in your place! Absalom, my son, my son!'

Happened about 1000 BC
Written down between about 600 and 500 BC

Absalom was David's third son.   *Absalom*

No wonder poor Absalom went astray. Famous or brilliant men have
often been a crushing problem to their sons, sometimes without
intending it or even noticing it. And quite ordinary parents have   *parents*
been known to cause as much trouble by lording it over their
children. Absalom may have been handsome but without the magic
spell of kingship he felt impotent in that society.

The ideal Hebrew leader was one who enticed the 'grace' of   *grace*
Yahweh to come among his people, his flocks and his pastures.
(See notes to 26.) In both Hebrew and Greek 'the Grace of God' was
connected with the idea of the flowing of seed, the pouring of
bounty, the generation of life. Moses the lawgiver had provided the   *Moses*
nation's bones and muscles but the beloved David became its flesh
and blood.

28 King Solomon

***
from 2 Samuel 12, and 1 Kings 2 to 5 : Jerusalem Bible

David consoled his wife Bathsheba. He went to her and slept with her. She conceived and gave birth to a son whom she named Solomon. Yahweh loved him and made this known through the prophet Nathan.

As David's life drew to its close he laid his charge on his son Solomon, 'I am going the way of all the earth. Be strong and show yourself a man. Observe the commandments of Yahweh your God, as it stands written in the Law of Moses, that so you may be successful in all that you undertake.' So David slept with his ancestors and was buried in the Citadel of David.

Then Zadok the priest and Nathan the prophet anointed Solomon king. They sounded the trumpet and all the people said, 'Long live King Solomon!' Solomon was seated upon the throne of David and his sovereignty was securely established. He allied himself by marriage with Pharaoh, king of Egypt; he married Pharaoh's daughter and took her to the Citadel of David until he could complete the building of his palace and the Temple of Yahweh. Solomon loved Yahweh: he followed the precepts of David his father.

At Gibeon Yahweh appeared in a dream to Solomon during the night. God said, 'Ask what you would like me to give you.' Solomon replied, 'Yahweh my God, I am a very young man, unskilled in leadership, in the midst of a people so many its number cannot be counted. Give your servant a heart to understand good and evil!' It pleased Yahweh that Solomon should have asked for this. 'Since you have asked for this,' Yahweh said, 'and not asked for long life for yourself or riches or the lives of your enemies, here and now I do what you ask. I give you a heart wise and shrewd as none before you has had and none will have after you. What you have not asked I shall give you too: such riches and glory as no other king ever had. And I will give you a long life, if you follow my ways.' Then Solomon awoke; it was a dream. He returned to Jerusalem and offered communion sacrifices before Yahweh and held a banquet for all his servants.

Yahweh gave Solomon immense wisdom and understanding, and a heart as vast as the sand on the seashore. He composed three thousand proverbs, and his songs numbered a thousand and five. He could talk about plants from the cedar in Lebanon to the hyssop growing on the wall; he could talk of animals, and birds and reptiles and fish. Men from all nations came to hear Solomon's wisdom, and he received gifts from all the kings of the world, who had heard of his wisdom.

So died David, the darling shepherd of Bethlehem. *Le roi est mort, vive le roi!* He would revive somehow or other. (See notes to 26 on 'shepherds', 'Tammuz', and 'life-formula', note to 27 on 'grace' and notes to 20 down to 'Bethlehem'.) *David*

The three main elements are, incidentally, to be found contained in Solomon's coronation, as they have been in English coronations over the past 1000 years: these are the king's promises to obey the laws of God, and the people's approval; the anointing; and the king's crowning, enthroning and communion with God. *coronation*

These people firmly believed that 'to observe the laws of God' automatically resulted in 'success in all that you undertake'. It was scientifically sound idea, for if their god was the creator and if their version of his laws was a true representation of his mind, what could go wrong?

Solomon however was not as brilliant as this reading suggests. He began his reign with a bloodbath, disposing of all possible enemies in his kingdom, including his own brother and the distinguished soldier Joab. He plunged vast numbers of his people into grinding slavery and the disastrous long-term effects only came when he himself was comfortably 'sleeping with his ancestors'. *Solomon* *slavery*

His dream however is of untouchable beauty: who, when offered the fulfilment of his dearest wish, would simply ask for 'a heart to understand good and evil'? *good & evil*

29 'Let the universe praise Yahweh!' —a Jewish song

from Psalm 148 : Jerusalem Bible

Let earth praise Yahweh:
sea-monsters and all the deeps,
fire and hail, snow and mist,
gales that obey his decree,

mountains and hills,
orchards and forests,
wild animals and farm animals,
snakes and birds,

all kings on earth and nations,
princes, all rulers in the world,
young men and girls,
old people, and children too!

Let them all praise the name of Yahweh,
for his name and no other is sublime,
transcending earth and heaven in majesty,
raising the fortunes of his people.

Alleluia!

Let heaven praise Yahweh:
praise him, heavenly heights,
praise him, all his angels,
praise him, all his armies!

Praise him, sun and moon,
praise him, shining stars,
praise him, highest heavens,
and waters above the heavens!

Let them all praise the name of Yahweh,
at whose command they were created;
he has fixed them in their place for ever,
by an unalterable statute.

Alleluia!

Psalms were sung from about 1000 BC
They were mainly written down between about 500 and 200 BC

This song was probably sung by two choirs, one representing Earth and the other Heaven. They probably faced each other and there were probably more complicated versions of it so that one choir spoke to the other as if in conversation. It was a lively conversation.

creation

'Alleluia' meant something like, 'Now *you* praise Yahweh!' and was a sort of challenge to the other choir to produce even more exuberant ideas! The singing of such psalms was a scene of mounting excitement. There was stamping and clapping, unrehearsed dances and uninhibited shouts of joy.

Alleluia!

psalms

Psalms were far more widely popular and better known than pop songs are in modern society. In Hebrew poetry there was intrinsic play on words, puns, parallelisms and symmetries. Most of the Hebrew puns are lost in English of course, but parallelisms are still plain as the version opposite shows: 'mountains and hills', 'wild animals and farm animals' and so on. And the whole piece is divided into two parallel statements, one about Earth, the other Heaven. This demonstrates their fundamental idea of worship, that it was a process of man imitating his god.

worship

Hebrew poetry had no use for the sort of rhymes and rhythms used, for example, in the poem in notes to 39.

poetry

30 The first temple

***
from 1 Kings 5, 6 and 8 : Jerusalem Bible

Solomon sent this message to Hiram the king of Tyre, 'You are aware that David my father was unable to build a temple because his enemies waged war on him from all sides. But now Yahweh has given me rest: not one enemy, no calamities. I therefore plan to build a temple for Yahweh. So now have cedars of Lebanon cut down for me; my servants will work with your servants, and I will pay for the hire of your servants at whatever rate you fix. As you know, we have no one as skilled in felling trees as the Sidonians.' When Hiram heard what Solomon had said, he was delighted. 'Blessed be Yahweh!' he said.

King Solomon raised a levy throughout Israel for forced labour. He sent thirty thousand men to Lebanon in relays; they spent one month in Lebanon and two months at home. At the king's orders they quarried huge stones for laying the temple foundations—quarry-dressed stones, so no sound of pick or any iron tool was to be heard in the Temple while it was being built.

The Temple that King Solomon built for Yahweh was sixty cubits long, twenty cubits wide and twenty-five in height. He also built an annexe against the side all round. And he made windows. He lined the inside of the walls with panels of cedar wood and laid the floor with juniper planks. All round the Temple walls he carved figures of cherubs. He made the door of olive wood and the leaves of juniper.

In the inner part of the Temple he designed the Holy of Holies to contain the ark of Yahweh, and he plated it on the inside with pure gold. He made an altar of cedar wood in front plated with gold. He plated the whole Temple with gold, the whole Temple entirely.

Solomon took seven years to build it exactly as it had been planned. Then Solomon called the elders of Israel together in Jerusalem. The priests brought the ark of Yahweh to its place in the Holy of Holies. Where the ark was placed the cherubs spread out their wings and sheltered the ark. There was nothing in the ark except the two stone tablets Moses had placed in it; they are still there today.

Then (in the presence of the whole assembly of Israel) Solomon stood before the altar of Yahweh and, stretching out his hands towards heaven, said, 'Yahweh, God of Israel, will you really live with men on earth? Why, the heavens and their own heavens cannot contain you. How much less this house that I have built! Yahweh my God, listen to the prayer of Israel your people as they pray in this place.'

Temples exist in many religions. They are intended to be places where people can meet their god. In some temples the god is thought actually to live.

Solomon seems to have followed the Canaanite pattern in building this, the first Israelite temple. Archaeologists have unearthed the remains of several like it. Pictures of it are fairly common in books about the Old Testament. It covered about the area of a tennis court. From primitive times it had been shaped like the human womb. Its entrance was a porch (the vulva) guarded by two lofty pillars. Inside there was a 'Holy Place' (the vagina) which led to a dark room called the 'Holy of Holies' (the uterus). The fundamental shape of Christian churches has been notably similar.

temple

womb

This Holy of Holies was an exact cube of sides approximately 9 metres (30 feet). Steps led up to its entrance which was covered by a curtain. It was windowless and without light. It was said to contain the Ark of the Covenant, that is, the box in which were kept the two slabs of stone on which were written the ten main rules in Moses-law (see reading 17). This ark was guarded by two cherubs — fierce lion-bodied, sphinx-headed, winged creatures. (It was the Renaissance artists who invented the chubby, flying babies.)

Holy of Holies

Ark

Moses-law cherubs

The Holy of Holies was only entered on special festivals of worship by the high priest. In primitive fertility symbolism he, of course, represented the reproductive organ of the creator-god, the divine phallus. They believed that by acting out his creative process in this way they would become at one with him and thereby share his powers of generation: then their crops and cattle and women would be fruitful. The priest was anointed with oils which represented the divine spermatozoa. The Moses-law, situated in the central vessel, was for them the 'Word of God' that vitalizing food of the life-giver, that 'bread of heaven'.

worship priests

atonement

word

Sacrifices were performed publicly outside on a sort of miniature ziggurat about 5 metres (15 feet) high (see notes to 5).

Solomon had a vast building programme besides the Temple. The farming communities which had to spend so much time in his service grew increasingly restless. His own palace was twice the size of this temple for Yahweh, and there were numerous other public buildings and, outside Jerusalem, many fortified towns. Megiddo, for example, was a 'chariot city' with stables to accommodate over 400 horses.

Solomon

building

Megiddo

31 'The house of Yahweh'—a Jewish song

***
from Psalms 87 and 84 : Jerusalem Bible

Yahweh loves his city
  founded on the holy mountain.
It is Yahweh who makes her what she is,
  he, the Most High, Yahweh.
All who were born in Zion
  call her 'Mother'.

How my soul yearns for Yahweh's courts!
My heart and my flesh sing for joy to the living God.

Happy those who live in your house
  and can praise you all day long!
The sparrow has found its home at last,
  the swallow a nest for its young!

A single day in your courts
  is worth more than a thousand elsewhere;
merely to stand on the steps of God's house
  is better than living with the wicked.

Yahweh!
Happy the man who puts his trust in you!

Psalms were sung from about 1000 BC
They were mainly written down between about 500 and 200 BC

'Psalms' were songs sung to the accompaniment of a harp (see notes to 24 and 42). The word *psallo* described the twanging of harps.

psalms

harps

To 'praise' someone or something meant to 'prize' him or it, that is to recognize openly the true value.

praise

'Yahweh' meant something like, 'He shows himself to be'. In Hebrew 'to be' was much stronger, than simply 'to exist'. It contained the idea of being PRESENT and ACTIVE. He was for them 'the Living God', the god of life, not simply the 'source of all existence'. He was the most real thing in all reality. He created the sun, the moon and stars, he ordered the procession of the seasons, he controlled wind, rain, dew and drought, he was the master of fertility, and the giver and taker of all life and growth. He paced across the raging seas, thunder was his voice, clouds clothed his heavenly form, the earth quaked at his approach.

Yahweh

presence

reality

On earth they made for him their temple at Jerusalem upon Mount Zion. It was his house. It was on a high place so that he could easily come among them and 'show himself to be'. In their temple they would play out what was going on in the whole universe: the praise of the creator by his creatures.

first temple
high places

Many people's idea of 'heaven' is a motherly sort of place where one is accepted, fed and protected. These people certainly felt in need of this sort of heaven, being surrounded by enemies and, they believed, evil spirits.

heaven

32 The end of Solomon

***

from 1 Kings 9 to 12 : Jerusalem Bible

King Solomon equipped a fleet at Ezion-geber on the shores of the Red Sea, in the land of Edom. His sailors went to Ophir and brought back gold which they delivered to King Solomon. And in Jerusalem he made silver common as pebbles, and cedars plentiful as the sycamores of the Lowlands. He built up a force of chariots imported from Egypt and horses from Cilicia.

The fame of Solomon reached the queen of Sheba. She brought immense riches to Jerusalem with her. On coming to Solomon she opened her mind freely to him; and Solomon had an answer for all her questions, not one of them was too obscure for the king to expound. When the queen of Sheba saw all the wisdom of Solomon, the palace he had built, the food at his table, the accommodation for his officials, the organization of his staff and the way they were dressed, his cup-bearers, and the holocausts he offered in the Temple, it left her breathless, and she said to the king, 'Until I came and saw it with my own eyes I could not believe what they told me, but clearly they told me less than half: for wisdom and prosperity you surpass the report I heard. How happy your wives are! How happy these servants of yours! Blessed be Yahweh your God.' And she presented the king with gold and great quantities of spices and precious stones. And King Solomon in his turn presented the queen of Sheba with all she expressed a wish for. Then she went home, she and her servants, to her own country.

King Solomon loved many foreign women: not only Pharaoh's daughter but Moabites, Edomites, Sidonians and Hittites. When Solomon grew old his wives swayed his heart to other gods; he was deeply attached to them.

Solomon's reign in Jerusalem over all Israel lasted forty years. Then Solomon slept with his ancestors and was buried in the Citadel of David his father. Rehoboam his son succeeded him. But Rehoboam rejected the advice given him by the elders and consulted the young men who had grown up with him. He took no notice of the people's wishes and Israel went off to their tents.

As soon as Jeroboam son of Nebat heard the news he returned from Egypt where he had taken refuge from King Solomon. When the people heard that Jeroboam had returned, they summoned him to the assembly and made him king of Israel.

No one remained loyal to Rehoboam except the tribe of Judah.

Solomon died in 922 BC
Written down between 600 and 500 BC

It is odd that the wisdom of Solomon should have been remembered, for he was a very imperfect king. He reduced many of his people to slavery, he abandoned the pure worship of Yahweh which his ancestors had fought so hard for, and he neglected the vital education of Prince Rehoboam. The result was disaster: the Kingdom of Israel split.

wise

In the South King Rehoboam with only the tribe of Judah held the capital, Jerusalem: they became known as JUDAH and survived through thick and thin to produce the JEWS of the first century AD.

Judah

Jew

In the North rebel Jeroboam with the other eleven tribes made Samaria his capital; they were called ISRAEL and lasted for 200 years becoming the despised SAMARITANS of the first century AD.

Samaria

Israel

King Solomon had certainly been a shrewd businessman. There was enormous prosperity in the land. But the prosperity had brought its weaknesses. As a well-known Jew of the first century AD said, the wild flowers were better off than 'Solomon in all his glory'.

Solomon

33   Elijah on Mount Carmel

***

from 1 Kings 16 to 18 : Jerusalem Bible

Ahab son of Omri became king of Israel and reigned in Samaria. Ahab son of Omri did what is displeasing to Yahweh: he married Jezebel, the daughter of the king of the Sidonians, and then proceeded to serve Baal and worship him in Samaria.

After a while the country had no rain and famine was severe in Samaria. A long time went by and Ahab called all Israel together and assembled the prophets of Baal on Mount Carmel.

The word of Yahweh came to Elijah the Tishbite: 'Go, present yourself to Ahab; I am about to send down rain on the land.' So Elijah went and stepped out in front of all the people. 'How long,' he said, 'do you mean to hobble first on one leg then on the other? If Yahweh is God, follow him; if Baal, follow him.' But the people never said a word. Elijah then said to them, 'I alone am left as a prophet of Yahweh, while the prophets of Baal are four hundred and fifty. Let two bulls be given us; let them choose one for themselves and I will prepare the other. You must call on the name of your god, and I shall call on the name of mine; the god who answers with fire is God indeed.' The people all answered, 'Agreed!' Then the prophets of Baal took the bull and prepared it, and from morning to midday they called on the name of Baal. But there was no answer as they performed their hobbling dance round the altar and Elijah mocked them. 'Call louder,' he said, 'for he is a god: he is busy, or he has gone on a journey; perhaps he is asleep and will wake up.' So they shouted louder and gashed themselves, as their custom was, until the blood flowed down them. But there was no attention given to them.

Then Elijah said to all the people, 'Come closer to me,' and all the people came closer to him. He took twelve stones and built an altar in the name of Yahweh. Round the altar he dug a trench. He then arranged the wood, dismembered the bull and laid it on the wood. Then he stepped forward. 'Yahweh, God of Israel,' he said, 'let them know today that you are God in Israel and are winning back their hearts.'

Then the fire of Yahweh fell and consumed the holocaust and when all the people saw this they fell on their faces. 'Yahweh is God,' they cried, 'Yahweh is God.' And now the sky grew dark with cloud and storm, and rain fell in torrents.

Happened in about 850 BC
Written down between 600 and 500 BC

The word 'god' emerged from the Aryan word *gheu* meaning 'to call down' (invite, invoke) or 'to offer up some gift' (sacrifice). It referred, therefore, to primitive human activities not to a definite object like, say, 'mountain'.

gods give sacrifice

Some people say that belief in a god is no more than a 'figment of the imagination'. They say that people, being afraid of things they do not know and cannot control, have to put their troubled minds at rest with ideas of 'gods' whom they can contact and sometimes even control. They say that this sort of relationship with these imagined gods has the crippling effect of a substitute for proper human relationships for it is easier to make friends with an idea than with real people. The atheist simply says, 'There are no gods.'

atheists

Thus, if 'God' were no more than a product of the imagination, the reading opposite could be as follows. There was a drought in the North and famine among the Israelites, so they tried to invoke their new god, Baal, but nothing happened until a wild man of the mountains, Elijah, arrived and offered a sacrifice to his god Yahweh. Elijah knew much about the weather in those parts. His timing was perfect. The sticks and the meat on his altar of rocks ignited and the rain came tumbling down. Yahweh was in, Baal was out, and Elijah slaughtered the 450 false prophets to teach everybody a lesson.

Elijah elements

These people believed that their god could be most likely found in mountains and clouds. These became symbols, among many others, of his presence. Writers used them as code words for centuries after this.

mountains

This story of Elijah, with his pure desert vision of the Father of Heaven, confounding the false prophets of Baal in Canaan is a misleading simplification. Elsewhere in the Bible it is clear that the Hebrews learnt much from these Canaanites. In fact, ultimately Yahweh was Baal in their minds, and the Jewish people became the feminine object of his love—as Astarte (later Aphrodite, or Venus) had been to Baal (later Adonis). The force of the culture of Canaan can be grasped from note to 30 on Temple worship.

Canaan

Yahweh

Adonis

34 Naboth's vineyard

from 1 Kings 21 and 22 : Jerusalem Bible

Naboth of Jezreel had a vineyard close by the palace of Ahab king of Israel. And Ahab said to Naboth, 'Give me your vineyard to be my vegetable garden; I will give you a better vineyard for it or, if you prefer, I will give you its worth in money.' But Naboth answered, 'Yahweh forbid that I should give you the inheritance of my ancestors!'

Ahab went home gloomy and out of temper at the words of Naboth of Jezreel. He lay down on his bed and turned his face away. His wife Jezebel came to him. She said, 'You make a fine king of Israel, and no mistake! Get up and eat; I will get you the vineyard of Naboth myself.'

So she wrote letters in Ahab's name to the elders who lived where Naboth lived. In the letters she wrote, 'Put Naboth in the forefront of the people. Confront him with a couple of scoundrels who will accuse him. Then take him outside and stone him to death.'

The men did what Jezebel ordered. They put Naboth in the forefront of the people; then the scoundrels came and made their accusation: 'Naboth has cursed God and the king': then they led him outside the town and stoned him to death. They then sent word to Jezebel. She said to Ahab, 'Get up! Take possession of the vineyard which Naboth of Jezreel would not give you, for Naboth is dead.' Ahab got up.

Then the word of Yahweh came to Elijah the Tishbite, 'Up! Go down to meet Ahab king of Israel, in Samaria. You will find him in Naboth's vineyard; he has gone down to take possession of it. You are to say this to him, "Yahweh says this: You have committed murder; now you usurp as well. For this—and Yahweh says this—in the place where the dogs licked the blood of Naboth, the dogs will lick your blood too".' When Ahab heard these words, he walked with slow steps.

There was a lull of three years with no fighting. Then Ahab king of Israel said to Jehoshaphat king of Judah, 'Will you come with me to fight at Ramoth-gilead? Ramoth-gilead belongs to us and yet we do nothing to wrest it away from the king of Aram.' So they went up against Ramoth-gilead. The king of Aram had given his chariot-commanders the following order: 'Do not attack anyone of whatever rank, except Ahab king of Israel.' But the king of Israel went into battle disguised.

Now one of the men, drawing his bow at random, hit the king of Israel, and in the evening he died; the blood from the wound flowed into the bottom of the chariot. In Samaria they buried the king. They washed the chariot at the Pool of Samaria; the dogs licked up the blood.

Happened in about 850 BC
Written down between 600 and 500 BC

As the first paragraph in reading 33 explains, Ahab was a weak and *Ahab* horrid king in the North, and Jezebel was the selfish and cruel power *Jezebel* behind his throne. In the end she also died a violent death under the wheels of a chariot. Her name however lives on: a 'Jezebel' is a brazen woman plastered with cosmetics, bent on seduction and random copulation or something like that! Jezebel, then, was 'a bad thing'.

The story about the death of Jezebel starts like this: 'When Jehu came to Jezreel, Jezebel heard of it; and she painted her eyes, and adorned her head, and looked out of the window . . . .' The word 'cosmetics' comes from the Greek cosmos meaning the 'ordered *cosmetics* universe'. Cosmetics, then were literally what put a girl 'right' — at *right & wrong* least she felt 'right'.

Following that tradition of cosmetic beauty, the Prophet *Mohammed* Mohammed in about AD 600 wrote that Paradise (the Garden of *Paradise* Eden, the place of delight) contained 'wide-eyed houris', adorned and submissive.

Aram was Syria. The Aramaic language became increasingly *Aram* popular in business and diplomacy until the time of Jesus when it *Jesus* was widely spoken. In fact Jesus probably spoke Aramaic himself and there is a possibility that the very first versions of the four Christian Gospels were written in Aramaic. *Gospels*

To damage someone's reputation by writing or saying scurrilous things about him was 'blasphemy' and, in the case of Naboth, his *blasphemy* accusers were violating Rule 9 of the Moses law. Ironically, they were accusing him of violating Rule 3, the worst kind of blasphemy which included even thinking ill of God. See reading 17 and its notes.

For land ownership see notes to 37.

35 Naaman

from 2 Kings 5 : Jerusalem Bible

Naaman, army commander of the king of Aram, was a man who enjoyed his master's respect and favour since, through him, Yahweh had granted victory to the Aramaeans. But the man was a leper.

Now, a servant of Naaman's wife said to her mistress, 'The prophet of Samaria would cure him of his leprosy.' Naaman went and told his master the king of Aram. He said to Naaman, 'Go by all means.' So Naaman left.

Naaman came with his chariot and drew up at the door of Elisha's house. And Elisha sent him a messenger to say, 'Go and bathe seven times in the Jordan, and your flesh will become clean once more.' But Naaman was indignant, saying, 'Surely the rivers of Damascus are better than any water in Israel? Could I not bathe in them?' And he turned round and went off in a rage, but his servants said, 'My father, if the prophet had asked you to do something difficult, would you not have done it?' So he went down and immersed himself seven times in the Jordan. And his flesh became clean once more like the flesh of a little child.

Returning to Elisha with his whole escort, he went in and stood before him. 'Now I know,' he said, 'that there is no God in all the earth except in Israel. Now please accept a present from your servant.' But Elisha replied, 'As Yahweh lives, whom I serve, I will accept nothing.'

Naaman had gone a small distance when Gehazi, the servant of Elisha, said to himself, 'My master has let this Naaman off lightly by not accepting what he offered. I will run and get something out of him.' So Gehazi set off in pursuit of Naaman. Naaman jumped down from his chariot to meet him. 'Is all well?' he asked. 'All is well,' he said. 'My master has sent me to say, "Two young men of the prophetic brotherhood have arrived from the highlands. Be kind enough to give them a talent of silver".' 'Please accept two talents,' Naaman replied tying up the silver in two bags. Gehazi took them and put them away in the house. He then went and presented himself to his master.

'Gehazi,' Elisha said, 'where have you been?' 'Your servant has not been anywhere,' he replied. But Elisha said to him, 'My heart was present when someone left his chariot to meet you; you have taken money.'

And Gehazi left his presence a leper, white as snow.

Happened in about 850 BC
Written down between 600 and 500 BC

Leprosy is a chronic infective disease. It affects the skin and the *leprosy*
nerves. The skin becomes discoloured and scabby, limbs can lose
their power and become senseless and deformed. It is sometimes
called 'the living death'. It grows gradually but it can heal quite
quickly.

Moses law had laid down strict rules about all diseases. A person
with suspected leprosy was to report to the local priest. Priests were *priests*
from earliest times doctors in the primitive sense, not unlike a *doctors*
modern homoeopathic doctor — they examined a patient's stars, *homoeo-*
determined his 'spiritual light and darkness', and they foretold future *pathy*
events. If the priest suspected an infectious disease he was to
isolate the patient for seven days and if leprosy was confirmed he
was to send the patient outside the town.

A leper had to tear his clothes, leave his hair untidy and shout
'unclean' if anyone came near. His stricken family would leave food *unclean*
for him outside the gate of the town each day. If he recovered the
priest had to go out to him and confirm that he was 'clean' again.
Recovery was rare.

Healing can be accelerated by the cooperation of the patient. If he *healing*
has faith in the cure or the curer he can join in the operation. People
like Naaman had primitive beliefs in the power of things like baptism *baptism*
and the number 7: emerging from water was like emerging from the
womb at birth, putting off the former fish-like existence and
changing into 'the new man'; and 7, signifying perfection, had a
magical value in several cultures.

The River Jordan from north to south is about 120 km (70 miles) as *Jordan*
the crow flies but because it twists its muddy way down the valley it
measures 320 km (200 miles) as the fish swims — not an attractive
river for foreigners (see map 2).

36 Hosea—'Come back to me my love'

**

from Hosea 1, 4, 11 and 14 : Jerusalem Bible

The word of Yahweh that was addressed to Hosea:

When Israel was a child I loved him,
and I called him out of Egypt.
I was like someone who lifts an infant close against his cheek;
stooping down to him I gave him his food.

Sons of Israel, listen to the word of Yahweh:
there is no fidelity, no tenderness,
no knowledge of God in the country,
only perjury and lies, slaughter, theft,
adultery and violence, murder after murder.
This is why the country is mourning, and all who live in it pine away,
even the wild animals and the birds of heaven;
the fish of the sea themselves are perishing.
Thus does a senseless people run to ruin.

I took them in my arms, yet they have not understood.
I led them with kindness and love,
but the more I called to them, the further they went from me.
My people are diseased through their disloyalty;
They call on Baal, but he does not cure them.
Israel, how could I give you up?
My heart recoils from it,
my whole being trembles at the thought,
I will not give rein to my fierce anger,
for I am God, not man:
I am the Holy One in your midst
and have no wish to destroy.

Yahweh will be roaring like a lion—
How he will roar!—
and his sons will come speeding from Egypt like a bird,
from Assyria like a dove,
and I will settle them in their homes
—it is Yahweh who speaks.

Let the wise man understand these words.
For the ways of Yahweh are straight,
and virtuous men walk in them
but sinners stumble.

In the Northern Kingdom from about 750 BC
Written at about the same time

The bad behaviour of the Northern people seemed to be connected *pollution*
with economic and ecological disintegration: the prophet claimed
that their unfaithful, selfish and violent ways of treating each other
were inseparable from the careless and ungodly treatment of their
surroundings; pollution would result and self-destruction, which
was all against 'the will of Yahweh'. But they took as much notice of
Hosea as people do of a sandwich-man in a busy market shouting, *Hosea*
'Repent!'

Hosea's wife had run off with other men and left him, so he knew all *adultery*
about the deadliness of being abandoned. (See note to 26 on
'adultery'.) Hosea's imagery made Yahweh the lover and the People
of Israel his wife. (Compare this with the conception of 'worship' in
notes to 30 and see 'Yahweh' in notes to 33.)

Hosea was against 'sin', the divine seed running to waste, and he
called for 'faithfulness'. See notes to 18 on 'sin' and 'faith'.

37   Micah—'Yahweh will reign'

from Micah 1, 3, 4 and 6 : Jerusalem Bible

The word of Yahweh that was addressed to Micah—his visions of Samaria and Jerusalem.

Listen now, you rulers of the House of Israel.
Are you not the ones who should know what is right,
you, enemies of good?

In the days to come
the Temple of Yahweh
will be lifted higher than the hills.
The peoples will stream to it; and they will say,
'Come, let us go up to the mountain of Yahweh,
to the Temple of God
so that he may teach us his ways.'
They will hammer their swords into ploughshares,
their spears into sickles.
Nation will not lift sword against nation,
there will be no more training for war.
Each man will sit under his vine and his fig tree,
with no one to trouble him.
The mouth of Yahweh has spoken it.

That day—it is Yahweh who speaks—
I will finally gather in the lame
and out of the lame and the weary
I will make a mighty nation.
Then will Yahweh reign over them
on the mountain of Zion
for ever.

Now listen to what Yahweh is saying;
stand up and listen.
This is what Yahweh asks of you:
only this, to act justly,
to love tenderly
and to walk humbly with your God.

The text of Micah was badly altered after his death but there still *Micah*
remains a clear outline of the man and his message. He was a
countryman with typical misgivings about town dwellers, rich
property owners, government orders and weak-willed priests. He *property*
had a red-hot social conscience. He condemned such social evils as
the expropriation of smallholders from their properties and of
peasants from the land; these had become widespread since King
Ahab's time (see reading 34). And he condemned child slavery,
money-grubbing priests and promotion-conscious prophets. To him *corruption*
the Holy City of Jerusalem was a sick joke.

The threat of the Assyrians from the north was, to Micah, the angry
hand of Yahweh out ot teach Israel a lesson. Living as he did in the
south on the Philistine border near Gath he was more aware of the
dangers of foreign powers than were the ruling classes in
Jerusalem. But they did not hear him. The exquisite simplicity of the
message in the last paragraph opposite fell on deaf ears.

Micah said destruction would come (see readings 38 and 41) and
that after a period of tears and humiliation (readings 42 to 46)
Yahweh would return to his holy mountain at Jerusalem (readings
47 and 48). There would be peace, other nations would turn to Israel
for guidance and Israel would produce a David-like hero, and he
would be a brave military deliverer, a god-sent 'Messiah' — see note *Messiah*
to 55.

38 Samaria falls

***

from 2 Kings 6, 12, and 16 to 18 : Jerusalem Bible

It happened after this that Ben-hadad king of Aram mustered his whole army and came to lay siege to Samaria. In Samaria there was a great famine, and so strict was the siege that one quarter-kab of wild onions sold for five shekels of silver. But Yahweh had caused the Aramaeans in their camp to hear the noise of a great army in the dusk and they had made off and fled for their lives.

Then the king of Aram prepared to attack Jerusalem. He besieged it but could not reduce it. It was then that Ahaz king of Judah reigned in Jerusalem. He sent messengers to Tiglath-pileser king of Assyria to say, 'Come and rescue me.' The king of Assyria granted his request and, going up against Damascus, he captured it and deported its population.

The king of Assyria invaded the whole country and, coming to Samaria, laid siege to it for three years. Then he captured Samaria and deported the Israelites to Assyria; he settled them in the cities of the Medes. (This happened because the Israelites had sinned against Yahweh their God who had brought them out of the land of Egypt.) And the king of Assyria brought people from Babylon and settled them in the towns of Samaria to replace the Israelites.

When Hezekiah son of Ahaz was twenty-five years old he became king of Judah and reigned in Jerusalem. He did what is pleasing to Yahweh, just as his ancestor David had done, keeping the commandments that Yahweh had laid down for Moses. And so Yahweh was with him, and he was successful in all that he undertook. He refused to serve the king of Assyria and he harassed the Philistines as far as Gaza.

Ben-hadad reigned in about 850 BC *and Samaria fell in 721* BC, *so this extract cover overs 100 years' history.*
It was written somewhere between 600 and 500 BC

The total effects of famine are difficult to imagine: there is no *famine* substitute for actually suffering it. To those who are cradled among people who talk of snacks and sweets and several courses and indigestion tablets, and many of whom fall ill and die of too much eating and drinking and smoking, 'famine' is a foreign word. It would be morbid to describe here the effects of starvation on the body, and consequently on the mind. It is enough to say that famine was common, and it was only one of many terrors. Add to it the fear *fear* of evil spirits and disease, and then add a siege with the eventual *evil spirits* prospect of losing everything and everyone you have grown up *disease* with. To guess at the daily terrors of their lives is difficult.

According to Assyrian records, almost 30 000 Samarian Israelites were carried off captive to Assyria, never to return. And in their place, captives from elsewhere in the Assyrian empire were brought to Samaria. So the Samaritans who descended from this mixed *Samaria* population were, in the eyes of the Hebrews down in Judah, bastards. They had neglected the pure worship of Yahweh and Yahweh had abandoned them to the rape of the Assyrian. They and their children were beyond the pale of God's mercy: that is what people said down in pure-blooded Judah.

39 Judah invaded

from Isaiah 36 and 37 : Jerusalem Bible

In the fourteenth year of Hezekiah king of Judah, Sennacherib king of Assyria attacked all the fortified towns of Judah and captured them. He sent a large force to King Hezekiah in Jerusalem. The cupbearer-in-chief took up a position near the conduit of the upper pool. The master of the palace, the secretary and the herald went out to him. The cupbearer-in-chief said to them, 'Say to Hezekiah, "The great king of Assyria says: What makes you so confident? Who are you relying on, to dare to rebel against me?" ' And to the people sitting on the ramparts he called out, 'Do not let Hezekiah delude you by saying: Yahweh will save you. Has any god of any nation saved his country from the power of Assyria? Where are the gods of Samaria? Did they save Samaria?'

They kept silence and said nothing in reply. They went to Hezekiah and reported this. King Hezekiah covered himself with sackcloth and went to the Temple of Yahweh. He sent the elders to the prophet Isaiah. They said to him, 'The king of Assyria has sent to insult the living God.'

Isaiah replied, 'Do not be afraid of the words you have heard or the blasphemies of the king of Assyria. He will return to his own country.'

The same night the angel of Yahweh went out and struck down 185 000 men in the Assyrian camp. In the early morning when it was time to get up, there they lay, so many corpses.

Sennacherib returned home.

Happened in 701 BC
Written at about the same time

More terrified people. Psychological warfare — those mind-twisting
megaphones across no man's land. Few soldiers deny they have   *propaganda*
prayed in the battlefield. The atmosphere was conjured up in these   *prayer*
verses from Byron's poem (written about 1800):

'The Assyrian came down like a wolf on the fold,
And his cohorts were gleaming in purple and gold;
And the sheen of their spears was like stars on the sea,
When the blue wave rolls nightly on deep Galilee.

'Like the leaves of the forest when Summer is green,
That host with their banners at sunset were seen.
Like the leaves of the forest when Autumn was blown,
That host on the morrow lay wither'd and strown.

'For the Angel of Death spread his wings on the blast,
And breathed in the face of the foe as he pass'd;
And the eyes of the sleepers wax'd deadly and chill,
And their hearts but once heaved, and for ever grew still!

'And there lay the rider distorted and pale,
With the dew on his brow and the rust on his mail;
And the tents were all silent, the banners, alone,
The lances unlifted, the trumpet unblown.'

Was it an epidemic among the Assyrians? The inhabitants of   *epidemic*
Jerusalem thanked their 'god of life'. No one was cynical about   *disease*
such things. Even the ideas of 'chance' and 'good luck' were in their   *luck*
minds connected with 'the bountiful gifts of the god of life' in those
days (see notes to 64 on 'luck').

For 'Isaiah' see notes to 45.

40 'There will be a return to integrity' —Jeremiah

*

from Jeremiah 23 : Jerusalem Bible

Doom for the shepherds who allow my flock to be destroyed and scattered — it is Yahweh who speaks! This is what Yahweh says about the shepherds of my people:

They are quick only in doing wrong
and powerful only in crime.
Yes, even prophet and priest are godless,
I have found their wickedness even in my own house.

In the prophets of Samaria
I have seen nauseating things:
they prophesied in the name of Baal
and led my people Israel astray.

And in the prophets of Jerusalem
I have seen horrors;
from the prophets of Jerusalem
godlessness has spread throughout the land.

Do not listen to what those prophets say:
they are deluding you,
they retail visions of their own,
and not what comes from the mouth of Yahweh.

Right, I will take care of you for your misdeeds—it is Yahweh who speaks! But the remnant of my flock I myself will gather and bring back to their pastures; no fear, no terror for them any more; not one shall be lost—it is Yahweh who speaks!

See, the days are coming—it is Yahweh who speaks—
when I will raise a virtuous Branch for David,
who will reign as true king and be wise,
practising honesty and integrity in the land.
In his days Judah will be saved
and Israel dwell in confidence.
And this is the name he will be called:
Yahweh-our-integrity.

This passage concerns the situation in the Southern Kingdom in about 600 BC
Written at about the same time

Jeremiah was the son of a country priest in a small town near Jerusalem. He, like Micah and other prophets, grew up in a society which offended him. He loved the country and did not want to enter public life but, after a vivid dream, he felt compelled. His message was similar to Micah's — see reading 37 — but his preaching of it got him into trouble. He was at first expelled from the temple. When he took to writing, his manifestos were publicly destroyed, he was put in the stocks, he was flogged, imprisoned, charged with treason and thrown into a muddy pit to die. He has often been connected with Isaiah's picture of 'the suffering servant' — see reading 46.

Jeremiah

Since about 650 BC bad King Manasseh had allowed too many Assyrian preoccupations to be imported — things like human sacrifices, necromancy and astrology. These had eclipsed much of the simple worship of Yahweh. King Josiah however had since cleared out the temple and discovered a book of ancient law (perhaps Deuteronomy — see below) and from it had started a religious reform. But Jeremiah said that this reform was only superficial and the heart of the people was still with the Assyrians. And he warned that, because of their schizophrenia, cruel King Nebuchadnezzar of Babylon would soon crush them.

law

Schizophrenia refers to a divided personality, the thoughts and feelings being divorced from the actions. In its mild form it can be recognized by most people in themselves. Its opposite is 'integrity' which means, literally, 'being undisturbed'. To integrate is to make into a unit. In mathematics, an integer is an unbroken number. In the Jewish mind, integrity meant 'health' (see notes to 63) and 'righteousness' (see notes to 16).

schizo-phrenia

integrity

'The Book of Deuteronomy'. For a sample of its laws see 'unclean' in notes to 143, and of its interpretations see 'Manna' in notes to 78, and for its famous summary of all Jewish laws see reading 102 with its notes.

Deutero-nomy

41 Jerusalem falls

***

from 2 Kings 24 and 25, and Jeremiah 29 to 31 : Jerusalem Bible

At that time the troops of Nebuchadnezzar king of Babylon marched on Jerusalem and the city was besieged. King Nebuchadnezzar himself came while his troops were besieging it. Then the king of Judah and his officers surrendered to the king of Babylon. King Nebuchadnezzar carried off all the treasures of the royal palace and of the Temple of Yahweh, and broke up the golden furnishings that Solomon had made. He carried off into exile in Babylon all the men of distinction, the blacksmiths and metalworkers and all men capable of bearing arms. Only the poorest people in the country were left behind. And he made Zedekiah king of Jerusalem.

This is the text of the letter that the prophet Jeremiah sent from Jerusalem to those elders whom Nebuchadnezzar had led away into exile: 'Yahweh the God of Israel says to all exiles deported to Babylon, "Build houses, settle down; plant gardens and eat what they produce; take wives and have sons and daughters. Work for the good of the country; pray on its behalf. For only when seventy years are over will I visit you and bring you back to this place." '

And Yahweh addressed this to Jeremiah: 'Write all the words I have spoken to you in a book, for the days are coming when I will make a new covenant with Israel, not like the one I made with their ancestors on the day I took them out of Egypt. They broke that covenant. No, this is the new covenant I will make: I will plant my Law deep within them, writing it on their hearts. Then I will be their God and they will know me, the least no less than the greatest.'

Zedekiah rebelled against Babylon. King Nebuchadnezzar came with his whole army, entered Jerusalem and burned down the Temple, the royal palace and all the houses, and the troops demolished the walls. He put out Zedekiah's eyes and carried him off with the remainder of the population to Babylon.

Thus Judah was deported from its land.

Jerusalem was captured in 597 BC and finally destroyed in 587 BC
Written some time before about 500 BC

This exile in Babylon was for Judah a blessing in disguise. During *exile* their exile they thought and wrote and rethought all that had happened from the beginning. Most of their writings or 'scriptures' *scriptures* were completed during this period.

These exiles from Judah crystallized the religion called Judaism. *Judaism* From this time the word 'Jew' appeared. Their understanding of the *Jew* nature of God deepened. They did not attempt to hide their primitive past. On the contrary, they told every detail in their Scriptures, good and bad. So at last the Jews emerged, the 'Yehudi', and the modern form of their religion is commonly considered to have begun during this period.

All that had been built in Jerusalem since Solomon during the past 400 years was now gone; worst of all, the two tablets of stone on which were written the Moses-law (said to be kept inside the Ark of *Moses-law* the Covenant, housed inside the Holy of Holies, that is the sacred centre of the Temple of Yahweh) were destroyed. Disaster. But out *Temple* of it a deeper understanding about laws: if their laws were truly *law* given by God, that is, if they were in tune with the mind of the creator, wouldn't they be written in the hearts of his creatures? They *heart* were more useful there, and safer: no one could interfere any more.

Prophets were now different from the days of Samuel. They were *prophets* still the keepers of the nation's conscience but now they turned their attention more to the future. They 'prophesied' in the modern sense of the word.

42   Lamentations over Jerusalem

from Lamentations 1 and 3: Authorized Version

How doth the city sit solitary, that was full of people! She that was princess among the provinces, how is she become a widow! She weepeth sore in the night and her tears are on her cheeks. Among all her lovers she hath none to comfort her; all her friends have dealt treacherously with her, they are become her enemies.

Judah is gone into captivity. She dwelleth among the heathen. She findeth no rest: all her persecutors overtook her.

The ways of Zion do mourn, because none come to the solemn feasts; all her gates are desolate; her enemies prosper.

And from the daughter of Zion all her beauty is departed: her princes are gone without strength. Is it nothing to you, all ye that pass by? Behold, and see if there be any sorrow like unto my sorrow.

The Lord's mercies fail not; they are new every morning. The Lord is good unto them that wait for him. It is good that a man should quietly wait for the Lord. He sitteth alone and keepeth silence if so be there may be hope.

This refers to the fall of Jerusalem between 597 and 587 BC
Possibly written during that time but may have been written nearer about 500 BC

The five poems in 'The Book of Lamentations' have been traditionally connected with Jeremiah. They were used in worship among the Jews in exile.

Jeremiah

See 'lament' in notes to 25.

The poetry and music of ritualistic lamentation among the Jews at this time was not melodious. Harp accompaniments gave a lop-sided 'rumbling' rhythm and the human voice expressed 'screeches, roars and wails'! The process was connected with the more ancient Sūmerian word meaning 'hurricane', and the voice of the storm of course had long indicated the waking of the fertility god from his slumber (see reading 33).

lament
harp

wind

In drama today the Greek word *catharsis* still describes the releasing and refreshing effect of a tragedy. And in medicine a 'cathartic' is a purgative. The Greeks were referring to the same lamentation formula as the Jews. And perhaps the same formula can be detected in people who crowd at an accident or an execution, wrestling and boxing, bull-fighting, hunting or murder trials. And, if newspapers are anything to go by, it looks as if the human species still has a fundamental need for the lamentation formula.

catharsis

43 'Remember Jerusalem'—a Jewish song

*

from Psalm 137 : Jerusalem Bible

Beside the streams of Babylon
we sat and wept
at the memory of Zion,
leaving our harps
hanging on the poplars there.

For we had been asked
to sing to our captors,
to entertain those who had carried us off:
'Sing' they said
'some hymns of Zion.'

How could we sing
one of Yahweh's hymns
in a pagan country?

Jerusalem, if I forget you,
may my right hand wither!

If I do not count Jerusalem the greatest of my joys
may I never speak again!

Psalms were sung from about 1000 BC
They were mainly written down between about 500 and 200 BC

Very little is known about the life of the Jewish exiles in Babylon. *exile*
Though they could not worship Yahweh in a temple any longer they *worship*
learned to worship him in other ways. They met on their Sabbath to
read their Scriptures and pray and sing songs. The psalm opposite
was one of their songs, though, as it shows, much of the hope
spoken of by prophets like Micah and Jeremiah seemed to have
been given up. It was more of a lament.

The type of worship developed during that period of exile was the
foundation of later synagogue worship which grew up in every *synagogue*
Jewish community when they returned to Judah.

Other Jews were dispersed in Egypt for example. In about 1900 *dispersion*
papyri were discovered which spoke in detail of a colony of them on
the island of Elephantine (modern Aswan) about 950 km (600 miles)
up the Nile. There was another at Alexandria. And there is evidence
of several others in the Armenian parts of Russia, Turkey and Iran.
But, unlike the Babylonian Jews, few if any of these colonies
returned to Judah.

'Pagan' for the Jews referred to any ethnic group outside their own *pagan*
nation. It was not very polite. It meant to the Jews 'rustic and rather
illiterate'. Heathens and Barbarians were pagans to them, yet, at the
other end of the scale, so were the more intellectual Greeks (reading
51).

Elsewhere non-Jews were called 'gentiles' which, in Hebrew, meant *gentiles*
roughly 'other nations'. Its equivalent in Aryan languages was
connected with 'procreation' and through Latin and Greek a whole
family of words has reached modern English: gentile, gentle
and gentleman; genitive, genitals and genesis; generous, generate
and general — to name but a few.

So the point is this: the word 'gentile' to Jews meant dim and pagan
yet to non-Jews is engendered a whole host of civilized ideas! The
Jews, in their turn, had treated the Egyptian word 'Hebrew' in
precisely the same way. (See note to 10 on 'Hebrews'.)

44 Ezekiel—'Dry bones'

***

from Ezekiel 1 and 37 : Jerusalem Bible

In the thirtieth year, as I was among the exiles on the bank of the river, heaven opened and I saw visions from God. The hand of Yahweh was laid on me, and he carried me away by the spirit and set me down in the middle of a valley, a valley full of bones. He made me walk up and down among them. There were vast quantities of these bones on the ground the whole length of the valley; and they were quite dried up.

He said to me, 'Son of Man, can these bones live?' I said, 'You know, Lord Yahweh.' He said, 'Prophesy over these bones. Say, "Dry bones, hear the word of Yahweh. The Lord Yahweh says: I shall cover you with skin and give you breath, and you will live; and you will learn that I am Yahweh." '

I prophesied as I had been ordered. While I was prophesying, there was a noise, a sound of clattering; and the bones joined together. I looked, and saw that they were covered with sinews; flesh was growing on them and skin was covering them, but there was no breath in them. He said to me, 'Prophesy to the breath; prophesy, son of man. Say, "Come from the four winds, breath; breathe on these dead; let them live!" I prophesied as he had ordered me, and the breath entered them; they came to life again and stood up on their feet, a great, an immense army.

Then he said, 'Son of man, these bones are the whole House of Israel. They keep saying, "Our bones are dried up, our hope has gone; we are as good as dead." So prophesy. Say to them, "The Lord Yahweh says this: I am now going to open your graves; I mean to raise you from your graves, my people, and lead you back to the soil of Israel. And I shall put my spirit in you, and you will know that I, Yahweh, have done this." '

The 'river' is the Euphrates in Mesopotamia.

'Son of man' in these Jewish writings usually meant no more than 'man'.

son of man

What is 'life'? Does it start at conception or at birth? Does it end when hearts stop beating or movement ceases? What exactly is it? In Hebrew a single word stood for 'breath' and 'wind' and 'spirit'. These three things, in their minds, were from the one source: the Living God.

life

breath

God

This vision (dream) contains the idea of the rising of a dead body to new life. It is in fact a very primitive notion. Long before the inception of the Hebrew Passover idea Canaanite tribes among others had been celebrating the miraculous revival of life in springtime. So the seeds of the idea of resurrection lay deep in the human mind.

visions
dreams

resurrection

Man, with all living creatures, animal and plant alike, is annually conditioned, whether he likes it or not, by nature's revival in spring. It is not surprising that he has learnt to be an optimist, to hope against hope in his daily affairs. His hope of some sort of resurrection is as natural as any other instinct.

In India soon after this time, Buddha was teaching that at death a man's soul migrated to another body and each life brought him nearer to complete purification. A similar doctrine was later popular in Greece and elsewhere (notes to 148) and today it is found among theosophists and spiritualists. It is called 'reincarnation'.

Buddha

reincar-
nation

45 Isaiah—'Comfort'

from Isaiah 40 and 52 : Authorized Version

Comfort ye, comfort ye my people, saith your God. Speak ye comfortably to Jerusalem, and cry unto her, that her warfare is accomplished, that her iniquity is pardoned.

How beautiful upon the mountains are the feet of him that bringeth good tidings, that publisheth peace.

The voice of him that crieth in the wilderness, 'Prepare ye the way of the Lord, make straight in the desert a highway for our God. Every valley shall be exalted, every mountain and hill shall be made low. The crooked shall be made straight, and the glory of the Lord shall be revealed.'

O Zion, O Jerusalem, that bringest good tidings, lift up thy voice with strength. Be not afraid. Say unto the cities of Judah, 'Behold, the Lord God will come.'

To whom will ye liken God? It is he that sitteth upon the circle of the earth, that stretcheth out the heavens as a tent to dwell in. Who hath measured the waters in the hollow of his hand, and comprehended the dust of the earth in a measure, and weighed the mountains and the hills in a balance? Behold, the nations are counted as the small dust of the balance. Hast thou not heard that the Creator of the earth giveth power to the faint? And they that wait upon him shall mount up with wings as eagles.

Jerusalem finally fell in 587 BC
Probably written during the following fifty years

Approximately three different authors wrote 'The Book of the Prophet Isaiah'. The first thirty-nine chapters 'Proto-Isaiah' were possibly largely written by the prophet himself (reading 39 is a sample). The next sixteen chapters, 'Deutero-Isaiah', were written more than fifty years later by an unknown hand for the exiles in Babylon just before their return to Judah. These chapters are among the most sublime in the whole of the Old Testament. (This and the next reading are examples.) The third section, written in about 500 BC, is less striking.

Isaiah

Prophets are said to be 'inspired teachers' or 'revealers of truth' or 'interpreters'. Anyone under the sun, therefore, is capable of prophecy. But it is a hard fact that a prophetic person, whether he is revealing truth to himself or to other people, will always be unpopular: and he will be most unpopular with the one he loves most: and if he is a normal person the one he loves most will be himself. (See the remarks on loving in reading 102, and also notes to 40 on 'Jeremiah' and the last saying in reading 60.).

prophets
revelation

true

The prophet's problem therefore was to stand aside from himself and to allow the truth to flow through him. He was not required to express his opinion about it. The reading opposite displays the majestic authority of a true prophet.

authority

opinion

Feet: the most neglected servants of the body; strong, faithful, long-suffering, painstaking, blind yet sensitive, obedient; always toeing the line for an avaricious body, always taken for granted, always bearing the brunt of progress in silence, standing in the dirt so that other members may be elevated from it; often ridiculed, usually kept out of sight, yet innocent. Perhaps the mysterious servant in reading 46 was a pair of feet!

feet

46   Isaiah—'The perfect servant'

***

from Isaiah 52, 42 and 53 : Authorized Version

Break forth into joy, sing together, ye waste places of Jerusalem; put on thy beautiful garments, O Jerusalem.

Behold my servant! He shall be very high. Kings shall shut their mouths at him; for that which had not been told them, shall they see and consider. Behold, I have put my spirit upon him.

When we see him, there is no beauty that we should desire him. He is despised and rejected; a man of sorrows, and acquainted with grief.

He was despised, and we esteemed him not. He made his grave with the wicked. He had done no violence, neither was any deceit in his mouth.

Yet the pleasure of the Lord shall prosper in his hands because he was wounded for our transgressions, and with his stripes we are healed.

Jerusalem finally fell in 587 BC
Probably written during the following fifty years

Who was this servant? There have been many theories. But no one *servant*
knows. These passages outlined the silhouette of a humble and
innocent servant who had been punished for someone else's crimes,
who was unpopular and physically unattractive, and yet because of *popular*
his suffering, in some unexplained way, had brought about healing *suffering*
and optimism among others so great that even the mighty were, or
would be, silenced. This mysterious unnamed figure has become a
familiar cipher in both the Jewish and the Christian equations.

'Behold!' meant, 'Take a look at this!' *behold*

'To esteem' meant 'to consider' or 'to weigh up the value of'. *esteem*

'Transgressions' were 'wanderings' beyond the bounds of the law, *trans-*
in this case the Moses law. *gressions*

'Sins', similarly, were any thoughts or deeds which were against the *sins*
wishes of God. And these 'wishes' of the Creator were written in the
hearts of his creatures — they knew them well enough.

47 Rebuilding Jerusalem

from Ezra 1 and 5, and Nehemiah 2 to 4 : Jerusalem Bible

Now in the first year of Cyrus king of Persia, Yahweh roused his spirit to fulfil the word spoken through Jeremiah. Thus Cyrus displayed a proclamation throughout the kingdom: 'Yahweh, the God of Heaven, has given me all the kingdoms of the earth; he has ordered me to build a Temple in Jerusalem, in Judah. Whoever there is among you of all his people, let him go up to Jerusalem to build the Temple of Yahweh. And let each survivor, wherever he lives, be helped by the people with voluntary offerings.'

Then the heads of families of Judah and the priests, and in fact all whose spirit had been roused by God, prepared to go and rebuild the Temple; and all their neighbours gave them every assistance with silver, gold, goods, cattle, quantities of costly gifts and with voluntary offerings of every kind.

King Cyrus took the Temple vessels which Nebuchadnezzar had carried away from Jerusalem, and handed them over to Sheshbazzar of Judah; he appointed Sheshbazzar high commissioner. Sheshbazzar therefore came and laid the foundations of the Temple on its original site in Jerusalem. So the Jews—the priests, the officials and other responsible persons—said, 'Let us start!' and with willing hands they set about the good work.

When Sanballet the Horonite came to know that repairs to the walls of Jerusalem were going forward, he flew into a rage. He ridiculed the Jews and in front of his kinsmen, the men of Samaria, he exclaimed, 'What are these pathetic Jews trying to do? Let them build; a jackal jumping on their wall will soon knock the stones down again!' And he conspired with the Arabs to come and attack Jerusalem.

From that day onwards, the men of Judah were armed. As each builder worked he wore his sword at his side, from break of day till the stars appeared.

The Jews began to return to Jerusalem from 538 BC *— following the Edict of King Cyrus.*
Probably written about half a century later
For 'the word spoken through Jeremiah' see reading 40.

The first temple built by Solomon (reading 30) had been destroyed fifty years before (reading 41.) This second temple was not nearly so splendid. The Book of Ezra records that when the old men who remembered the first temple saw the foundations of this one they wept aloud. It stood for about 350 years till it was sacked by Syrian soldiers (reading 51). The third and much larger temple started by Herod the Great in 20 BC was destroyed in AD 70 by Roman soldiers. (It is the temple of New Testament writings — see reading 58 onwards.)

Temple

Today the site is occupied by a magnificent Moslem mosque which has dominated the Holy City for the past thirteen centuries. Known as the Dome of the Rock, its dome covers the rock from which the Prophet Mohammed was said to have ascended into heaven in about AD 630, (see Map 4). The real 'Zion' of the Islam religion is of course in Mecca. However, their Jerusalem shrine serves to remind everyone that Mohammedan roots spring from deep in the hearts of the Jewish and Christian religions: these three equations have very many common factors.

Mohammed

Sanballet and his Samaritan countrymen could not be blamed for their contempt. These Jews had labelled them a bastard nation (see notes to 32 and 38 on Samaria).

Samaria

48 'The city of peace'—a Jewish song

**

from Psalm 122 : Jerusalem Bible

How I rejoiced when they said to me,
  'Let us go to the house of Yahweh!'
And now our feet are standing
  in your gateways, Jerusalem.

Jerusalem restored! The city,
  one united whole!
Here the tribes come up,
  the tribes of Yahweh,

they come to praise Yahweh's name,
  as he ordered Israel,
here where the tribunals of justice are,
  the royal tribunals of David.

Pray for peace in Jerusalem,
  'Prosperity to your houses!
Peace inside your city walls!
  Prosperity to your palaces!'

Since all are my brothers and friends,
  I say, 'Peace be with you!'
Since Yahweh our God lives here,
  I pray for your happiness.

Psalms were sung from about 1000 BC
They were mainly written down between about 500 and 200 BC

The modest new second temple of Jerusalem (see reading 47) served as the centre of Israel's life after the return from Exile. Little is known about its size or construction but it is certain that the people had a great affection for it. Yahweh for them was enthroned in his temple.

second temple

The 'Book of Psalms', the 'Psalter', was the hymn book of the second temple. It has nourished the thoughts of Jews and Christians to this day. It was the musical foundation of congregational worship and, although small provincial synagogues sprang up elsewhere, none were ever considered to touch the dramatic scenes of priestly sacrifice which these psalms sustained.

Psalms

worship synagogues

There are 150 Psalms. One-third of them praise the creator for his excellent handiwork (see readings 22, 29, 31 and 48) or thank him for his virtues. Another third beg him to come and help (see reading 43). The remaining third are a mixture of these two and difficult to classify. It is interesting that the two main types of psalm correspond to the very primitive double-thought about gods: on the one hand 'to offer up' and on the other 'to call down'. See notes to 33 on 'gods' and notes to 7 on 'give'.

Psalms

Happiness was considered to be a gift (see notes to 64).

happy

49 The story of Job

from Job 1 to 3 and 42 : Jerusalem Bible

There was once a man of Uz called Job: a sound and honest man who feared God and shunned evil. Seven sons and three daughters were born to him. And he owned sheep, camels, oxen and donkeys, and many servants besides. He was a man of mark among all the people.

One day, Yahweh said to Satan, 'Where have you been?' 'Round the earth,' he answered, 'roaming about.' So Yahweh asked him, 'Did you notice my servant Job? There is no one like him on the earth.' 'Yes,' Satan said, 'but Job is not God-fearing for nothing, is he? You have blessed all he undertakes, and his flocks throng the countryside. But, lay a finger on his possessions: I warrant you, he will curse you to your face.' 'Very well,' Yahweh said, 'all he has is in your power. But keep your hands off his person.' So Satan left the presence of Yahweh.

A messenger came to Job. He said, 'The Sabaeans swept down on your oxen at the plough and carried them off. Your servants they put to the sword: I alone escaped to tell you.' He had not finished speaking when another messenger arrived. 'Fire,' he said, 'has burnt up all your sheep and your shepherds too: I alone escaped.' Another messenger arrived and said, 'The Chaldaeans have raided your camels and made off with them; they put your servants to the sword: I alone escaped to tell you.' And another messenger arrived and said, 'Your sons and daughters were at their meal, when suddenly from the wilderness a gale sprang up and the house fell on the young people. They are dead: I alone escaped to tell you.'

Job rose and tore his gown and, falling to the ground, he worshipped and said, 'Naked I came from my mother's womb, naked I shall return. Yahweh gave, Yahweh has taken back. Blessed be the name of Yahweh!' In all this misfortune Job offered no insult to God.

Once again Yahweh said to Satan, 'Did you notice my servant Job?' Satan replied, 'Lay a finger on his flesh, and he will curse you.' 'Very well,' Yahweh said, 'he is in your power. But spare his life.' So Satan left the presence of Yahweh. He struck Job down with malignant ulcers from the sole of his foot to the top of his head. Job took a piece of pot to scrape himself and went and sat in the ash pit.

His friends, looking at him from a distance, could not recognize him; they wept and spoke never a word, so sad a sight he made. In the end it was Job who broke the silence and said to Yahweh, 'I know that you are all powerful: what you conceive, you can perform. I have been holding forth on matters I cannot understand, with my empty-headed words. I retract all I have said, and in dust and ashes I repent.'

Yahweh restored Job's fortunes and his friends. After his trials, Job lived on until he was old and saw his children's children. Then he died, an old man and full of days.

The story of Job (pronounced jobe), the dramatization of a well-known Hebrew cipher—the persecuted man whose humble patience was eventually rewarded. It has also been found in the folk tales of several other religions.

Job

What Job said in the fourth paragraph opposite has been a familiar saying among mourners burying their dead. The key note is 'thanks'.

death
thanks

The last sentence of the fourth paragraph is perhaps the key to the whole of the Job story—though there is disagreement about it. The problem of human pain has always been a difficult one—see notes to 46, 80 and 152 on 'suffering'. Much may be learnt from people who work in hospitals.

pain

'Satan'—see notes to 68 on the Devil.

'Worship'—see notes to 7.

'Repent'—see notes to 59.

50 The story of Jonah

**

from Jonah 1 to 3 : Jerusalem Bible

The word of Yahweh was addressed to Jonah: 'Up!' he said, 'Go to Nineveh, the great city, and inform them that their wickedness has become known to me.' Now Nineveh was a great city beyond compare. And Jonah decided to run away from Yahweh. He went down to Joppa and found a ship bound for Tarshish; he paid his fare and went aboard. But Yahweh unleashed a violent wind on the sea, and there was such a great storm at sea that the ship threatened to break up. The sailors took fright, and each of them called on his own god. Jonah, however, had gone below and fallen fast asleep. The boatswain came upon him and said, 'Get up! Call upon your god! Perhaps he will spare us a thought.' Then they said to him, 'Where do you come from?' He replied, 'I am a Hebrew and I worship Yahweh, the God of heaven, who made the sea and the land.' The sailors said, 'What have you done?' He told them that he was trying to escape from Yahweh. They were seized with terror at this and said, 'What are we to do with you, to make the sea grow calm for us?' For the sea was growing rougher and rougher. He replied, 'Throw me into the sea, for it is my fault that this violent storm has happened to you.' They then called on Yahweh and said, 'O Yahweh, do not let us perish for taking this man's life.' And taking hold of Jonah they threw him into the sea; and the sea grew calm again.

Yahweh had arranged that a great fish should be there to swallow Jonah; and Jonah remained in the belly of the fish for three days. From the belly of the fish he prayed to Yahweh.

Then Yahweh spoke to the fish, which vomited Jonah onto the shore.

The word of Yahweh was addressed a second time to Jonah: 'Up!' he said, 'Go to Nineveh, the great city, and preach to them as I told you to.' Jonah set out and went to Nineveh in obedience to the word of Yahweh.

Story written about 400 BC

Since they had returned from Babylon and resettled securely in their fortified town, these Jews had become rather self-righteous, telling each other that they were Yahweh's chosen race and that everyone else was wicked.

righteous

For 'righteous' see notes to 16. 'Self-righteousness' was the process of measuring oneself up against oneself rather than up against a lofty conception of the creator. It was easier to succeed and it led to smugness.

The author of this reading objected to this smugness. He said that, if his fellow Jews were really blessed with an enlightened vision of the creator's mind, they should share it with other nations, not keep it to themselves. The reading is therefore a satire. 'Jonah' meant 'dove' and stood for Israel. Nineveh, in the minds of the Jews at that time, stood for gentile irreligion. In the satire, Jonah did not want to enlighten the gentiles. He wanted to see them liquidated if possible! In fact he would sooner have died than share the Jewish vision with them.

Jonah

gentile

So the story of Jonah was a sort of 'parable', that is, a subtle device to expose a hidden meaning.

parable

The dove was widely regarded as a symbol of peace and reconciliation (readings 4 and 59). That idea of peace was not a passive pacifism but, in terms of the old fertility philosophy, it was an active fruitfulness, a state of bioplasmic balance within the self and the world. So the word-play of the story was clear: Jonah the dove tried to fly away from his duty and caused a storm, but learnt his lesson in a fish's belly (the word could also mean womb) and emerged to bring peace to the world at large.

dove

peace

51 The Greeks

from 1 Maccabees 1 : Jerusalem Bible

Alexander of Macedon defeated Darius, king of the Persians and Medes. And he undertook many campaigns, gained possession of many fortresses, and put the local kings to death. So he advanced to the ends of the earth, and subdued provinces, nations and princes, and they became his tributaries. But the time came when Alexander took to his bed, in the knowledge that he was dying. He summoned his comrades, who had been brought up with him from his youth, and divided his kingdom among them while he was still alive. Each of his comrades established himself in his own region. All assumed crowns after his death, they and their heirs after them for many years, bringing increasing evils upon the world.

From these there grew a sinful offshoot, Antiochus Epiphanes. He became king of the Greeks. Once Antiochus had seen his authority established, he determined to make himself king of Egypt. And he invaded Egypt in massive strength, with chariots and elephants and a great fleet. He engaged Ptolemy, king of Egypt, in battle. And Ptolemy turned and fled. The fortified cities of the land of Egypt were captured, and Antiochus plundered the country.

After his conquest of Egypt, Antiochus turned about and advanced on Israel. He pillaged Jerusalem and set it on fire, tore down its houses and wall, took the women and children captive and commandeered the cattle. Breaking into the Temple he stripped it of everything. He then went back to his own country, uttering words of extreme arrogance and leaving the place a shambles.

He issued a proclamation that all were to become a single people, each renouncing his particular customs. All the pagans conformed to the king's decree, and many Israelites chose to accept his religion. He appointed inspectors and anyone not obeying the king's command was put to death.

Yet there were many in Israel who stood firm. They chose death rather than profanation of the holy covenant, and they were executed. It was a dreadful wrath, forcing Israel into hiding.

Alexander the Great, at the age of 22 inspired by his beloved poet Homer, spread Greek civilization over the known western world and across Asia to India.

Alexander civilization

Note the gap of 150 years between the first two paragraphs opposite. It was then, in about 250 BC, that the Jews' Bible was translated at Alexandria from Hebrew into Greek. That 'Old Testament' was called the 'Septuagint' because it was said to have employed the work of seventy-two translators.

*Bible
Alexandria
testament*

Now the Ptolemies centred in Alexandria fought the Seleucids centred in Antioch: thus the territory around Judaea became the apple of discord between the Greeks of Egypt and the Greeks of Syria during this period.

Antioch

For the Greeks, the supreme god of the heavens was Zeus. His majesty is roughly represented in notes to 31 by the description of 'Yahweh'. Zeus inhabited not Mount Zion but Mount Olympus. This similarity between Zeus and Yahweh was not an accident. It was a simple process of evolution: the Greeks being of Aryan stock and the Hebrews being of Semitic stock had both inherited their funandmental thought-forms from Sūmer (in the Euphrates-cum-Tigris basin) since the Neolithic period (approximately 6000 to 3000 BC). Both 'Zeus' and 'Yahweh' derived from the Sūmerian god-word meaning 'juice of fecundity' or 'spermatazoa' or 'seed of life'. Though by 100 BC the conception of such names was less raw, still the thought-forms remained.

Zeus

Aryans

Sūmer

The two groups of races which appeared to have been influenced by that distant Sūmerian culture were 'Semitic' including Assyrians, Syrians, Phoenicians, Hebrews and Arabs; and 'Aryan' or 'Indo-Europeans' including Sanscrit-speaking Indians, Persians, Greeks and Latins. There were others, but the line is very difficult to draw. 'Sūmerian' should not be confused with 'Samarian' or 'Samaritan' (see note to reading 32 and others).

By the time of the third paragraph opposite Antiochus Epiphanes thought he himself was Zeus incarnate. When the Jews of Jerusalem refused to worship an erection of his image in their temple, he lost his temper. (It was the second temple — see note to 47.) Guerrilla warfare developed (reading 53); and alongside it, an aggressive belief in the incarnation of a military and political 'Messiah' — of Jewish stock (see notes to 55).

Antiochus

second temple

Messiah

'Pagan' — see note to 43.

52 'Let us now praise famous men'—a lecture

from Ecclesiasticus 44 : Authorized Version

Let us now praise famous men, and our fathers that begat us. The Lord hath wrought great glory by them through his power from the beginning. Such as did bear rule in their kingdoms, men renowned for their power, leaders of the people by their counsels and by their knowledge of learning, wise and eloquent in their instructions; such as found out musical tunes and recited verses in writing; rich men furnished with ability, living peaceably in their habitations: all these men were honoured in their generations and were the glory of their times.

And some there be which have no memorial, who are become as though they had never been born, and their children after them. But these were merciful men whose righteousness hath not been forgotten. Their seed shall remain for ever and their glory shall not be blotted out. Their bodies are buried in peace, but their name liveth for ever more.

Written in about 200 BC

This reading together with readings 51 and 53 comes from the *Apocrypha* 'Apocrypha' or 'hidden writings'. They were included by the Greek translators of the Old Testament (see notes to 51) but they were rejected by those purist Jews who would not speak Greek and who regarded them as 'pagan' (see notes to 43).

The value of the Apocrypha is that it fills in much of the hidden background between the end of the Old Testament and the *Testament* beginning of the New. The 'New Testament' is, of course, all writings between about AD 50 and 100 by people who believed that Jesus was the christ (see notes to 55 and readings 55 to 160). The apocryphal writings came from that vitalizing period of Greek supremacy. (The success of the Christian religion in the Roman Empire was borne within the language and thought-forms inherited from Greece.)

The writer of the Book of Ecclesiasticus was Ben Sira, a Jerusalem *Ben Sira* Jew, by trade a teacher with Greek ideas. He believed with the Greeks that a good man was a knowledgeable man, and the idea *good* harmonized with the Hebrew belief that a godly man was a law-abiding man (see note to 41 on laws). More is known about Ben Sira than any other scriptural writer BC.

With the authority of wisdom he gave pithy advice about friendship, *authority* children, giving, swearing, lying, adultery, scandalmongery, *wise* borrowing, moderation, money, parties, alcohol, dreams, doctors, prayer, work, death, astrology and the scriptures.

It was such liberal-minded Jews as Ben Sira who later formed the sect called the 'Sadducees', a political party which stood for the *Sadducees* interests of the priestly aristocracy (see notes to 11) and the rich. They were possibly named after Zadok the priest (readings 27 and 28).

53 The Romans

from 1 Maccabees 2, 3 and 8 : Jerusalem Bible

In those days Mattathias, the son of a priest, left Jerusalem. He saw the blasphemies that were being committed and said, 'Alas that I should have been born to witness the overthrow of my people, and the overthrow of the Holy City, and to sit by while she is delivered over to her enemies.' Raising his voice, Mattathias said, 'Even if every nation obeys the king, each forsaking its ancestral religion, I and my sons and my brothers will still follow the covenant of our ancestors. Heaven preserve us from forsaking the Law. We will not swerve either to right or to left.' As he finished speaking, he was fired with zeal and went through the town shouting at the top of his voice, 'Let everyone who has a fervour for the Law come out and follow me.' Then he fled with his sons into the hills, leaving all their possessions behind. He had five sons.

Soon they were joined by stout fighting men of Israel and they organized themselves into a fighting force. As the days of Mattathias were drawing to a close, he said to his sons, 'This is the time, my children, to have a burning fervour for the Law of our ancestors.' Then he blessed them, and died. And all Israel mourned him deeply.

Then his son Judas, called Maccabaeus, took over his command. All his brothers and all who had attached themselves to his father supported him, and they fought for Israel with a will. He was like a lion in his exploits, he engaged in battle after battle. He went through the towns of Judah and all evildoers were utterly confounded. His name resounded to the ends of the earth. His name even reached the king's ears.

Now Judas Maccabaeus had heard of the reputation of the Romans, their military strength, and their benevolence towards all who made common cause with them. They had subdued kings far and near, making themselves masters: the Gauls, the province of Spain, Asia, the Indian territory with Media, and the Greeks. Their influence was paramount. They had set up a senate where three hundred and twenty councillors debated daily how best to regulate public affairs. Judas sent envoys to Rome to conclude a treaty of peace and to enrol as allies and friends. The proposal met with the approval of the senators. Their alliance said: 'Good fortune attend the Romans and the Jewish nation by sea and land for ever; may sword and enemy be far from them.'

The Maccabaean Revolt started in 167 BC
Written in about 100 BC

The Maccabees like hammers, fired with zeal for the pure religion of   *Maccabees*
Moses, forged for themselves about seventy years of precarious
independence from the Syrians, and in smouldering cooperation
with the Romans who gave away nothing much. But in the process,
their compromises with the un-Jewish ways of the gentile world
cooled and split the affections of their followers.

By 100 BC two political parties had started to take shape. Each had
contempt for the other, which was a pity because their contribu-
tions to Jewish society were complementary. On the one hand, the
Sadducees (notes to 52), conservative in politics, wished to keep   *Sadducees*
the aristocratic priesthood (notes to 10 and 11) centred at the
Jerusalem temple (notes to 48) and for them the anointed 'Messiah'
(notes to 23 and 55) was to be the High Priest, and the 'Kingdom of
God' would come there and then in Judaea (notes to 137).

On the other hand, the Pharisees (notes to 63), socially separated   *Pharisees*
from the central priesthood, taught in the provincial synagogues
that those who followed their complex interpretations of the Moses-
law would be rewarded with resurrection from death and offered
membership of a Kingdom of Heaven ruled by a David-like warrior-
king (notes to 137 again).

These two parties tore the people apart in fierce and fruitless arguments so that the simple teaching of people like Jesus of Nazareth   *Jesus*
went by largely unheard.

54 'The burning fiery furnace' —a political cartoon

*

from Daniel 3 : Jerusalem Bible

King Nebuchadnezzar had a golden statue made which he erected in the province of Babylon. King Nebuchadnezzar then summoned the satraps, prefects, governors, counsellors, treasurers, judges, men of law, and all the provincial authorities to assemble and attend the dedication of the statue. The herald then made this proclamation: 'Men of all peoples, nations, languages! This is required of you: the moment you hear the sound of horn, pipe, lyre, trigon, harp, bagpipe, or any other instrument, you must prostrate yourselves and worship the golden statue erected by King Nebuchadnezzar. Those who do not prostrate themselves and worship shall be immediately thrown into the burning fiery furnace.'

And so the instant the people heard all the instruments they worshipped the statue. Some then came forward and laid information against the Jews. They said to King Nebuchadnezzar, 'O king, live for ever! You have issued a decree, O king, to the effect that everyone on hearing the sound of horn, pipe, lyre, trigon, harp, bagpipe or any other instrument is to prostrate himself and worship the golden statue; and anyone who does not worship is to be thrown into the burning fiery furnace. Certain Jews have ignored your command, O king; these men are Shadrach, Meshach and Abednego.'

Furious with rage, Nebuchadnezzar gave orders for the furnace to be made seven times hotter than usual, and he sent for Shadrach, Meshach and Abednego. They were then bound and thrown into the burning fiery furnace. The king's command was so urgent and the heat of the furnace was so fierce, that the men carrying Shadrach, Meshach, and Abednego were burnt to death by the flames from the fire.

Shadrach, Meshach and Abednego fell, still bound, into the burning fiery furnace, and they stood and walked in the heart of the flames. Then all three in unison began to sing, glorifying and blessing God. King Nebuchadnezzar sprang to his feet in amazement and shouted, 'Servants of the Most High God, come out, come here!' And from the heart of the fire out came the three men. The advisers of the king crowded round to examine them: the fire had had no effect on their bodies: not a hair of their heads had been singed, their cloaks were not scorched, no smell of burning hung about them. Nebuchadnezzar exclaimed: 'Blessed be the God of Shadrach, Meshach and Abednego, for there is no other god who can save like this.'

Antiochus Epiphanes reigned from 175 to 163 BC
This propaganda was probably written during the last years of his reign

The 'Book of Daniel' was the last of the Old Testament to have been written. It is rather peculiar. It is plain propaganda against Antiochus Epiphanes (see reading 51) but its characters are disguised as Babylonians like 'King Nebuchadnezzar' (see reading 41) at the time of the Exile four hundred years before.

Out of 'Daniel' have come several famous phrases in our language: 'feet of clay', 'the writing on the wall', 'a Belshazzar's feast'. It is a colourful story book.

The prophets had talked of a golden age to come after returning from Exile (e.g. readings 37, 40, 44 and 45). But it had not come. In fact what Antiochus was doing now was worse than anything during the past four centuries. Encouraged by Greek-minded Jews in Jerusalem (see notes to 52 and 53 on 'Sadducees') he set about importing by force Greek and Syrian customs (reading 51, paragraph 4). He housed his troops in the Jerusalem temple (notes to 48), he banned the Sabbath rest (reading 17) and the worship of Yahweh, he burned the scriptures publicly and killed all who were found in possession of them. Throughout Judaea and at the Jerusalem temple he erected altars for the worship of Zeus 'the Lord of Heaven' (see notes to 51) — the Jews were able to twist this title round in Hebrew so that it meant something like 'the Abominable Exterminator'! And he forced the Jews to drink pig stew — that may have been the origin of their belief that the swine was an 'unclean' animal.

In this un-golden age it was not surprising that propaganda like 'Daniel' was put about — there was much more of it than is contained in the Bible. It was called 'apocalypse' or 'revealing writing' and pointed to a future and spiritual golden age in the heavens, a place of mystery and miracle, supernatural wonders, and strange words, symbols, numbers and people — this story of 'the burning fiery furnace' is quite straight forward compared with some apocalypses. They were still being written in AD 100 (see readings 158 and 159) and were most popular among the faction of the Pharisees (notes to 53).

Daniel
Antiochus

Nebuchad-
nezzar

Belshazzar

Sadducees

second
temple
Sabbath
scriptures
Zeus

pigs

propaganda

apocalypse

Pharisees

55   John the Baptist—'Be prepared!'

***

from Matthew 3 and Luke 3 : Jerusalem Bible

In the fifteenth year of Tiberius Caesar's reign, when Pontius Pilate was governor of Judaea, and Herod tetrarch of Galilee, and during the pontificate of Annas and Caiaphas, the word of God came to John, son of Zechariah, in the wilderness. He went through the whole of Jordan district proclaiming a baptism of repentance. And this was his message: 'Repent, for the kingdom of heaven is close at hand.'

This was the man the prophet Isaiah spoke of when he said: 'A voice cries in the wilderness: Prepare a way for the Lord, make his paths straight.'

This man John wore a garment made of camel-hair with a leather belt round his waist, and his food was locusts and wild honey. People from Jerusalem and all Judaea and the whole of the Jordan district made their way to him, and as they were baptized by him in the river Jordan they confessed their sins.

When people asked him, 'What must we do, then?' he answered, 'If anyone has two tunics he must share with the man who has none, and the one with something to eat must do the same.'

A feeling of expectancy had grown among the people, who were beginning to think that John might be the Christ. So John declared before them all, 'I baptise you with water, but someone is coming—someone who is more powerful than I am, and I am not fit to undo the strap of his sandals. He will baptise you with the Holy Spirit.'

There were many other things he said to the people as well as this.

Probably happened between AD *25 and 30*
From various writings between AD *50 and 85*

A strange man by modern standards but a fairly common type of prophet at the time of the reading opposite.

John the
Baptist

This reading should come between readings 58 and 59 chronologically, but it fits better here as a hinge between the 'scriptures' of the Jews and the earliest writings of the so-called 'Christian' Jews, that is between the Old and New Testaments.

scriptures
Testaments
Bible

There was by this time in Judaea an electric sense of expectation. Since their return from Exile in Babylon, the Jews had been invaded first by the Greeks and now by the Romans. The prophets had increasingly forecast a visit to Earth from God in human guise. He would save them from all their enemies and establish a heavenly kingdom on Earth. Their word for this kingly visitor was 'Messiah'. When the translation of the Hebrew Scriptures into Greek was ordered in about 250 BC, 'Messiah' became *Christos*, in English 'The Christ'. (Subsequently, those people who claimed that Jesus of Nazareth was 'The Christ' were called 'Christians'.)

expectation

prophets

Messiah

The Christ
Christians

At this time there were many prophets about like this son of a Jerusalem priest. They had various messages. There were plenty of anxious people who would listen to them. It was common practice to persuade people to change course and, having been persuaded, these people would undergo a 'baptism' that was a ceremonial ducking in water. This ceremony was thought to wash away the effect of their 'sins' and make new men of them.

baptism

The quotation from Isaiah is in reading 45. The Christian document called 'The Gospel according to Saint Matthew' was written by a Jew who was particularly anxious to make every possible link with Jewish Scriptures so that his Jewish readers would be happy to accept his authority as a writer.

Isaiah
Matthew

56   Mary discovers she is going to have a baby

***

from Luke 1 : New English Bible

In the sixth month, the angel Gabriel was sent from God to a town in Galilee called Nazareth, with a message for a girl betrothed to a man named Joseph, a descendant of David; the girl's name was Mary. The angel went in and said to her, 'The Lord is with you, most favoured one!'

But she was deeply troubled by what he said and wondered what this greeting might mean. Then the angel said to her, 'Do not be afraid, Mary, for God has been gracious to you; you shall conceive and bear a son, and you shall give him the name Jesus. He will be great; he will bear the title 'Son of the Most High'; the Lord will give him the throne of his ancestor David, and his reign shall never end.'

'How can this be,' said Mary, 'when I have no husband?'

The angel answered, 'With God nothing will prove impossible. The Holy Spirit will overshadow you; and for that reason the child to be born will be called holy, "Son of God".'

Mary said, 'I am the Lord's servant. As you have spoken, so be it.' Then the angel left her.

Happened between 7 and 5 BC
From writings between about AD *50 and 80*

Nothing is known to have been written about Jesus of Nazareth *Jesus*
until twenty years or so after the death of the man. Most of these
early writers believed him to be the long-awaited 'Messiah', the
'Christ'.

The name 'Jesus' was the Greek version of the Hebrew name
'Joshua' which meant 'Yahweh saves'. (See note to 19 on
'Joshua'.)

The reading opposite was for practical Roman minds. Luke who *Luke*
wrote it, was alone among the four main writers (Matthew, Mark,
Luke and John) to refer to the practical details of both the arrival on
Earth and the departure from Earth of the 'Son of the Most High
God': he wrote that Jesus had been fathered by the Spirit of God
and, at the end of his time on Earth, he had been removed in the
clouds of Heaven (reading 134).

But these details were not so important as the lesson they taught:
that the gracious creator can conceive in his creatures miraculous *grace*
new life when they are obedient and receptive to him. In this way, if
not in other ways too, Mary was a 'virgin'. This virgin conception *virgin*
was not new. Its germ lay deep in the religions of the ancient world
(notes to 19).

There is no doubt that Jesus had been a lovable person, whatever *love*
else they believed he was. Whoever talks of the person he loves is a
poet. That is why Luke and others used the poetical terms of their *poetry*
time: 'angels', 'I am with you', 'fear not', and 'clouds' in the
Scriptures had always indicated the presence of God. *presence*

Loving and believing are very close to each other in meaning. *believe*

'Gabriel' in Hebrew meant 'man of God'. He also appeared in the *Gabriel*
Book of Daniel and was considered next in rank to the Archangel
Michael.

'To conceive' can be to formulate a new idea in the mind or to start *conceive*
the life of a new baby in the womb of a woman. (See note on 74.)

'Annunciation' has been the traditional name given to the *Annuncia-*
announcing of the birth of Jesus. It is celebrated on 25 March and is *tion*
sometimes called Lady Day. There has been a lingering belief
among some farmers and gardeners that seeds sown on that day
will flourish.

'Gracious' meant 'kindly' and 'benevolent'. *grace*

57 The birth of Jesus

***
from Luke 2 : New English Bible

In those days a decree was issued by the Emperor Augustus for a general registration throughout the Roman world. This was the first registration carried out while Quirinius was governor of Syria. For this purpose everyone made his way to his own town; and so Joseph went from the town of Nazareth in Galilee, to Judaea to be registered at the city of David, called Bethlehem, because he was of the house of David by descent. And with him went Mary. While they were there the time came for her child to be born, and she gave birth to a son, her first-born. And because there was no room for them to lodge in the house, she wrapped him round, and laid him in a manger.

Happened between about 7 and 5 BC
From writings between AD 50 and 80

About 500 years after the birth of Jesus, a monk in Rome was told to calculate the year in which it had taken place. But he got it wrong. It is likely to have occurred at least four years earlier than he reckoned, so that the year AD 1984 will be more like 1990. 'AD stands for *Anno Domini*, Latin for 'Year of the Lord'. This was the 'Christian era', the new age in which Jesus was generally accepted as 'the Christ'. And all that happened before Christ was considered to be BC. 'Nativity', derived from another Latin word, is the traditional name for the birth of Jesus.

Jesus nativity

AD
time
Christian

BC

The Romans periodically made all Jews report to the home towns of their ancestors, so that they could keep a check on them for tax purposes; a compulsory census. No one was excused.

Romans
tax

Joseph, Mary's husband, came from Bethlehem which had also been the home of King David a thousand years before. Bethlehem was 8 km (5 miles) from Jerusalem, and about 135 km (85 miles) from Nazareth.

Jesus'
family

Compare this with reading 56. One is mainly plain history, the other pure poetry — two sides of the same coin.

history
poetry

58 The boy Jesus

from Luke 2 : New English Bible

Now it was the practice of his parents to go to Jerusalem every year for the Passover festival; and when he was twelve, they made the pilgrimage as usual.

When the festival season was over and they started for home, the boy Jesus stayed behind in Jerusalem. His parents did not know this; but thinking that he was with the party, they journeyed on for a whole day, and only then did they begin looking for him among their friends and relations.

As they could not find him, they returned to Jerusalem to look for him; and after three days they found him sitting in the Temple surrounded by the teachers, listening to them and putting questions; and all who heard him were amazed at his intelligence and the answers he gave.

His parents were astonished to see him there, and his mother said to him, 'My son, why have you treated us like this? Your father and I have been searching for you in great anxiety.'

'What made you search?' he said. 'Did you not know that I was bound to be in my Father's house?' But they did not understand what he meant.

Then he went back with them to Nazareth, and continued to be under their authority; his mother treasured up all these things in her heart.

As Jesus grew up he advanced in wisdom, and in favour with God and men.

'A man who loves his son will beat him frequently' — according to Ben Sira in the Book of Ecclesiasticus, chapter 30 (see notes to 52). The ten rules of the Moses-law (reading 17) included 'honour your father and mother so that you may have a long life . . .' and see also note to 140 on 'stoning'. A father's authority was believed to be a microcosm of Yahweh's authority. 'Spare the rod and spoil the child' was a hard fact of life to them.

authority

parents

children

In the reading opposite the boy seems by modern standards to be a bit precocious and perhaps in need of a good hiding. But children matured much earlier then and in the country districts education such as it was ceased at about twelve, words like 'adolescent' and 'leisure' did not exist, the father's work had to be learnt quickly and carried on. The expectation of life in the Roman Empire was about thirty-five. (It is above sixty-five today in Europe.)

education
work
life

Education began at mother's knee, learning prayers and graces, Sabbath customs and psalms by heart. Then at five or six to school, often in the open air by the synagogue, to learn reading and writing and to study the Old Testament (like the Koran in modern Moslem schools), and to be instructed by the local rabbi (like Buddhist monks in modern Burma and Tibet). What the boy lacked in mathematics, science and sport he gained in practical ways working with his father to earn a living, in most cases a very meagre living. Idleness was unpardonable. Unemployment was the kiss of death.

synagogue
Mohammed
rabbi
Buddha

The third temple, that of Herod the Great, covered an area thirty times larger than Solomon's had done (notes to 30). The central building with its Holy of Holies (now with nothing inside it at all) was much the same as Solomon's had been but it was now surrounded and served by an enormous complex of extra buildings: palaces, courtrooms, formal yards, gateways and porches, domes, tall towers, butcheries, altars of sacrifice, barracks, prison cells, a hippodrome, a treasury, libraries and the Sanhedrin. Several thousand priests and levites worked there in shifts — there was never a dull moment! Its atmosphere was not unlike a large and busy continental cathedral surrounded by a thriving market place. (See Map 4.)

third temple
Herod the
Great

Sanhedrin

At Passover there was heavy congestion everywhere. Anyone could get lost at Passover (notes to 92 and 103).

59   Jesus is baptized

***
from Mark 1, Matthew 3 and 4, Luke 3 and John 1 : New English Bible

And so it was that John the Baptist appeared as a preacher in the Judaean wilderness; his theme was: 'Repent! Prepare a way for the Lord! Clear a straight path for him!'

The people were on the tiptoe of expectation, all wondering about John, whether perhaps he was the Messiah. They flocked to him from all Judaea and were baptized by him in the River Jordan.

It happened at this time that Jesus came from Nazareth in Galilee and was baptised in the Jordan by John during a general baptism of the people. After baptism Jesus came up out of the water at once, and was led away by the Spirit into the wilderness, to be tempted by the devil.

John testified: 'I saw the Spirit coming down from heaven and resting upon him like a dove. I did not know him, but he who sent me had told me, 'When you see the Spirit coming down and resting upon someone, you will know that it is he who is to baptize in the Holy Spirit.' I saw it myself, and I have borne witness. This is God's Chosen One.'

Probably happened in about AD *25*
From writings between AD *50 and 95*

Compare this with readings 55 and 45.

'To repent' was 'to change one's mind'; the mind was the power of reasoning which could redirect the will.

repent
mind

'Baptism', the ceremony of ducking in water, was to symbolize the putting aside of one's self-centred ways, and emerging clean and refreshed to a new way of life.

baptism

'Messiah' was the Hebrew word for 'God's Chosen One', anointed and set aside for the special mission of saving Judaea from her enemies. Though Jesus seemed at this stage to remain in the crowd, incognito and his baptism was a symbolic anointing for the work which lay ahead.

Messiah

To be 'tempted' was to be tested.

tempt

'To testify' was 'to bear witness' or 'to give evidence'.

testify

A dove in the Jewish mind symbolized various things. In this case it was the PRESENCE of God, his 'Holy Spirit'. It brought peace and reconciliation.

dove
Spirit of
God

60 Jesus leaves Nazareth

**

from Luke 4, John 7, and Matthew 13 : New English Bible

So he came to Nazareth where he had been brought up, and went to synagogue on the Sabbath day as he regularly did. He stood up to read the lesson and was handed the scroll of the prophet Isaiah. He opened the scroll and found the passage which says, 'The spirit of the Lord is upon me because he has anointed me; he has sent me to announce good news to the poor, to proclaim release for prisoners and recovery of sight for the blind.'

He rolled up the scroll, gave it back to the attendant, and sat down; and all eyes in the synagogue were fixed on him.

He began to speak. 'Today,' he said, 'in your very hearing, this text has come true.'

The Jews were astonished: 'How is it,' they said, 'that this untrained man has such learning?' Jesus replied, 'The teaching that I give you is not my own; it is the teaching of him who sent me.'

In amazement they asked, 'Where does he get his wisdom from? Is he not the carpenter's son? Is not his mother called Mary?'

'I tell you this,' he went on, 'no prophet is recognized in his own country.'

At these words the whole congregation were infuriated. They leapt up, threw him out of the town, and took him to the brow of the hill on which it was built, meaning to hurl him over the edge. But he walked straight through them all, and went away.

The local synagogue was used like a local chapel or church. It was   *synagogue*
either circular or rectangular and retained the threefold partition of
temple design though it was no longer used for sacrifices (notes to
30). It was also the local school and library, and if the rabbi (notes to   *education*
61) was a good man the people would go to him for advice and for
the settlement of arguments and debts. And there were sometimes   *law*
meetings and community meals in the synagogue. Wherever there
was a Jewish community of ten or more, there would be a
synagogue. In larger towns the rabbi's work was shared by priests
and scribes. In Jerusalem there were more than four hundred
synagogues.

Galilean synagogues were almost always directed southwards
towards Jerusalem, just as most European churches have faced
east. Women were separated and out of sight behind a screen. In   *women*
the centre was a platform with a reading desk and one or two seats.
The reader stood. A preacher sat. The main object in the building   *preaching*
was a chest containing the papyrus scrolls of Hebrew Scripture, and
above it a lamp which was never extinguished.

There were no sacrifices at synagogues. Their services were usually   *worship*
of a set form: singing psalms and rocking to and fro in time, reading
the Old Testament, explaining it and praying aloud together. The
people sat throughout, except during the central act which was
'Rejoicing in the Law'—it was the reading of the Moses-law and   *Moses-law*
sometimes having excited processions with it. The emotion
surrounding this ceremony had replaced the emotions that used to
be aroused with sacrifices.

In the reading opposite, the passage which Jesus read was from the
third part of Isaiah (notes to 45).   *Isaiah*

Jesus did not worry about his popularity. He had his message to
give. He did not give it apologetically—if he had done so, they might
not have noticed what he was saying. See note to 45 on 'prophets':
the true prophet was always made to feel least 'at home' with   *prophets*
himself and in his homeland.

The crowd imagined he was making a fool of the Holy Scriptures
and them. Fierce argument: there was nothing magical about his   *miracles*
unnoticed departure.

61 Jesus chooses his first followers

***
From Mark 1, Matthew 4 and 8, John 1 and Luke 4 : New English Bible

Jesus was walking by the shore of the Sea of Galilee when he saw two brothers: Simon (called Peter) and his brother Andrew, on the lake at work with a casting net; for they were fishermen. Jesus said to them, 'Come with me, and I will make you fishers of men.' At once they left their nets and followed him.

The next day Jesus met Philip who, like Andrew and Peter, came from Bethsaida, and said to him, 'Follow me.' Philip went to find Nathanael. When Jesus saw Nathanael coming, he said, 'Here is an Israelite worthy of the name; there is nothing false in him.' Nathanael asked him, 'How do you come to know me?' Jesus replied, 'I saw you under the fig tree before Philip spoke to you.'

'Rabbi,' said Nathanael, 'you are the Son of God; you are the king of Israel.' Jesus answered, 'Is this the ground of your faith, that I told you I saw you under the fig tree? You shall see greater things than that.'

Jesus then went to Peter's house and found Peter's mother-in-law in bed with fever. So he took her by the hand; the fever left her, and she got up and waited on them.

At the sunset all who had friends suffering from one disease or another brought them to him; and he laid his hands on them one by one and cured them.

The news spread rapidly, and he was soon spoken of all over the district of Galilee.

Happened between about AD *26 and 27*
From writings between AD *50 and 95*

A 'rabbi' was a Jewish teacher. He was usually to be found in the   *rabbi*
village synagogue where his duty was to lead the worship and
studies of the local people and sort out their problems. In small
villages he was a sort of teacher, minister, priest, solicitor, doctor
and psychiatrist all in one! There were also travelling rabbis and
Jesus seems to have been regarded as one of these. They collected
about a dozen close followers around them; these were called
'disciples' or learners. If they sent them out on teaching missions   *disciples*
they were called 'apostles' or messengers. (See note to 62 on   *apostles*
'saint'.)

Jesus was sometimes called *Rabbi*, sometimes the more formal title
Rabbuni. Sometimes he was called 'Master' which meant simply   *master*
someone who was greater than the speaker ('Mr' or 'Mister' is the   *Mr*
weakened form of 'Master'). And again he was sometimes called
'Lord' which was very respectful indeed: a slave would use it when   *Lord*
speaking to his master.

There was unbelievable disease among these people. All fevers and   *disease*
illnesses were thought to be evil spirits which had come to live in
and devour the body — usually as a punishment. Sick people were
terrified as much by their pain as by their merciless consciences.
Others kept their distance. Therefore when someone like Jesus
came close to them, unafraid, like a brother who really loved them in
spite of everything, it is not surprising that they recovered quickly.
He was not a magic man, but simply a champion lover.

The fish has been a symbol of life among peoples of this part of the   *fish*
world for countless ages. The Jewish Friday meal of fish was   *symbol*
possibly adopted during their Exile in Babylon and, again possibly,
the Babylonians learnt it from Indian cults. The exact reasons for
fish becoming a secret symbol among early Christians are also
uncertain. It had been a sacred animal among the primitive Syrians
and they had always influenced Jewish culture in the north of
Galilee.   *Galilee*

Jesus started life in the North Country, the open hills of Galilee and
Samaria. Southerners of Judaea clustering around their capital   *Samaria*
Jerusalem despised the Northerners saying they had been mongrels   *Judaea*
and traitors ever since the rebellion of Jeroboam (reading 32).

62 Jesus shows himself to his followers

from Mark 1, 4 and 6, Luke 4 and 5, Matthew 4 and 13: New English Bible

Jesus went round the whole of Galilee preaching the gospel of the Kingdom.

One day he began to teach by the lake-side. The crowd that gathered round him was so large that he had to get into a boat on the lake, and there he sat, with the whole crowd on the beach right down to the water's edge. He spoke to them at some length.

When he had finished speaking, he said to Simon, 'Put out into the deep water and let down your nets for a catch.' Simon answered, 'Master, we were hard at work all night and caught nothing at all; but if you say so, I will let down the nets.'

They did so and made a big haul of fish; and their nets began to split. So they signalled to their partners in the other boat to come and help them. This they did and loaded both boats to the point of sinking. When Simon saw what had happened he fell at Jesus' knees and said, 'Go Lord, leave me, sinner that I am!' For he and all his companions were amazed at the catch they had made.

'Do not be afraid,' said Jesus. 'Come with me.'

When they came ashore, he was immediately recognized; and the people scoured the whole countryside and brought the sick on stretchers. Wherever he went, to farmsteads, villages, or towns, they laid out the sick in the market-places and begged him to let them simply touch the edge of his cloak.

Happened between about AD *26 and 28*
From writings between AD *50 and 85*

For 'preaching', see the first three paragraphs of reading 60. *preaching*
That represents the mission or business of Jesus in its elemental *Jesus*
form. *mission*

A 'messenger' in Greek was an 'angel', and a messenger with good *message*
news was an 'ev-angel-ist'. (The four main 'evangelists' of the Jesus *angel*
Event have been known as Saint Matthew, Saint Mark, Saint Luke *evangelist*
and Saint John.) Subsequently, from Anglo-Saxon times, good
news or a good story was 'good-spel' or 'god-spel', and this grew *gospel*
into 'gospel'.

The English word 'saint' represents the original idea of 'holiness', *saint*
that is 'set apart for a special reason'. (See also note to 7 on
'sacrifice'.) After the death of Jesus, those people who believed
he was the Christ set themselves apart from society and were simply
known as 'the saints'. It was not a special title in those days. The
Pharisees for other reasons also separated themselves (notes to 53).
And so did certain other sects. (Compare with notes to 61 on
'rabbi', 'disciples' and 'apostles'.)

For 'Kingdom' see notes to 64.

Understanding the elements had always been a sign of the power of *elements*
the creator at work (notes to 17 and 33). So had the understanding
and healing of sickness (reading 35). The aggressiveness of the *healing*
elements in agriculture and the aggressiveness of evil spirits in sick
people were among the many 'crooked' things that prophets like
Isaiah had said would be 'straightened out' (reading 45). *Isaiah*

For the symbolism of 'fish' see notes to 61.

This enormous catch of fish had a profound effect on Simon. He felt *Peter*
he had been wasting his time — he was supposed to be an expert!
Somewhere he had been missing the point, or he had been
'sinning'. 'Sin' was a technical term — see notes to 18 on 'faith' and
'atonement'.

63   A tax-collector joins Jesus

***

from Mark 2, Matthew 9, and Luke 5: New English Bible

Once more Jesus went away to the lake-side. As he went along, he saw a man named Matthew, a tax-gatherer at his seat in the custom-house. He said to him, 'Follow me.' And Matthew rose to his feet, left everything behind, and followed him.

When Jesus was at table in his house, many bad characters (tax-gatherers and others) were seated with him and his disciples; for there were many who followed him.

The Pharisees noticed this and said to his disciples, 'Why is it that your master eats with tax-gatherers?'

Jesus overheard, and said to them, 'It is not the healthy that need a doctor. I did not come to invite virtuous people, but sinners.'

Happened between about AD *27 and 28*
From writings between AD *50 and 85*

The Romans who occupied the country of the Jews imposed a tax *Romans*
on certain essential foods like meat and salt, and on land. They *tax*
employed Jews to collect these taxes. These tax-collectors were *tax-*
permitted to keep whatever money they could squeeze out above *collectors*
the fixed amounts. So, of course, they were regarded by their
fellow-countrymen as vile traitors, sinners to be despised.

It is a mistake to assume for certain that this tax-collector later wrote *Matthew*
what is called 'The Gospel according to Saint Matthew'.

'Pharisees' had become a distinct party within Judaism by 100 BC. *Pharisees*
(The word meant 'separated ones'.) They encouraged a strict
obedience to the Laws of Moses and added a web of complicated
rules. They also encouraged synagogue worship and, partly
because of their hatred of the Romans and all interfering foreigners,
they were influential among the common people.

'Health' meant 'wholeness' in the thinking of the Jews. For them, *health*
the body and the non-physical part of a man (his mind, his emotions
and his will) were all one. If he obeyed the Laws of God, they
thought he would be healthy. A similar connection has existed in the
English language: heal, hale, whole, holy and hallow all come from *homoeo-*
the same Anglo-Saxon origin. *pathy*

Thus Jewish law-breakers were 'sinners'. 'Sin' was 'crime against *sin*
God'. Their Laws, they maintained, were the very Laws of God. Any
form of sickness was caused, they said, by human sin — falling away
from God's Laws and allowing evil spirits to come into the body.
And if a good and holy person fell sick, they said, he was suffering
for the sins of others.

64 Jesus talks about a kingdom of heaven

***

from Luke 6 and 12, and Matthew 5: New English Bible

During this time he went out one day into the hills to pray, and spent the night in prayer to God. When day broke he called his disciples to him, and from among them he chose twelve and named them Apostles: Simon, to whom he gave the name Peter, and Andrew his brother, James and John, Philip and Bartholomew, Matthew and Thomas, James son of Alphaeus, and Simon who was called the Zealot, Judas son of James, and Judas Iscariot who turned traitor.

He came down the hill with them and took his stand on level ground. Then turning to his disciples he began to speak, and this is the teaching he gave:

'Have no fear, little flock; for your Father has chosen to give you the Kingdom. Sell your possessions and give in charity. Provide for yourselves purses that do not wear out, and never-failing wealth in heaven, where no thief can get near it, no moth destroy it. For where your wealth is, there will your heart be also.

'How blest are those who know that they are poor; the kingdom of Heaven is theirs.

'How blest are you who weep now; you shall laugh.

'How blest are those who hunger and thirst to do what is right; they shall be satisfied.

'How blest are those whose hearts are pure; they shall see God.

'How blest are the peacemakers; God shall call them his sons.'

'Blessed' or 'how blest' meant 'how happy and to be envied'. A *blessed* happy person was one who 'happed upon good luck'. An unhappy *happy* person was a 'hapless' one—nothing ever seemed to happen! So *luck* happiness was considered to be a gift from heaven. It was not a marketable commodity; modern advertising is misleading!

Jesus taught these people that the mechanics of gaining happiness were simple: they had to accept the poverty and sorrows of their lives heartily, striving only to make peace and do the right thing—that was their own responsibility. Laughter and satisfaction were divine gifts, and a vision of their closeness to the heart and mind of God would follow. That brought undestroyable happiness.

When people were involved in this process they became members of that secret society called the Kingdom of Heaven. It was an *Kingdom* active and organic process.

For 'Apostles' see notes to 61.

The Philip here is not the later evangelist mentioned in reading 139 *Philip the* and notes to 141. *Apostle*

65   Jesus teaches : salt and light

from Luke 14, and Matthew 5 : New English Bible

'If you have ears to hear with, hear.'

'Salt is a good thing; but if salt itself becomes tasteless, what will you use to season it? It is now good for nothing but to be thrown away and trodden under foot.

'You are salt to the world.

'A town that stands on a hill cannot be hidden. When a lamp is lit, it is put on the lamp stand where it gives light to everyone in the house.

'You are light for all the world. And you, like the lamp, must shed light among your fellows, so that, when they see the good you do, they may give praise to your Father in heaven.'

Compared with the political arguments between Scribes and
Pharisees, and the complicated religious arguments everywhere
else, this simple sort of preaching was a very refreshing thing — for   *preaching*
those who had time to listen (see notes to 53 on Sadducees and   *deaf*
Pharisees).

Note, at the end, the duty of the prophet was not to draw attention   *prophets*
to himself but to his creator (see note to 45 on truth). Even this
powerful man Jesus was not trying to draw attention to himself.

66 Jesus teaches : murder

**
from Matthew 5 : New English Bible

'Do not suppose that I have come to abolish the Law. I did not come to abolish, but to complete.

'You have learned that our forefathers were told, "Do not commit murder; anyone who commits murder must be brought to judgement."

'But what I tell you is this: Anyone who nurses anger against his brother without good cause must be brought to judgement. If he abuses his brother, if he sneers at him, he must answer for it to the court.

'If someone sues you, come to terms with him promptly while you are both on your way to court.'

'If, when you are bringing your gift to the altar, you suddenly remember that your brother has a grievance against you, leave your gift where it is before the altar. First go and make peace with your brother, and only then come back and offer your gift.

'Again, you have learned that they were told, "Love your neighbour, hate your enemy."

'But I tell you this: Love your enemies, bless those who curse you, do good to those who hate you; only so can you be children of your heavenly Father.

'You must therefore be all goodness, just as your heavenly Father is all good.'

The Moses-law (reading 17) was, on the whole, negative. Certainly *Moses-law*
the Pharisees' interpretation of it (notes to 53) was negative,
prohibitive. It resulted in people saying to themselves: 'I'm all right,
I've never killed or cursed anyone, I've never lied or stolen.' Jesus
was against this attitude (see his story in reading 89).

Jesus urged people to have a positive attitude to godliness. (See *righteous*
also reading 102.)

Another point. Between positively loving someone and killing them, *love*
there were many degrees of hatred. The real crime of hatred in its
many disguises was far more common than people realized. Murder *murder*
was simply one of the forms it sometimes took. Others were spite,
greed, deceit, spreading scandal and similar unseen crimes. But the
central crime was hatred, and it was committed daily by all sorts of
self-righteous people (see notes to 50).

67 Jesus teaches : secrecy

***
from Matthew 5 and 6 : New English Bible

'Be careful not to make a show of your religion before men.

'When you do some act of charity, do not let your left hand know what your right hand is doing. Your good deed must be secret, and your Father who sees what is done in secret will reward you.

'Thus, when you do some act of charity, do not announce it with a flourish of trumpets, as the hypocrites do in synagogue and in the streets to win admiration from men: they have their reward already.

'Again, when you pray, go into a room by yourself, shut the door, and pray to your Father who is there in the secret place; and your Father who sees what is secret will reward you.

'Do not be like the hypocrites. They love to say their prayers standing up in synagogue and at the street corners, for everyone to see them. I tell you this: they have their reward already.

'Unless you show yourselves far better men than the Pharisees and the doctors of the law, you can never enter the kingdom of Heaven.'

Secrecy was one of the key words of the Kingdom of Heaven. The *secret* joke about the hands contained the vital point: just doing good did not win automatic membership of the Kingdom—it had to be so *Kingdom* secret that the do-gooder himself hardly knew he was doing it.

A 'hypocrite' was an 'actor'; among the Jews he was the religious *hypocrite* type who obeyed all the rules perfectly while his heart was elsewhere. The 'open reward' he was after was admiration from people—and all sorts of popularity. *popular*

'Charity' was kindness, affection, trustfulness, leniency, generosity, *charity* sympathy and things like that.

'Doctors of the Law' were expert teachers of the Jewish Law. *Doctors of* ('Doctor' in English originally meant a teacher or a learned man; *the Law* 'Doctor of Medicine' is a more recent development.) Jewish doctors of the law were also employed as 'scribes' to copy the scriptures and as secretaries to draw up legal documents. They tended to 'know all'.

68 Jesus teaches : prayer

***
from Luke 11 and Matthew 6 : New English Bible

One of his disciples said, 'Lord, teach us to pray.'

He answered, 'When you pray, do not go babbling on like the heathen, who imagine that the more they say the more they are likely to be heard. Do not imitate them. Your Father knows what your needs are before you ask him. (If you know how to give your children what is good for them, how much more will the heavenly Father give good things to those who ask him!)

'This is how you should pray:

"Our Father in heaven,
Thy name be hallowed.

Thy kingdom come upon us:
Thy will be done on earth as in heaven.

Give us today our daily bread.

Forgive us the wrong we have done,
For we too forgive all who have wronged us.

And save us from the evil one." '

This is the only actual prayer that Jesus is said to have *prayer*
recommended. It is the famous 'Lord's Prayer'.

'Heavenly Father' was a valuable way of approaching the idea of *father*
'God' because it led to the idea of the 'Brotherhood of Man'. It was *brother*
not by their own efforts or virtue that they were brothers, but by
'The Grace of God'.

'To hallow' was to set apart and keep purely for a special use. It was *hallow*
'to make holy'. For them God's name was 'holy', his Spirit was
'holy', the Scriptures were 'holy'. Kings, prophets and priests, being
set aside in the anointing ceremony for a special job, were also
'holy'. A special place at a table being kept empty for a special guest
would be 'holy'.

'The Devil' in the Old (Jewish) Testament was considered to be the *Devil*
chief of evil spirits in the world who tried to mislead people but who
seems to have been less powerful than God himself. Origins are
uncertain. The Aramaic word 'Satan' meant 'Enemy'; 'Beelzebub',
another name for the Devil, meant 'Lord of the Flies' and may have
been connected with a Phoenician sun-god. The Greeks called him
'the Slanderer'.

By the first century AD, the Devil was thought to be well established
on Earth as the powerful 'Tempter', infiltrating human minds and
violently sabotaging human lives with physical pain, diseases and
madness. All forms of self-centredness were the will of the Devil. To
run with the Devil was to go to Hell. Hell was the furthest point from *Hell*
Heaven, a place of darkness and misery where the will of God was *Heaven*
unknown. (See, for example, the end of reading 3.)

69 Jesus teaches : criticizing

***
from Luke 6 : New English Bible

'Pass no judgement, and you will not be judged.

'Whatever measure you deal out to others will be dealt to you in return.

'Can one blind man be guide to another? Will they not both fall into the ditch?

'How can you say to your brother, "My dear brother, let me take the speck out of your eye." You hypocrite! First take the plank out of your own eye, and then you will see clearly to take the speck out of your brother's.'

There was a type of double-think in many of the things Jesus said. On the one hand he would be talking about this physical world of the body's five senses, contained in space, movement and time; on the other hand there was a spiritual dimension. And in one short sentence he would switch from talking about the one to talking about the other. The result was often puzzling to the careless listener.

double-think

The first sentence opposite is an example; others follow. He was saying in effect, 'Do not criticize people either in talking or thinking on this earth, because there is no room in the Kingdom of Heaven for people who busy themselves in that way.' Behaviour in the physical sphere affected life in the spiritual sphere: they were two sides of the same coin.

criticize

Among the thoughts of Chairman Mao Tse Tung there is similar teaching: 'To indulge in irresponsible criticism in private instead of actually putting forward one's suggestions to the organizaton . . . to say nothing to people to their faces but . . . to gossip behind their backs . . . to say nothing at a meeting . . . but to gossip afterwards . . . . The result is that both the individual and the organization are harmed.'

Communism

This type of heavy elaboration however was probably not the technique used by Jesus: of the sayings which are more likely to have been his very own words, most were short and pithy.

Jesus

The third sentence about blind guides was probably intended for some Pharisees or Scribes who were present. It was another of his techniques to say something slightly puzzling like that. It would tease their minds into active thought.

(For another illustration of this teaching about criticism see the parable of the vineyard workers in reading 91.)

70 Jesus teaches : action

***

from Matthew 7 and Luke 6 : New English Bible

'Beware of false prophets. You will recognise them by the fruits they bear. For each tree is known by its own fruit: you do not gather figs from thistles. A good man produces good from the good within himself; and an evil man produces evil. For the words that the mouth utters come from the overflowing of the heart.

'Why do you keep calling me "Lord, Lord"—and never do what I tell you? Everyone who comes to me and hears what I say and acts upon it—I will show you what he is like. He is like a man who, in building his house, dug deep and laid the foundations on rock. When the flood came, the river burst upon that house, but could not shift it, because it had been soundly built. But he who hears and does not act is like a man who built his house on sand. As soon as the river burst upon it, the house collapsed and fell with a great crash.'

When Jesus had finished this discourse the people were astounded at his teaching; unlike their own teachers, he taught with a note of authority.

There were plenty of false prophets about, opportunists who were
cashing in on the atmosphere of expectation in the land.   *expectation*

The 'authority' of Jesus which appealed to so many ordinary people   *authority*
was, roughly speaking, the authority of common sense. That is,
provided that (a) the Mind of the Creator was perfectly reproduced
in nature and history, and (b) the whole Moses law was a genuine
representation of that Divine Mind, and (c) both these ideas were
common knowledge among people, it is then true to say that the
way of life which Jesus preached appeared to those people at that
time the pure fruit of 'common sense'. And if all this was so, it   *common*
follows that Jesus had what theologians call 'divine authority'.   *sense*

Compared with the exhausting and dry repetition of so much public
worship and the dead language of political speeches and the deceit-
ful advertising of false prophets, Jesus with his stimulating words
was divine. Anyone who was not stirred to action by his words was   *action*
lost.

71   Jesus in a storm

from Mark 4 and 5, Matthew 8 and Luke 8 : New English Bible

That day in the evening, Jesus said to them, 'Let us cross over to the other side of the lake.' So they left the crowd and took him with them in the boat where he had been sitting; and there were other boats accompanying him.

A heavy squall came on and the waves broke over the boat until it was all but swamped. Now he was in the stern, asleep on a cushion; they roused him and said, 'Master, we are sinking! Do you not care?'

'Why are you such cowards?' he said; 'how little faith you have!' Then he stood up and rebuked the wind and the sea.

The storm subsided and all was calm. 'Where is your faith?' he asked.

So they came to the other side of the lake and the men were astonished at what had happened. They said to one another, 'What sort of man is this, that even the wind and the sea obey him?'

Compare this story with Jonah (reading 50). Storms since primitive *elements*
times had symbolized the presence of the creator (readings 4, 17, *presence*
33). And the understanding and sometimes pacifying of them
indicated a 'Man of God', a prophet. Another primitive motif was
the necessity from time to time to wake a god up (especially reading
33).

Sudden squalls like this still today swirl down from the hills around
the Galilee lake and vanish as suddenly. Something like this story
probably happened. But the story-tellers, writing some years afterwards, were not concerned with writing an exact report for the
police! They were talking about a man who demonstrated
impressive power and authority. Matthew, Mark and Luke all went *power*
on to describe a healing which was another well-understood symbol
of divine power and authority. (See reading 72.) *authority*

See also notes to 62 on 'elements' and 'healing'.

A ship on a rough sea became an early Christian symbol: safety *boat*
surrounded by danger. *symbol*

In modern psychology, both Freud and Jung have regarded raging
seas as a universal symbol of the womb. It is not surprising, for the *womb*
human animal spends his first and vitally formative nine months
floating fish-like in his mother's womb — the experience is bound to
have conditioned his mind. There seems to be universal formula:
womb=heaven=divine presence (see 'fish' in notes 61, 'temple' in
notes to 30 and 31, and 'Heaven' and Yahweh' in notes to 31 — and *Heaven*
of course the readings opposite those notes). The event described
opposite was therefore a variation on a familiar pattern.

Stories like this were remembered and recorded because, to the *history*
story-tellers, they meant much more than at first meets the eye.
They were not plain history.

72 Jesus meets a mad man

***

from Mark 5, Luke 8, and Matthew 8: New English Bible

So they came to the other side of the lake into the country of the Gadarenes. As Jesus stepped ashore, he was met by a man who was possessed by devils so violent that no one dared pass that way. For a long time he had neither worn clothes nor lived in a house, but stayed among the tombs. No one was strong enough to master him. And so unceasingly, day and night, he would cry aloud among the tombs and on the hill-sides and cut himself with stones.

When he saw Jesus he cried out, and fell at his feet shouting, 'You son of God, what do you want? Have you come here to torment me?'

Jesus asked him, 'What is your name?' 'Legion,' he replied. This was because so many devils had taken possession of him.

Now there happened to be a large herd of pigs feeding on the hill-side. And the herd, of about two thousand, rushed over the edge into the lake and were drowned.

The men in charge of them saw what happened and carried the news to the town. When the people came out to see for themselves, they found the mad man sitting there clothed and in his right mind; and they were afraid. The spectators told them how the mad man had been cured and what had happened to the pigs.

Then they begged Jesus to leave the district for they were in the grip of a great fear. As he was stepping into the boat, the man who had been possessed begged to go with him. But Jesus sent him away: 'Go back home,' he said, 'and tell them everything that God has done for you.' The man went all over the town spreading the news of what Jesus had done for him.

Happened between about AD *27 and 28*
From writings between about AD *50 and 85*

A few wealthy people had family tombs and sometimes these were   *tombs*
situated in the courtyards of their houses. But most burials were in
common graves and hillside caves outside the town.

Madness was not uncommon. It had many forms from depression   *mad*
to raving lunacy. The causes were numerous: hunger, under-
nourishment, deformity, poverty, inactivity, religious and social
oppression, disease, pain and loneliness. Worse than all these were
primitive superstitions about sin, guilt, death and damnation.   *superstition*

'Legion' was a Roman military division of between 3000 and 6000   *Romans*
soldiers.   *legion*

Pigs had been regarded as unclean and their meat as unfit to eat by   *pigs*
Judaean Jews ever since the Northern kingdom had rebelled and
mixed with foreign Canaanite customs (reading 32).

It may be easier to think of the stampede of swine in this story
simply as a strange coincidence which nonetheless fed the story-   *myth*
tellers' superstitions.

Much healing is a simple process, as every modern doctor knows.   *healing*
Jesus showed a fearless and unconditional love. The man had never
before met anything like it.

73 Jesus heals a paralytic man

from Mark 2, Luke 5 and Matthew 9: New English Bible

When after some days Jesus returned to Capernaum, the news went round that he was at home; and such a crowd collected that the space in front of the door was not big enough to hold them. He was teaching, and Pharisees and teachers of the law were sitting round.

And a man was brought who was paralysed. Four men were carrying him but because of the crowd they could not get him near. So they went up on to the roof and let him down through the tiling, bed and all, into the middle of the company in front of Jesus.

Seeing their faith, Jesus said to the man, 'Take heart; your sins are forgiven.'

Now the lawyers and the Pharisees thought to themselves, 'Who is this fellow with his blasphemous talk? Who but God alone can forgive sins?'

Jesus knew that this was what they were thinking, and said to them, 'Is it easier to say, "Your sins are forgiven," or to say, "Stand up and walk?" '

He now addressed the paralytic: 'Stand up, take your bed, and go home.' At once he rose to his feet before their eyes, took up the bed he had been lying on, and went home praising God. They were all lost in amazement: 'You would never believe the things we have seen today,' they said.

'Paralysis' is nervous and muscular powerlessness. It comes after several types of illness, and sometimes it can heal, especially if the patient exercises strong will-power.

disease

will

This 'bed' was a litter, a sort of stretcher.

For 'housetops' see notes to 19, and for 'lawyers' see notes to 67 and 102.

Illness, they feared, was the result of sin (notes to 63). 'Sin' was a crime against or neglect of the excellent plans of the creator. And they were certain that the only way to become 'at one' with him again was to persuade him by some means to 'forgive' them. This then was the magic formula in their minds:

sin

forgive

SIN – SICKNESS – ATONEMENT – FORGIVENESS – HEALING.

atonement

It was a chain of events but ultimately it was the creator only, they believed, who could take the initiative (see the end of reading 42). They could try to persuade him to heal or forgive but it was his gracious choice whether and when to act. (See 'Job', reading 49.)

initiative

'Blasphemy' meant 'insulting God' (notes to 34). But Jesus was concerned with healing the man, not arguing about complicated thought-forms.

healing

By now Jesus had a reputation for this power of healing. The patient had heard about him before he arrived and was already 'confident' or 'full of faith' in him. The healer only had to say the word. The man's faith did the trick. It was immaterial whether he had faith in the exorcism of devils or the swallowing of antibiotics or the whispered breathing of a holy name. The mechanics of healing are very, very simple, not in fact magical.

faith

name

74 The family of Jesus

***
from Luke 8 and 11, John 15, and Matthew 12: New English Bible

After this he went journeying from village to village, proclaiming the good news of the kingdom of God. With him were the Twelve and a number of women who had been set free from infirmities: Mary (known as Mary of Magdala), Joanna (the wife of a steward of Herod's), Susanna, and many others. These women provided for them out of their own resources.

People were now gathering in large numbers, and as they made their way to him, he said, 'I call you servants no longer. I have called you friends because I have disclosed to you everything that I heard from my Father. You are my friends if you do what I command you. This is my commandment: love one another, as I have loved you.'

He was still speaking to the crowd when his mother and brothers appeared; they stood outside wanting to speak to him. Someone said, 'Your mother and your brothers are here outside; they want to speak to you.'

Jesus turned to the man who brought the message and, pointing to the disciples, he said, 'Here are my mother and my brothers. Whoever does the will of my heavenly Father is my brother, my sister, my mother.'

While he was speaking thus, a woman in the crowd called out, 'Happy the womb that carried you!'

He rejoined, 'No, happy are those who hear the word of God and keep it.'

Apparently after the Annunciation (reading 56) Joseph quickly married Mary so that the neighbours who did not know what had happened would not wag their tongues and shake their heads; and after the Nativity (reading 57), Joseph and Mary are thought to have produced a family which included four sons. All these details are interesting but unimportant for this reading. This is another example of Jesus' double-think technique (see notes to 69).

Jesus'
family

double think

'Father' — see notes to 68.

The woman's remark about 'the womb' here was a pregnant one! The generative activity of the womb is remarkably similar to that of the brain: both are organs of conception — see notes to 56; the receptiveness of the womb is encouraged by the art of the lover, and the receptiveness of the mind is wooed by the words of the speaker; the desire to conceive a baby is like the will to propagate an idea; conception in the womb is followed by a period of gestation (that is 'carrying'), and in the mind by meditation (that is thinking both conscious and unconscious): growth results from both of these: the womb gives birth to a baby after nine months, and after a period of assimilation the mind also projects an image: and finally, just as the baby shows a likeness to the parent, so the image resembles the modified shape of the original idea.

womb

minds

For a miniature of all this, see the last two sentences opposite.

75   In a cornfield, a point of law

from Luke 6, Matthew 12 and 23, and Mark 2: New English Bible

One Sabbath Jesus was going through the cornfields and his disciples were plucking the ears of corn, rubbing them in their hands, and eating them.

The Pharisees noticed this and said to him, 'Look, your disciples are doing something which is forbidden on the Sabbath.' Jesus answered, 'The Sabbath was made for man, and not man for the Sabbath.'

He also said to them, 'Have you not read in the Law that the priests in the Temple break the Sabbath and it is not held against them?

'Alas for you lawyers and Pharisees! You are like tombs covered with whitewash: outside, you look like honest men, but inside you are full of dead men's bones and hypocrisy.'

The law about resting on the sabbath (reading 17) was intended to *sabbath*
make sure that people had a rest once a week, doing no work, just
sitting about and tuning their hearts to the re-creational majesty of
the creator (reading 1). But certain petty minds had woven a web of *law*
complicated extra rules: for example, if a man rubbed an ear of corn
in his hands and chewed up the grain on the sabbath, he was doing
the work of a miller and that was insulting behaviour which would
disturb God on his rest-day; but if a priest in the temple on the
Sabbath did the work of a miller it would not disturb God. This is
what was taught under the heading of 'God's Law'. Jesus did not
like it.

A 'hypocrite' was originally simply an 'actor'. But it came to mean *hypocrite*
'someone who outwardly made a show of being a religious man but
was empty in fact of true godliness'. (For 'godly' see 'righteous' in
notes to 16). Today it loosely means 'someone who pretends to be
better than he really is'.

Some thoughts of Chairman Mao Tse Tung are similar: 'To be *Communism*
aware of one's own mistakes and yet make no attempt to correct
them, taking a liberal attitude towards oneself . . . is . . . a
corrosive which undermines cohesion.' (With 'cohesion' compare
'integrity', reading 40.)

Jesus was very rude about hypocrisy — see reading 96. It really cut a *integrity*
man off from himself.

76 Why parables?

from Matthew 13, and John 18 : New English Bible

The disciples went up to Jesus and asked, 'Why do you speak to them in parables?'

He replied, 'I utter things kept secret since the world was made. My kingdom does not belong to this world. (If it did, my followers would be fighting to save me from arrest by the Jews.) My kingly authority comes from elsewhere. It has been granted to you to know the secrets of the kingdom of Heaven; but to those others it has not been granted. For this people has grown gross at heart; their eyes are closed, their ears are dull and they listen without hearing or understanding. That is why I speak to them in parables.

'Here is a picture of the kingdom of Heaven. A merchant looking out for fine pearls found one of very special value; so he went and sold everything he had, and bought it.

'Have you understood all this?' he asked; and they answered, 'Yes.'

For the definition of 'parable' see notes to 50. It is useful to remember that most parables, however long, contain only one main teaching point. *parables*

Jesus was a master teacher: he usually wrapped up his message so that people had to hunt for it. Education handed out on a plate has never nourished anybody substantially, and too much spoon-feeding weakens will-power. *education*

will

There had been a primitive conception that learning about the creator involved a process of eating (see 'Moses-law' and 'worship' in notes to 30); and now, in synagogue worship, there was an echo of that conception (see 'Moses-law' and 'worship' in notes to 60). To feed on and digest the 'Word of God' and to use its nourishment in everyday life was the highest possible service, they believed. It gave their lives a rare quality — 'fabulous', 'heavenly', 'eternal', 'immortal'. That was what they believed, and many of them really got 'turned on' or 'tuned in' — see the opening of notes to 75. *word*

life
eternal

Nevertheless, although the 'Word of God' was treated as if it were food, care was needed to ensure a digestible sequence, a healthy quantity, a balanced diet, and so on. In this analogy, a parable was simply one of several culinary devices.

77 Jesus teaches : the coming of the kingdom

**

from Luke 10, 13 and 17, Mark 4, and Matthew 9 and 10 : New English Bible

The Pharisees asked Jesus, 'When will the kingdom of God come?' He said, 'The kingdom of God is among you. It is like yeast which a woman mixed with flour. Or it is like a mustard seed which a man sowed in his garden: once sown, it springs up and forms branches so that the birds settle in its shade.'

And Jesus said to his disciples, 'The kingdom is like this: a man scatters seed on the land and the seed grows. The ground produces a crop by itself—he does not know how, but as soon as the crop is ripe he sets to work with the sickle.'

He said to them, 'The crop is heavy but the labourers are scarce. You must therefore be on your way; I am sending *you*. Heal the sick, cast out devils and proclaim the message: The kingdom of Heaven is upon you.'

Happened between about AD *27 and 29*
From writings between about AD *50 and 85*

A collection of sayings about the Kingdom of Heaven probably   *'Q'*
written down at Antioch in about AD 50 (in a document called 'Q')
and quoted only by Matthew and Luke: it is thought to be as close
as anyone can be certain of getting to the actual words which Jesus   *Jesus*
possibly spoke. The first paragraph opposite comes from 'Q'.

The whole reading opposite is thought to say something like this:
'Fermentation is complete. The period of hidden growth is over. The
situation in which the Kingdom of Heaven can flourish is HERE, it is   *Kingdom*
here NOW.
    It is a CRITICAL situation.'   *expectation*

('Crisis' calls for decisions; it is fraught with dangers, but at the
same time it offers opportunities.) 'The situation must be exploited
AT ONCE by people who are brave enough to put themselves at the
disposal of the King of Heaven.' (See 'faith' in notes to 81).
'Through them he can put the world of man in tune with himself
again.' (See the famous 'at-one-ment' formula in notes to 73.)   *atonement*

78   A hungry crowd

**

from Mark 6, Luke 9, Matthew 14 and John 6 : New English Bible

The apostles now rejoined Jesus and they set off privately by boat to a lonely place. But many saw them leave and recognized them, and came round by land, hurrying from all the towns towards the place, and arrived there first. When Jesus came ashore, he saw a great crowd; and his heart went out to them, because they were like sheep without a shepherd; and he had much to teach them.

As the day wore on, the Twelve approached him and said, 'This is a lonely place and it is getting very late; send the people off to the farms and villages round about, to buy themselves something to eat.' He answered, 'There is no need for them to go; give them something to eat yourselves.' But they said, 'Are we to go and buy provisions for all this company?' (There were about five thousand.)

Then Andrew said to him, 'There is a boy here who has five barley loaves and two fishes; but what is that among so many?' Jesus said, 'Let me have them.' He told the people to sit down on the grass; then, taking the five loaves and the two fishes, he looked up to heaven, said the blessing, broke the loaves, and gave them to the disciples; and the disciples gave them to the people.

They all ate to their hearts' content; and the scraps left over, which they picked up, were enough to fill twelve great baskets. Then he made the disciples embark and go on ahead to the other side, while he sent the people away. After doing that he went up the hillside to pray alone.

Here is the repeat of a very primitive conception. Round about 3000 BC men in the area of the Persian Gulf appear to have believed that since rain made the crops grow it must contain within it the seed of life: dew and rain were the divine spermatazoa of the god of heaven. (See 'anthropomorphism' in notes to 3 and 22); sometimes the rain came with thunder and the shrieking wind—and these were his voice ('Yahweh' in notes to 31 and 'wind' in notes to 42). *element*

The unfamiliar fungus found among the dew by the Children of Israel (reading 16) had been 'the bread of heaven' germinated during the night (see 'manna' in notes to 16). They ate it and it sustained their life. *Manna life*

But the writer of 'Deuteronomy' (see notes to 40) in about 650 BC pointed out to the Israelites that there was more to that food than met the eye: 'He humbled you, he made you feel hunger, he fed you with manna which neither you nor your fathers had known, to make you understand that man does not live on bread alone, but on everything that comes from the mouth of Yahweh.' *Deuteronomy*

Jesus was said to have quoted this verse soon after his baptism (reading 59) when he was in the desert without food.

In this reading Jesus appeared to be trying to teach that, 'Man does not live by bread alone.' He wanted his close followers to feed the people with 'the Word of God' but they were only thinking of their stomachs! They missed the point. *logos*

Next time he tried to teach this point (reading 80) he was much more direct, and it caused trouble!

If stories like 'the feeding of the 5000' are read as plain history many of the hidden thought-forms remain undiscovered. Christian creeds have never demanded belief in the so-called 'miracles'. Yet there are people today who insist that 5000 people were actually fed on five loaves and two fishes. *history*

miracles

79 People ask for a 'sign from heaven'

from Matthew 12 and 16, and Mark 8 : New English Bible

The Pharisees and Sadducees came and, to test Jesus, they asked him to show them a sign from heaven. His answer was, 'It is a godless generation that asks for a sign. And the only sign that will be given it is the sign of the prophet Jonah. Jonah was in the sea-monster's belly for three days and three nights, and in the same way the Son of Man will be three days and three nights in the bowels of the earth.'

He sighed deeply to himself and said, 'Why does this generation ask for a sign? You know how to interpret the appearance of the sky; in the evening you say, 'The sky is red: it will be fine weather'; and in the morning you say, 'The sky is red and lowering: it will be stormy today.' You know how to interpret the appearance of the sky—can you not interpret the signs of the times? Are your minds closed? You have eyes—can you not see? You have ears—can you not hear?'

So he went off and left them.

Happened in about AD *28*
From writings between about AD *50 and 85*

'Signs' or 'signals' communicate orders from a higher authority. The *miracles*
Pharisees and Sadducees both reckoned they were in touch with
the divine authority of heaven. Like foreign police inspectors they *authority*
demanded from Jesus proof of his authority. But if he had given
them proof, they would not have had to decide for themselves who
he was (and they would not have discovered him).

Perhaps they were expecting him to 'perform a miracle' for them like
a magician. But 'miracles' and 'wonders' and 'significant events'
were gifts for open-hearted people at the right time. He would not
hand out undignified peep-shows.

Jesus was not a magician. He was not an entertainer. He was an *education*
educator, a teacher, and he treated them to a soufflé of riddles.
(See 'education' in notes to 76.)

'Jonah' — see notes to 50.

For 'the signs of the times' see 'expectation' in notes to 55 and 70
and especially notes to 77.

80 Two sides of Simon Peter

***

from John 6, Mark 8, Luke 9, and Matthew 16 : New English Bible

When Jesus was teaching in the synagogue at Capernaum, the Jews began to murmur disapprovingly because he said, 'I am that living bread which comes from heaven: if anyone eats this bread, he shall live for ever.' This led to a fierce dispute among the Jews and many of his disciples exclaimed, 'This is more than we can stomach: why listen to such words?'

From that time, many of his disciples withdrew and no longer went about with him. So Jesus asked the Twelve, 'Do you also want to leave me?' Simon Peter answered him, 'Lord to whom shall we go? Your words are the words of eternal life.'

Then Jesus and his disciples set out for the villages of Caesarea Philippi. On the way he asked his disciples, 'Who do people say I am?' They answered, 'Some say John the Baptist, others Elijah, others Jeremiah, or that one of the old prophets has come back to life.'

'And you?' he asked. 'Who do you say I am?' Simon Peter replied, 'You are the Messiah.' Then Jesus said, 'Simon, you are favoured indeed!—that was revealed to you by my heavenly Father. And I say this to you: You are Peter the Rock; and on this rock I will build my church—I will give you the keys of the kingdom of Heaven.'

Then he gave them strict orders not to tell anyone that he was the Messiah. And he began to teach them that he had to go to Jerusalem and there to suffer much from the chief priests, to be put to death and to be raised again on the third day. He spoke about it plainly. At this Peter took him by the arm and began to rebuke him. But Jesus turned round and, looking at his disciples, rebuked Peter: 'Away with you, Satan,' he said; 'You think as men think not as God thinks.'

Happened in about AD 28
From writings between about AD 50 and 95

'Simon' was a Hebrew name. His new name was Greek: *Petros*   *Peter*
was Peter and *petra* was a rock. A play on words. A nick-name.

Among the key qualities in the Kingdom of Heaven were things like   *Kingdom*
enthusiasm, spontaneity and generosity.

'Church' originally referred to a group of people meeting together.   *church*
There was no special building. The first assemblies of the so-called
Christians only started after the death of Jesus, secretly in each
other's houses. (See readings 131 onwards.)

'To suffer' is to experience things like grief, wrong, pain,   *suffer*
punishment, loss or change. The sufferings of Jesus (readings 110
to 122) came to be known by the Latin word 'Passion'. Hence, 'to   *passion*
have compassion for' someone meant 'to suffer with' them or 'to   *compassion*
pity' them deeply. Anyone who is passionately in love, suffers a lot.   *pity*
And from Greek, 'to sympathize' meant exactly the same.   *love*
   sympathy

'The Chief Priests' were those Jerusalem priests who were members
of the Sanhedrin. They were very powerful in the Jewish world.   *priests*
They were at this time mainly of the Sadduceean party, and
descendants of Aaron.

This conception of 'feeding on the Words of the Creator' was not at
all new — see 'Moses law' in notes to 60.

And for 'eternal life' see 'life' in notes to 76.

81 Jesus heals an epileptic boy

**
from Luke 9, Matthew 17, and Mark 9: New English Bible

Next day when Jesus came down from the hills with Peter, James and John, they saw a large crowd. All at once a man in the crowd came up to Jesus, fell on his knees before him, and said, 'Have pity on my son, sir: he is an epileptic. He is possessed by a spirit which makes him speechless. Whenever it attacks him, it dashes him to the ground, and he foams at the mouth, grinds his teeth, and goes rigid. Have pity, sir. I brought him to your disciples but they could not cure him.' Jesus answered, 'What an unbelieving generation! Bring your son here.'

But before the boy could reach him he fell on the ground and rolled about foaming at the mouth. Jesus asked the father, 'How long has he been like this?' He replied, 'From childhood. But if it is at all possible for you, take pity upon us and help us.'

'If it is possible!' Jesus said. 'Everything is possible to one who has faith.'

'I have faith,' cried the boy's father; 'help me where my faith falls short.'

Jesus spoke sternly to the boy. Then the devil, after crying aloud and racking him fiercely, came out, and the boy looked like a corpse—in fact many said, 'He is dead.' But Jesus took his hand and raised him to his feet, and he stood up. Jesus gave him back to his father. And they were all struck with awe at the majesty of God.

Afterwards the disciples came to Jesus and asked him privately, 'Why could we not cast him out?' He answered, 'Your faith is too weak. I tell you this: if you have faith no bigger than a mustard seed, you will say to this mountain, "Move!", and it will move; nothing will prove impossible for you.'

'Epilepsy' is a nervous disease. Usually without any warning the patient falls unconscious and sometimes with convulsions, that is, violent and irregular movement due to involuntary contraction of the muscles. These fits often leave him frothing at the mouth and very exhausted. An 'epileptic' is someone who periodically suffers from these fits.

disease

At the time of the story opposite people believed evil spirits inhabited the body of the patient — see 'disease' in notes to 61.

'Sir' or 'Sire' comes from the Latin *Senior*, a man of superior age and therefore superior wisdom. In Italy they still say *Monsignor*, that is 'My Senior', and in France the same, *Monsieur*. And so on elsewhere. It is a term of respect. It translates in this reading from the Greek, 'My Master', often used for slave owners — see 'master' and 'Lord' in notes to 61.

Sir
Senior

Kneeling, for centuries past, had been the most respectful gesture of a slave, with hands clasped in front as if manacled, head bowed and eyes lowered, awaiting the 'pleasure' of his master (which 'pleasure' had been known to include chopping the slave's head off!)

kneel
slave

'Faith' was a catalyst in human relationships. Without 'an act of faith' from at least one party, no developments could follow. A 'faithful servant' was always 'sticking his neck out' and putting himself 'at the mercy of' someone else.

faith

In healing there are no hard and fast rules. It is a commerce of love. It is an organic realm in which faithful intercourse takes place (see 'Kingdom of Heaven' in notes to 80). Sometimes the healer's faith is needed (as in the case opposite), sometimes the patient's faith does the trick (as in reading 93) and sometimes it is the friends of the patient (as in reading 73). There are no hard and fast rules.

healing

As no cases of healing in the Bible provide a reliable medical record of the patient's continued good health after the cure, care must be taken not to draw the wrong conclusions from these stories. If extra evidence of true healing is required, it will have to be sought in the present age.

82 A story—'the good Samaritan'

**

from Luke 10, Mark 12, and Matthew 13 and 22 : New English Bible

On one occasion a lawyer came forward to put this test question to Jesus: 'Which is the greatest commandment?' He answered, "Love God with all your heart"—that commandment comes first; the second is like it: "Love your neighbour as yourself." '

The lawyer said to him, 'Well said, Master; but who is my neighbour?'

Jesus replied, 'A man was on his way from Jerusalem down to Jericho when he fell among robbers, who stripped him, beat him, and went off leaving him half dead. It so happened that a priest was going down by the same road; but when he saw him he went past on the other side. So too a Levite came to the place, and when he saw him he went past on the other side.

'But a Samaritan who was making the journey came upon him and, when he saw him, was moved to pity. He went up and bandaged his wounds, bathing them with oil and wine. Then he lifted him on to his own beast, brought him to an inn, and looked after him there. Next day he produced two silver pieces and gave them to the innkeeper and said, "Look after him; and if you spend any more I will repay you on my way back."

'Which of these three do you think was neighbour to the man who fell into the hands of the robbers?' The lawyer answered, 'The one who showed him kindness.'

Jesus said, 'Go and do as he did.'

Told between about AD 28 and 29
From writings between about AD 50 and 85

'Lawyer' — see 'Doctors of the Law' in notes to 67.

'Love' — see the whole of notes to 102.

This is a long parable but, like most parables, it only contains one main teaching point.

parables

In Jerusalem the lofty worship of the creator was carried out by priests (thoroughbred descendants of Aaron — notes to 11) and by assistant priests (thoroughbred descendants of Levi — note 10), but in this story the work of the creator was carried out by a mongrel (because Samaritans were reckoned by purist southern Jews to be of illegitimate descent — notes to 38 and reading 32).

priests
worship
Levite
Samaria

The 25 km (15 miles) from Mount Zion through the hills down to the Jordan valley was plagued by highwaymen — it was a familiar setting for such a story.

The oldest known city in the world is Jericho. Radiocarbon dating has indicated a population of about 3000 as early as 7800 BC. That means that, at the time of the parable of the Good Samaritan, Jericho was more than five times older than the venerated Jerusalem priesthood!

Jericho

83   Jesus turns towards Jerusalem

*

from Luke 9 and 13, Matthew 7, and Mark 10: New English Bible

Now Jesus set his face resolutely towards Jerusalem and sent messengers ahead. They went into a Samaritan village to make arrangements for him, but the villagers would not have him because he was making for Jerusalem. When James and John saw this they said, 'Lord, may we call down fire from Heaven to burn them up?—as Elijah did?' But he turned and rebuked them: 'I did not come to destroy men's lives but to save them.' And they went on to another village.

He continued his journey through towns and villages teaching as he made his way towards Jerusalem. Someone asked him, 'Sir, are only a few to be saved?' His answer was, 'The road that leads to life is narrow and the gate is small; those who find it are few. Struggle to get in through the narrow door, for I tell you that many people will come from north, south, east and west for the feast with Abraham, Isaac and Jacob, and all the prophets in the kingdom of Heaven. But many who are now first will be last.'

At that time a number of Pharisees said, 'You should leave this place and go on your way.' He replied, 'I must be on my way today because it is unthinkable for a prophet to meet his death anywhere but in Jerusalem.' They said, 'Herod is out to kill you.' He replied, 'Go and tell that fox, "On the third day I shall reach my goal".'

Happened between about AD *28 and 29*
From writings between about AD *50 and 85*

A passage of double-meanings! A talking at cross-purposes. *meaning*
Predictions, but of what?

A gathering of momentum, a gathering of clouds, a growing *expectation*
excitement, no one listening, fiery tempers, questions, narrow
paths, people sent ahead, nervous agents with veiled threats,
awkward doors, wild animals with cruel appetites, uncertainty all
round but, at the centre, resolution.

There was a popular vision (see 'apocalypse' in notes to 54) *apocalypse*
encouraged by groups like the Pharisees (notes to 53 and 63). There
would be a Belshazzar's Banquet in the Holy City. Corrupt leaders *Belshazzar*
would be destroyed. Foreigners would be expelled. The national
heroes would rise from their graves and greet the down-trodden
people who would rise from their miserable toil and march to the
capital, to the great feast, to the inauguration of a new age, a new
kingdom of eternal splendour, and heaven at last would come down
to earth!

All that was what most of the common people roughly believed at
this time. Their rulers knew it and were afraid. King Herod Antipas *Herod*
of Galilee, second son of Herod the Great, was no exception: *Antipas*
troublemakers must be encouraged to wander abroad, he felt.

(But Jesus had been talking about something quite different — see
readings 60 to 82.)

84 Jesus teaches : the meaning of humility

from Luke 14, and Matthew 18 : New English Bible

One Sabbath Jesus went to have a meal in the house of a leading Pharisee. When he noticed how the guests were trying to secure the places of honour, he spoke to them: 'When you are asked by someone to a feast, do not sit down in the place of honour. No, when you receive an invitation, go and sit down in the lowest place. For everyone who exalts himself will be humbled; and whoever humbles himself will be exalted.'

Then the disciples asked, 'Who is the greatest in the kingdom of Heaven?' He said, 'Let a man humble himself till he is like a child and he will be the greatest in the kingdom of Heaven.'

Then Jesus said to his host, 'When you give a lunch or dinner party, do not invite your friends, your relations or your rich neighbours; they will only ask you back again, and so you will be repaid! But when you give a party, ask the poor, the crippled, the lame and the blind; and so find happiness. For they have no means of repaying you, but you will be repaid.'

One of the company, after hearing all this, said to him, 'Happy the man who shall sit at the feast in the kingdom of God!'

A bizarre scene, if it is to be taken as plain history!   *history*

Again there was the Belshazzar fixation which gripped their minds   *Belshazzar*
(notes to 83). But he used it to make his point. The Kingdom of   *Kingdom*
Heaven was inhabited by humble people who accepted each other's
weaknesses (see 'love' in notes to 102), who put themselves last
and who were child-like (not childish!), and they were already repaid   *children*
with happiness, not plastic and commercial happiness, but
fabulous, heavenly, eternal, boundless happiness, bursting at the   *eternal*
seams with life, THERE AND THEN! (See 'happy' in notes to 64, 'life' in
notes to 76 and 'expectation' in notes to 77.)

'The Kingdom of Heaven' has often proved to be a deceptive   *Kingdom*
phrase. It has often encouraged the Belshazzar fixation where it
ought not to have done. A better translation would have been 'The
Sovereignty of Heaven', or

'A STATE OF AFFAIRS WHERE HEAVENLY VALUES FLOURISH'

85   A story—'the prodigal son'

from Luke 15 : New English Bible

Another time, the Pharisees and the doctors of the law began grumbling among themselves: 'This fellow,' they said, 'welcomes bad characters, and eats with them.'

Jesus answered them with this parable: 'There was once a man who had two sons; and the younger said to his father, "Father, give me my share of the property." So he divided his estate between them. A few days later the younger son turned the whole of his share into cash and left home for a distant country, where he squandered it in reckless living.

'When a severe famine fell upon that country, he began to feel the pinch. So he went and attached himself to one of the local landowners, who sent him on to his farm to mind the pigs. He would have been glad to fill his belly with the pods that the pigs were eating: no one gave him anything.

'Then he came to his senses and said, "How many of my father's paid servants have more than they can eat, and here am I, starving to death!" So he set out for his father's house.

'But while he was still a long way off, his father saw him, and his heart went out to him. He ran to meet him, flung his arms round him and kissed him. The son said, "Father, I have sinned against God and against you; I am no longer fit to be called your son; treat me as one of your paid servants."

'But the father said to his servants, "Quick! fetch my best robe, put it on him and put shoes on his feet. And let us celebrate! For this son of mine was lost and is found; he was dead and has come back to life." And the festivities began.'

'Prodigal' means 'recklessly wasteful'.   *prodigal*

Parables were double-decker fables, a popular vehicle for images of   *parables*
the double-thinker (notes to 69). A more conventional definition has   *double-think*
been 'an earthly story with a heavenly meaning'.

The point of the story opposite was to present a sketch of THE
CREATOR'S DELIGHTED RECOVERY OF A MISERABLE CREATURE. It was a
development of the saying in reading 64: 'How blest are those who   *Kingdom*
know that they are poor; the Kingdom of Heaven is theirs'.

This was a hard doctrine for people like the Scribes to swallow for   *Doctors of*
they imagined they were the pillars of society, the intelligentsia, the   *the Law*
faithful agents of philanthropy and organized charity. Jesus was   *philanthropy*
suggesting that they should 'repent' (notes to 59), that is, that they
should change their minds from the proud idea that they were doing   *repent*
rather well to the ACCEPTANCE-of-the-FACT of their natural self-   *pride*
centredness. But most of them dared not admit such 'poverty'
because they did not believe in the generous wealth of their creator
who was ACHING to come out and recover them!

All so-called 'sins' stemmed from this proud refusal to repent. Pride
was the most deadly of deadly sins.   *sin*

The translators of this reading have for some reason put 'God'
instead of 'heaven'. It is a pity because in this particular chapter   *God*
Luke avoided calling the Heavenly Father 'God'. It was the
respectful instinct of the Jew to find some title for him rather than
breathe his name (see notes to 95 on 'name'). In modern English the
word 'God' does seem a bit inadequate to describe such a majestic
and generous conception, in the same way that the word 'sex'
sometimes seems a silly little plastic word for those who wish to   *sex*
speak of love.

86   Jesus teaches : the treatment of money

from Luke 16 : New English Bible

Jesus said to his disciples, 'No servant can be the slave of two masters; for either he will hate the first and love the second, or he will be devoted to the first and think nothing of the second. You cannot serve God and Money.'

The Pharisees, who loved money, heard all this and scoffed at him. He said to them, 'You are the people who impress your fellow men with your righteousness; but God sees through you; for what sets itself up to be admired by men is detestable in the sight of God.

'The man who is dishonest in little things is dishonest also in great things. If then you have not proved trustworthy with the wealth of this world, who will trust you with the wealth that is real?'

Happened between about AD *28 and 29*
From writings between about AD *50 and 80*

There is a theory that the so-called Pharisees in the New Testament did not represent the true Pharisees of their day. On paper their manifesto was impressive but, as so often when people put politics and religion into practice, they accumulated a large number of unenterprising followers. These were the sort of middle-class passengers whom Jesus was always clashing with. In local life they enjoyed almost total control. Though their 'manifesto' was spelt out in religious terms—that was the complex interpretation of the Moses law—they applied it as a moral code which gave them great social influence but which also trapped them. They suffered from every sort of xenophobia and suffocated within a self-made shell of dogmatism.

Pharisees

xenophobia

There was a proverb of this time which said, 'The *love of* money is the root of all evil.' It has often been misquoted as, 'Money is the root of all evil,' and, if this is the sort of thing people think today, no wonder the teaching of Jesus is a closed book to so many.

love
money
rich
Bible

On the contrary, see the third paragraph of this reading: money certainly had a face value but it also had a secret value, for when it was in circulation it was a representation of relationships; if their dealings with each other were dishonest, so would they be with their creator.

money

'Money' here was the word for possessions and property.

87 Jesus teaches : the question of divorce

*

from Mark 10 and Matthew 19 : New English Bible

On leaving those parts, Jesus came into the regions of Judaea and Transjordan, and when a crowd gathered round him once again he followed his usual practice and taught them. And he healed them.

Some Pharisees came and tested him by asking, 'Is there any ground on which it is lawful for a man to divorce his wife?' He answered, 'Because God made them male and female, a man shall be made one with his wife. The two shall become one flesh—they are no longer two individuals.'

And he added, 'Whoever divorces his wife and marries another commits adultery against her. So too, if she divorces her husband and marries another, she commits adultery. It was because you were so unteachable that Moses gave you permission to divorce your wives; but I tell you, they are one flesh and what God has joined together, man must not separate.'

The disciples said to him, 'If that is the position, it is better to refrain from marriage.' To this he replied, 'Let those accept it who can.'

The people brought children for him to touch and the disciples scolded them for it. But when Jesus saw this he was indignant and said, 'Let the children come to me, for the kingdom of Heaven belongs to such as these.' And he put his arms round them and blessed them.

See reading 17, Moses law Rule 7: 'You shall not commit adultery.' *adultery*
(And see notes to 17 and, especially, 26 on 'adultery'.)

See note to 40 on 'Deuteronomy': it was generally believed that this   *Deuteron-*
'Book of the Law' had been written by Moses himself. Here is the   *omy*
passage this reading refers to: 'Supposing a man has taken a wife   *women*
and consummated the marriage; but . . . he has found some
impropriety of which to accuse her; so he has made out a writ of
divorce for her and . . . dismissed her from his house; she leaves
. . . to become the wife of another man. If this other man takes a
dislike and . . . dismisses her . . . or . . . happens to die, her first
husband who had repudiated her may not take her back as his wife
. . .'—and so on. This complex sort of legislation was the happy
hunting ground of anyone who wanted a good argument!   *divorce*

Divorce was terribly easy at the time: among the Jews one school of
the rabbis taught in practice that the husband might divorce his wife
if he got tired of her (though not, incidentally, she him); among non-
Jews, divorces were also becoming common at this time even
though the tradition of republican Rome had 'strictly upheld the
sanctity of marriage'.   *marriage*

Jesus referred to the biological fact of the matter: the process of
copulation like everything else had evolved from the mysterious   *copulation*
Source of Life and, in that perspective, it invited the respect of
every body — the two performers as well as the various legislative
bodies.

See 'sin', 'faith' and 'atonement' in note to 18.

The Kingdom of Heaven was said to belong to people of child-like   *Kingdom*
character. The cynic would say that a child was an exceedingly
'selfish' animal. But perhaps it would be more constructive to think   *children*
of a child's almost infinite capacity for 'receptiveness'! If heaven
was womb-like (notes to 71) then the prime function of its offspring
would be 'the capacity to receive'. (See the great theological leap
forward in notes to 148.)

88   An incident in the temple

from John 8: New English Bible

At daybreak Jesus appeared again in the temple and all the people gathered round him. He had taken his seat and was engaged in teaching them when the doctors of the law and the Pharisees brought in a woman. Making her stand out in the middle, they said to him, 'Master, this woman was caught in the very act of adultery. In the Law, Moses has laid down that such women are to be stoned. What do you say about it?'

They put the question as a test, hoping to frame a charge against him. Jesus bent down and wrote with his finger on the ground. When they continued to press their question, he sat up straight and said, 'That one of you who is faultless shall throw the first stone.' Then once again he bent down and wrote on the ground.

When they heard what he said, one by one they went away convicted by their conscience, the eldest first. And Jesus was left alone with the woman standing there.

Jesus again sat up and said to the woman, 'Where are they? Has no one condemned you?'

'No one, sir,' she said.

Jesus replied, 'No more do I. You may go; do not sin again.'

Happened between about AD *28 and 29*
Written between about AD *90 and 95*

A rich man was an owner and absolute ruler of property, cattle and women. A poor man was the same in theory. He owned his wife. He could divorce her if he wished to very easily. He was a father by the time he was about nineteen and a grandfather by about thirty-eight — if he lived that long. There was not a word in Hebrew for 'bachelor'. He could sell naughty daughters if he wished as slaves.

women
authority

A woman's place was in the home. She had been married off at an early age, and when the first baby arrived she was a busy woman. She was usually up before dawn. She brought all the water to the house from the community well. She did the milking, made cheese and butter, made the fire, baked every day, and boiled meat and vegetables. She used perfumes and the odd cosmetics and kept up with fashion in her dress and hairstyle. There were no drains or running water. The word 'leisure' was meaningless. She was often pregnant. Those babies that survived she breast-fed for two or three years. She taught them their first prayers and songs. She also taught them to work very hard indeed.

houses

cosmetics

family
education
work

Because of this busy domestic structure, adultery was considered to be rather extravagant! In fact since the early days in Canaan (readings 19—21) it had become unlawful (reading 17), partly because the early Israelites had automatically objected to many Canaanite customs, one of which had been religious prostitution in their temples. The Jews' most vital social unit was the family and all their laws and customs protected it. The average family at this time had probably four or five children.

adultery

family

This reading is almost certainly not the work of the writer of 'John's Gospel' (notes to 108) — some scholars have detected the style of Luke.

John the
Evangelist
Luke?

89   A story about humility

*

from Luke 18 : New English Bible

And here is another parable that Jesus told. It was aimed at those who were sure of their own goodness and looked down on everyone else.

'Two men went up to the temple to pray, one a Pharisee and the other a tax-gatherer. The Pharisee stood up and prayed thus privately: "I thank thee, O God, that I am not like the rest of men, greedy, dishonest, adulterous, or for that matter like this tax-gatherer. I fast twice a week; I pay tithes on all that I get."

'But the other kept his distance and would not even raise his eyes to heaven, but beat upon his breast saying, "O God, have mercy on me, sinner that I am." It was this man I tell you, and not the other, who went home acquitted of his sins. For everyone who exalts himself will be humbled; and whoever humbles himself will be exalted.'

Told between about AD *28* and *29*
From writings between about AD *50* and *80*

For 'Pharisee' and 'tax-collectors' see notes to 63.

'Fasting' meant going without food. The over-night fast is broken at *fast* 'breakfast'. Fasting was a religious exercise. It could last for days. It helped to purge a man and focus him.

'Tithes' were taxes paid for the upkeep of the temple. *tax*

To 'exalt someone' was to 'lift him up high into the air' and to *exalt* 'humble him', was to 'put him on the ground among the humus'! *humble* But of course, Jesus was 'double-talking' — see 'double-think' in notes to 69 and 'the Kingdom of Heaven' in notes to 84.

Compare this parable also with the process of 'repentance' in notes to 85.

90 A rich young man

from Mark 10, Matthew 19 and Luke 18: New English Bible

As Jesus was starting out on a journey, a stranger came up, a young man of the ruling class, and asked him, 'Master, what good must I do to gain eternal life?' 'Good?' said Jesus. 'Why do you ask me about that? No one is good except God alone. But if you wish to enter life, keep the commandments.'

'Which commandments?' he asked. Jesus answered, 'Do not murder; do not commit adultery; do not steal; do not give false evidence; do not defraud; honour your father and mother.'

The man answered, 'I have kept all these since I was a boy. Where do I fall short?' Jesus looked straight at him; his heart warmed to him and he said, 'There is still one thing lacking. If you wish to go the whole way, sell your possessions, give to the poor and follow me.'

When the young man heard this, he went away with a heavy heart; for he was a man of great wealth.

When Jesus saw it he said, 'How hard it is for the wealthy to enter the kingdom of God! It is easier for a camel to go through the eye of a needle!' They were amazed that he should say this, but Jesus insisted, 'Children, how hard it is to enter the kingdom of God!' They were more astonished than ever and said to one another, 'Then who can be saved?'

Jesus looked them in the face and said, 'Everything is possible for God.'

Happened between about AD *28 and 29.*
From writings between about AD *50 and 85*

'Good' — the most colourless of all words; 'goodness' — the most *good*
unrewarding of all qualities; 'the good life' — whatever it may mean,
the most boring possible existence! That was the verdict of the rich
young man opposite.

The opinion about the Bible, incidentally, among most people today *Bible*
is very similar. And this is almost certainly because it has been used *education*
by teachers — and still is by many — as a device for turning out 'good
girls and boys'. The Bible is for many a colourless, unrewarding and
boring Aunt Agatha. And it remains a closed book for many.

The young man wanted to come alive — the writer called it 'eternal *eternal*
life' (see notes to 76 on 'eternal' and notes to 84 on the 'Kingdom of
Heaven'). He had been to the synagogue and all that (see notes to
76 on 'will') but it had not turned him on.

In this particular case Jesus diagnosed 'love of money' (note to 86), *money*
and prescribed 'poverty'. Notice, this advice was given to an
individual person at a particular time, not to the world at large.

The choice lay with the young man. His free will was the vital switch *will*
and he alone could operate it. His own authority was supreme. *authority*

This price for 'life' however proved too high for the man — at the *hope*
time of the story, anyway. But the end of this reading hints at 'divine
initiative' (see the end of reading 42 and notes to 73 on
'atonement'); there was still hope. *atonement*

91   A story about vineyard workers

*

from Matthew 19 and 20 : New English Bible

Jesus said to his disciples, 'There was once a landowner who went out early one morning to hire labourers for his vineyard; and after agreeing to pay them the usual day's wage he sent them off to work. Going out three hours later he saw some more men standing idle in the market place. "Go and join the others in the vineyard," he said, "and I will pay you a fair wage": so off they went.

'At noon and at three in the afternoon he went out again and made the same arrangement. An hour before sunset he found another group standing there, so he said to them, "Go and join the others in the vineyard."

'In the evening, those who had started work an hour before sunset came forward and were paid the full day's wage. When it was the turn of the men who had come first, they expected something extra, but were paid the same amount as the others. As they took it they grumbled at their employer: "These late comers have done only one hour's work, yet you have put them on a level with us who have sweated the whole day long in the blazing sun!"

'The owner turned to one of them and said, "My friend, I am not being unfair to you. You agreed on the usual wage for the day, did you not? Surely I am free to do what I like with my own money. Why be jealous because I am kind?"

'Thus,' said Jesus, 'the last will be first, and the first last. The kingdom of Heaven is like this.'

Imagine the surprise and sweaty anger! Imagine the late-comers with their fat pay-packets nipping smartly round the corner, avoiding conversation! A delicious story of bizarre injustice. It was a parable with, as usual, a single main teaching point: heavenly values were surprisingly different from plain human values (see notes to 84 on the 'Kingdom of Heaven').   *values*

One of the secondary or incidental points in the parable was the idea that criticism was not 'a good thing' — see reading 69. The only useful comparison for a person to make was between himself and his creator. Everybody was unique and so comparison with other people's fortunes was an unrealistic and sterile preoccupation.   *criticize*

92   Jesus forecasts his death

***

from Mark 10 and Luke 18 : New English Bible

They were on the road going up to Jerusalem, Jesus leading the way; and the disciples were filled with awe, while those who followed behind were afraid. He took the twelve aside and began to tell them what was to happen to him. 'We are now going to Jerusalem,' he said, 'and the Son of Man will be given up to the chief priests and the doctors of law. They will condemn him to death and hand him over to the foreign power. He will be mocked and spat upon, flogged and killed; and three days afterwards, he will rise again.'

But they understood nothing of all this; they did not grasp what he was talking about; its meaning was concealed from them.

'Awe' was a mixture of respectful fear and speechless wonder. A *awe*
person who was filled with awe by something on the one hand kept
his distance and on the other hand felt a powerful attraction (see
reading 11). The modern word 'awful' is exhausted now and no
longer means 'full of awe'.

Passover week was approaching. Thousands of Jews were *Passover*
converging upon Jerusalem. Estimates of the number of pilgrims
vary between 125 000 and a million. The City measured no more
than 1½ sq. km (½ sq. mile) at that time.

There was the excitement usual in such crowds. But there was also
this Jewish sense of expectation: the Messiah must surely come *expectation*
soon: Rome, 'the foreign power', could not last for ever: even the
Jews' own crooked leaders would be brought to their knees. But
how long? And what would the consequences be? The fear of the
unknown was also among the crowds.

Most of Jesus' followers had come from the North. Few, if any,
understood what was really going on. There were so many rumours,
so many theories, so many unsolved puzzles. As he approached
Jerusalem, the number of his followers was erupting and so were
their expectations.

93 Blind Bartimaeus

from Mark 10: New English Bible

As Jesus was leaving Jericho with his disciples and a large crowd, Bartimaeus son of Timaeus, a blind beggar, was seated at the roadside. Hearing that it was Jesus of Nazareth, he began to shout, 'Son of David, Jesus, have pity on me!' Many of the people rounded on him: 'Be quiet,' they said; but he shouted all the more, 'Son of David, have pity on me.'

Jesus stopped and said, 'Call him.' So they called the blind man and said, 'Take heart; stand up; he is calling you.' At that he threw off his cloak, sprang up and came to Jesus. Jesus said to him, 'What do you want me to do for you?' 'Master,' the blind man answered, 'I want my sight back.' Jesus said to him, 'Go; your faith has cured you.' At once he recovered his sight and followed him on the road.

Happened between about AD *28 and 29*
Written in about AD *65*

This short scene was put in here as if it were intended to be an acted parable. It said, 'Open your eyes now if you really want to know what I have been trying to teach you. Words will fall short. Follow me on this road and I will act it all out for you'.

parable

silence

The blind man invoked the powerful name of David. His mind contained the popular thought-forms about David and his illustrious descendants — see notes to 24, 25, 26 and, especially, 27; also the last paragraph in reading 40.

David
expectation

For 'healing' and 'faith' see notes to 81.

94 The Jewish Council makes plans

**

from John 11 and 7: New English Bible

Now many of the Jews who had seen what Jesus did, put their faith in him
But some of them went off to the Pharisees and reported what he had done.

Thereupon the chief priests and the Pharisees convened a meeting of the
Council. 'What action are we taking?' they said. 'This man is performing
many signs. If we leave him alone like this the whole populace will believe in
him. Then the Romans will come and sweep away our temple and our nation.'
Then Caiaphas, who was High Priest that year, said, 'It is more to your
interest that one man should die for the people, than that the whole nation
should be destroyed.'

But one of their number, Nicodemus, intervened. He asked them, 'Does our
law permit us to pass judgement on a man unless we have first given him a
hearing and learned the facts?' 'Are you a Galilean too?' they retorted
'Study the scriptures and you will find that prophets do not come from
Galilee.'

So from that day on they plotted his death.

The Jewish Passover was now at hand, and many people went up from the
country to Jerusalem. They looked out for Jesus, and as they stood in the
temple they asked one another, 'What do you think? Perhaps he is not
coming to the festival.' Now the chief priests and the Pharisees had given
orders that anyone who knew where he was should give information, so that
they might arrest him.

Happened between about AD *28 and 29*
Written between about AD *90 and 95*

The 'chief priests' in Jerusalem were mainly Sadducees. They must   *priests*
have been extremely anxious if they were prepared to work with   *Sadducees*
their arch-enemies the Pharisees. They had heard alarming rumours   *Pharisees*
about 'the signs and wonders' surrounding this Jesus, but none
among them seemed to have actually witnessed any (see reading
79).

The 'Council' was the Sanhedrin, the supreme court of justice in   *Sanhedrin*
Jerusalem. It consisted of about seventy members, mainly the
aristocratic Sadducees, but it also included some Scribes and
Pharisees. It dealt with the religious problems of the whole Jewish
world, collected taxes, and acted as the civil court of Jerusalem   *tax*
itself.

The 'High Priest' almost certainly presided over the Sanhedrin.
Caiaphas (pronounced kye-er-fass) had been appointed in about AD   *Caiaphas*
18. He was eventually deposed in AD 37. He was the son-in-law of
Annas (see notes to 111).

'Nicodemus' — see notes to 123.

Note the xenophobic attitude to Galileans (see note to 86 on   *xenophobia*
'Pharisees'.)

95 Jesus enters Jerusalem

***
from John 12, Mark 11, and Luke 19 : New English Bible

The next day the great body of pilgrims who had come to the festival, hearing that Jesus was on the way to Jerusalem, took palm branches and went out to meet him, shouting, 'Hosanna! Blessings on him who comes in the name of the Lord! God bless the king of Israel!'

So they brought the colt to Jesus and spread their coats on it, and he mounted. And people carpeted the road with their cloaks, while others spread brushwood which they had cut in the fields, in accordance with the text of Scripture: 'Fear no more, daughter of Zion; see your king is coming, mounted on an ass.'

And now, as he approached the descent from the Mount of Olives, the whole company of his disciples in their joy began to sing aloud the praises of God for all the things they had seen: 'Blessings on him who comes as king in the name of the Lord! Peace in heaven! Glory in highest heaven!'

Some Pharisees who were in the crowd said to him, 'Master, reprimand your disciples.' He answered, 'I tell you, if my disciples keep silence, the stones will shout aloud.'

Happened between about AD *28 and 29*
From writings between about AD *50 and 95*

The words shouted by the people look odd in English translation but they were popular Hebrew songs which everyone knew well. These particular songs were from Psalm 118 which was sung each year during the actual Passover sacrifice in the Temple. 'Hosanna!' meant roughly, 'God save us!'

Hosanna

The Pharisees were objecting partly to the careless use of the phrase 'King of Israel'. It is impossible to tell how many of the crowd were in dead earnest but that was not the Pharisees' point. The Messiah movement was far too explosive an affair to jest with.

kings
Messiah

But worse still was the use of 'the name of the Lord'. To claim that he was a king was 'subversion', a civil crime. But this was 'blasphemy', a religious crime and far worse in the eyes of a Jew. The point about a name was that it stood for the person himself, and it *was* almost that person himself. If the name of the person was invoked, so was his character and his authority. This crowd was therefore welcoming Jesus as 'the Messiah', the divine deliverer of heaven. Many of them may have been unaware of what they were saying. However, Jesus did not deny it when the Pharisees challenged him to.

name

Messiah

The 'text of Scripture' referred to is the latter part of Zechariah written after about 500 BC. An ass was a symbol of peace. A horse would have meant war.

ass

Was there the mark of a cross on the back of a donkey before this time? Powerful and evocative legends have followed him a long way.

96 Jesus against hypocrisy

from Matthew 23 : New English Bible

Jesus then addressed the people and his disciples in these words: 'The doctors of the law and the Pharisees sit in the chair of Moses, therefore do what they tell you—pay attention to their words. But do not follow their practice, for they say one thing and do another.

'They make up heavy packs and pile them on men's shoulders but will not raise a finger to lift the load themselves. Whatever they do is done for show. They like to have places of honour at feasts and the chief seats in synagogues, to be greeted respectfully in the street and to be addressed as "rabbi".

'Alas, alas for you lawyers and Pharisees, hypocrites that you are! Alas for you blind guides! You travel over land and sea to win one convert, and when you have won him you make him twice as fit for hell as you are yourselves. You do not enter the kingdom of Heaven yourselves, and when others are entering you stop them—you shut the door in their faces.

'Alas for you lawyers and Pharisees, hypocrites: you clean the outside of cup and dish which you have filled inside by self-indulgence! Blind guides! You strain off a midge yet gulp down a camel! What blindness!

'You snakes, you vipers' brood, how can you escape being condemned to hell? You will receive the severest sentence.

'O Jerusalem, Jerusalem, the city that murders the messengers sent to her! How often have I longed to gather your children, as a hen gathers her brood under her wings—but you would not let me. Your temple is forsaken by God.

'Alas for you!' meant, 'How wearying it is to think about you!' and, 'How pitiful you are!'   *Alas!*

For 'hypocrites' see notes to 67; 'done for show', notes to 75; 'places of honour', reading 84; 'Rabbi', notes to 61; 'blind guides', reading 69; 'lawyers', notes to 67; 'Pharisees' notes to 63. 'Heavy packs' were loads of incomprehensible laws.

For the idea of a 'forsaken temple', see the prophet Micah in reading 37; for the idea of 'hell', see notes to 68.

'Messengers' here were the 'prophets' — see notes to 45.

And for 'the Kingdom of Heaven' see notes to 84.

It may be comfortable to think of the child Jesus as being 'meek and mild', but there is no evidence for such a sentiment, and this document shows a very different image!   *Jesus*

97 He weeps over Jerusalem

*

from Luke 19: New English Bible

When Jesus came in sight of the city, he wept over it and said, 'If only you had known, on this great day, the way that leads to peace! But no; it is hidden from your sight. For a time will come upon you, when your enemies will set up siege works against you; they will encircle you and hem you in at every point; they will bring you to the ground, you and your children within your walls, and not leave one stone standing on another, because you did not recognize God's moment when it came.'

Happened between about AD *28 and 29*
From writings between about AD *50 and 80*

His lamentation — many echoes here from the Old Testament: see   *lament*
especially reading 42. It had all happened before.

There lay Jerusalem, beautiful and desirable as ever (reading 48),   *expectation*
but abandoned by her heavenly lord, her temple worship no longer
responding to the pulse of his divine love (reading 29 and notes to
30), oblivious of the approaching crisis (notes to 77 on
'expectation').

In AD 66 the Jews rebelled against Roman occupation. It was the
result of the turbulence of the people and the misgovernment of the
Roman procurators after Pontius Pilate. Four years of siege   *siege*
followed. In AD 70 Jerusalem fell, most of the population was either   *third temple*
exterminated or removed, and the city with its temple was utterly
destroyed. In about AD 130 the Emperor Hadrian rebuilt it. He   *Hadrian*
erected in the temple area statues of himself and Jupiter. To the
Romans, Jupiter (or Jove) was the god of the sky, their version of   *Jupiter*
the Greek Zeus (notes to 54). Since then, Jewish visions of a   *Zeus*
peaceful City of God have suffered many miserable modifications.

98 He goes to the temple

from Matthew 21 and John 2 : New English Bible

When Jesus entered Jerusalem the whole city went wild with excitement.
'Who is this?' people asked, and the crowd replied, 'This is the prophet
Jesus, from Nazareth in Galilee.'

Jesus then went into the temple and drove out all who were buying and
selling in the temple precincts; there he found in the temple the dealers in
cattle, sheep and pigeons, and the money-changers seated at their tables.
Jesus made a whip of cords and drove them out of the temple, sheep, cattle,
and all. He upset the tables of the money-changers, scattering their coins.
Then he turned on the dealers in pigeons: 'Take them out,' he said; 'you must
not turn my Father's house into a market. Scripture says, "My house shall
be called a house of prayer"; but you are making it a robbers' cave.'

The Jews challenged Jesus: 'What sign,' they asked, 'can you show as
authority for your action?'

'Destroy this temple,' Jesus replied, 'and in three days I will raise it again.'

They said, 'It has taken forty-six years to build this temple. Are you going
to raise it again in three days?'

But the temple he was speaking of was his body.

Happened between about AD *26 and 29*
From writings between about AD *50 and 95*

The father of each family (or the senior member of each community of up to about ten or twelve) had to bring a lamb (or sometimes a smaller animal) and, in relays before the priests, slaughter it without breaking any bones, offer its blood to the altar (the priests collecting the blood in gold and silver bowls and flinging it at the foot of the altar which had special drains), flay it, give the fat to the priests for the Passover Sacrifice, prepare it for cooking, take it home and roast it for the Passover Feast.

sacrifice

priests

Passover

Many thousands of Jews were there — see 'Passover' in notes to 92. There was consequently a roaring trade in the temple precincts: not just in animals but in all the necessary and unnecessary things people buy when away from home in a festive mood.

third temple

'The Jews' in this reading were the temple authorities. They had shares in the Passover markets. They also ensured that all the foreign currencies coming in from all over the Roman Empire, being of course 'unclean', did not enter the temple precincts: hence the money-changers, with often dishonest rates of exchange, and the money-lenders, with often exorbitant rates cf interest.

money

Pilgrims also paid their temple tax at this time and it could only be handed over in temple coinage. It was a high time for crooks. (See the first two paragraphs of notes to 103.)

tax

The authorities, imprisoned in their bureaucracy, could not permit irregular practices — they had to be in receipt of a valid 'sign' (notes to 79). But he gave them another riddle.

99 A widow's gift

from Mark 12 and Luke 21 : New English Bible

His days were given to teaching in the temple and in the early morning people flocked to listen to him. Once he was standing opposite the temple treasury, watching as people dropped their money into the chest. Many rich people were giving large sums. Presently there came a poor widow who dropped in two tiny coins. He called his disciples to him. 'I tell you this,' he said, 'this poor widow has given more than any of the others; for those others had more than enough, but she, with less than enough, has given all that she had to live on.'

Happened between about AD *28 and 29*
From writings between about AD *50 and 80*

Modern and rather tired folklore says about giving, 'It's the thought   *give*
that counts,' and about money, 'Quality comes before quantity.'   *money*
But perhaps the story opposite is more penetrating.

100 Jesus talks of a 'Judgement' to come

*

from Matthew 25 : New English Bible

And Jesus said: 'When the Son of Man comes in his glory and all the angels with him, he will sit in state on this throne, with all the nations gathered before him. He will separate men into two groups, as a shepherd separates the sheep from the goats. Then the king will say to those on his right hand, "You have my Father's blessing; come, enter and possess the kingdom that has been ready for you since the world was made. For when I was hungry, you gave me food; when thirsty, you gave me drink; when I was a stranger you took me into your home, when naked you clothed me; when I was ill you came to my help, when in prison you visited me."

'Then he will say to those on his left hand, "The curse is upon you—go from my sight to the eternal fire that is ready for the devil and his angels. For when I was hungry and thirsty, you gave me nothing; when I was a stranger you gave me no home; when I was naked and ill and in prison, you did not come to my help." And they will reply, "Lord, when was it that we saw you and did nothing for you?" And he will answer, "I tell you this: anything you did not do for one of these, however humble, you did not do for me".'

Jesus put his picture into the popular apocalyptic framework. See   *apocalypse*
notes to 83.

'Son of Man' was a tricky title. In the Old Testament it had usually   *Son of Man*
meant 'mankind', and later 'an ideal figure representing mankind'.
Christian interpreters have usually insisted of course that in the New
Testament it referred to Jesus.

101 The question of 'tribute to Caesar'

**

from Mark 12, Matthew 22 and Luke 20: New English Bible

A number of Pharisees and men of Herod's party were sent to trap Jesus with a question. They came and said to him, 'Master, you are an honest man, we know, and truckle to no man whoever he may be. You teach in all honesty the way of life that God requires. Are we or are we not permitted to pay taxes to the Roman Emperor?'

He saw how crafty their question was and said, 'Why are you trying to catch me out? Fetch me a silver piece and let me look at it.'

They brought one and he said to them, 'Whose head is this? And whose inscription?'

'Caesar's,' they replied.

Then Jesus said, 'Pay Caesar what is due to Caesar, and pay God what is due to God.'

This answer took them by surprise and they fell silent. Thus their attempt to catch him out in public failed and they went away.

Herod Antipas (notes to 83) was in Jerusalem for Passover — being half-Jew through his mother. He had a sizeable palace in the city, inherited from his great and silly father. He was the Herod who, with his sadistic second-hand wife Herodias, had recently beheaded John the Baptist by mistake at a birthday party. But he had a conscience because, for a time, he had imagined Jesus to be the ghost of John: there had been quite a scare about it (reading 80, paragraph 3). For John the Baptist, see readings 55 and 59.

Herod
Antipas

John the
Baptist

The Roman emperor at this time was Tiberius. His predecessor had been Augustus (reading 57). All emperors were now called 'Caesar' after the famous Julius Caesar, first dictator of about 45 BC. At this time every inhabitant of Judaea had to pay a special tax directly to the emperor's privy purse and it had to be paid in Roman coinage. The mere mention of it therefore infuriated Jews because it symbolized their subjugation to Rome; they held that their only real allegiance should be to Yahweh.

Emperor
Tiberius
Augustus
tax

If Jesus had said it was right to pay the imperial tax, they would have reported him to the High Priest, Caiaphas, and he would have been charged with blasphemy. And if he had said it was wrong to pay it, they would have reported him to the Roman Procurator, Pontius Pilate, and hoped to see him charged with treason.

blasphemy
Caiaphas

treason
Pilate

102 The Great Commandment

***
from Mark 12 : New English Bible

Then one of the lawyers who had been listening to these discussions and had noticed how well Jesus answered, came forward and asked him, 'Which commandment is first of all?' Jesus answered, 'The first is, "Hear, O Israel: the Lord your God is the only Lord; love the Lord your God with all your heart, with all your soul, with all your mind, and with all your strength." The second is this: "Love your neighbour as yourself". There is no other commandment greater than these.' The lawyer said to him, 'Well said, Master. You are right in saying that God is one and beside him there is no other. And to love him with all your heart, your understanding, and your strength, and to love your neighbour as yourself—that is far more than any burnt offering or sacrifices.'

When Jesus saw how sensibly he answered, he said to him, 'You are not far from the kingdom of God.'

Happened between about AD *28 and 29*
Written in about AD *65*

This lawyer was one of the 'scribes'. They tended to know everything about complicated Jewish law. To challenge someone to an argument about legal matters was a national sport and scribes were generally champions.

Doctors of the Law

The answer Jesus gave was a quotation from writings which had been known for at least 500 years. It was the famous summary of the Moses-law (reading 17) from the 'Book of Deuteronomy' (notes to 40). 'Loving God' covered the first four commandments and 'Loving Man' covered the other six. No one could quarrel with his reply. It was neat.

Moses-law

Deuteron-omy

'Heart' meant the physical organ which they believed contained personality, character, intentions and will power.

heart

'Soul' meant the pure body of flesh and blood and breath, with its senses, emotions and desires.

soul

'Mind' meant understanding and powers of reasoning.

minds

'Strength' meant physical powers and abilities, physical health, energy and vigour.

strength

'Neighbour' meant people generally. 'Love' in this context meant roughly speaking, 'affection', positive and uncomplicated affection; people who gave it were 'philanthropic', that is, they loved mankind without prejudice.

neighbour

philanthropy

'Loving God', however, meant simply reflecting his love. He was said to be LOVE itself. So to love him involved turning towards him, picking up his vibrations, focusing on him, recognizing his true worth, realizing his 'worthship', worshipping him, that is, reflecting as much as possible to him and allowing all that overflowed to spill among other people. (It is, technically speaking, the divine love called 'charity'—the complement to the three 'natural' loves mentioned in notes to 157. But the popular word 'charity' today has blurred this original meaning.)

love

charity

'Contemplation' is unworded prayer based upon this sort of love. It is a religious exercise used in several religions. The Hindus call it 'yoga' and have practised it since about 500 BC.

contempla-tion
Hindu
yoga

This sort of analysis can go on for too long however, and it can destroy the thing it is trying to discover! When all these details are put back into 'the neat reply' opposite, the key word which sustains it is 'integrity' (see again notes to 40).

integrity

103 The chief priests plot

***

from Matthew 26 and Luke 22 : New English Bible

When Jesus had finished this discourse he said to his disciples, 'You know that in two days' time it will be Passover, and the Son of Man is to be handed over for crucifixion.'

Then the chief priests and the elders of the nation met in the palace of the High Priest, Caiaphas; and there they conferred together on a scheme to have Jesus arrested by some trick and put to death. 'It must not be during the festival,' they said, 'or there may be rioting among the people.'

Then Satan entered into Judas Iscariot, who was one of the Twelve; and Judas went to the chief priests and officers of the temple police to discuss ways and means of putting Jesus into their power. They were greatly pleased and undertook to pay him a sum of money. They weighed him out thirty silver pieces. He agreed, and began to look out for an opportunity to betray him to them without collecting a crowd.

Happened in about AD *29 in the Spring*
From writings between about AD *50 and 85*

Vast crowds in Jerusalem. Many of the more easy-going Jews from *Passover*
Samaria and Galilee. Springtime, season of riots and revolutions. *riots*
Annual festival. Excitement and expectation among the people. *expectation*
Guilt and fear among their leaders who presided over so many
crooked practices in public places. Rumours everywhere. Much
money changing hands. Quick money. Swindlers. Lies. No time for
upright politics — too much at stake.

(Yet there were also, of course, good people who were going quietly *history*
through the annual ceremonies and really making contact with the
source of their goodness. They did not draw attention to
themselves. They were not making history. See, for example,
reading 99.)

There was at this time a political movement among the more hot- *Zealots*
blooded Jews to bring on by force the birth of a new age: Rome
would be banished for ever and those Jewish leaders who had
compromised with Rome in any way would be deposed. The
movement appealed to the fiery-tempered. Their zeal was fed by the
common belief that God would send a special messenger to the
rescue, 'the Messiah', who would lead them to victory. They were *Messiah*
called the Zealots.

Several of Jesus' disciples may have belonged to this party. If Judas *Judas*
Iscariot belonged, it would explain his motive: he loved the man *Iscariot*
Jesus as the others did, but he believed Jesus would be the Messiah
only if he were less humble; someone, thought Judas, must force a
confrontation between Jesus and Caiaphas, and then his unique
genius would come to light.

The fourth Gospel says Judas was a mean-hearted thief who would
do anything for money. The other Gospels give no reason for his
treachery. The other eleven disciples may have been prejudiced *prejudice*
against him from the start since he was probably a Judaean and
they were all Northerners. If so, they would for ever see this 'plot' as
the work of a traitor. Their horror would never allow them to suspect
the zeal of a misguided friend.

104 Preparations for the Passover

**

from Luke 22 and Mark 14 : New English Bible

Then came the day of Unleavened Bread, on which the Passover victim had to be slaughtered, and Jesus sent Peter and John with these instructions: 'Go and prepare for our Passover supper.' They said, 'Where would you like us to make preparations?' He replied, 'As soon as you set foot in the city a man will meet you carrying a jar of water. Follow him into the house that he enters and give this message to the householder: "The Master says, 'Where is the room in which I may eat the Passover with my disciples?' " He will show you a large room upstairs all set out: make the preparations there.'

Then the disciples went off, and when they came into the city they found everything just as he had told them. So they prepared for Passover.

Happened in about AD *29 in the spring, on the Thursday of Passover week before 6 p.m.*
From writings between about AD *50 and 80*

For the 'slaughter of the Passover victim', see note to 98 on 'Passover'. 'Preparations' meant getting the food bought and prepared and also clearing out the house, a spring clean, decorations, seeing there was plenty of lamp oil in stock and putting on clean clothes. 'A man carrying a jar of water' would have been very easy to spot since the women did all that (notes to 88); it must have been a pre-arranged signal, for Jesus wanted to avoid arrest — until he was ready for arrest, it seems.

time

The Jewish twenty-four-hour day started at 6 o'clock in the evening (marked ■ in the table). The chart below should help to plot the course of the narrative during the next three days. The arrangement is however more traditional than historically conclusive. There are technical problems (see notes to 105 on 'Last Supper' for example).

Modern time		Jewish time	these readings	
Thursday	noon			
	3		104	preparations
	6	■————		
	9		105 - 9	supper
	midnight		110 - 12	trials at night
	3	Preparation	113	death of Judas?
		day for the		
	6	Sabbath	114 - 15	to Pilate, then Herod
	9		116 - 19	to Pilate again
Friday	noon		120 - 1	crucifixion
	3		122 - 3	death
	6	■————	124 - 5	burial
	9			
	midnight			
	3			
	6	Sabbath		
	9			
Saturday	noon			
	3			
	6	■————		
	9			
	midnight			
	3	The day		
	6	after	126 - 8	empty tomb
	9	the Sabbath		. . . and so on
Sunday	noon			

105 The last supper together

***
from Mark 14, Luke 22, John 13, Matthew 26 and 1 Corinthians 11:
  New English Bible

In the evening he came to the house with the Twelve. As they sat at supper Jesus said, 'How I have longed to eat this Passover with you before my death! My children, for a little longer I am with you; then you will look for me, and , I tell you now, where I am going you cannot come. I give you a new commandment; love one another. If there is love among you, then all will know that you are my disciples.'

During supper Jesus took bread and, having said the blessing, he broke it and gave it to the disciples with the words: 'This is my body, which is for you. Do this as a memorial of me.'

In the same way, he took the cup after supper and, having offered thanks to God, he gave it to them with the words: 'Drink from it, all of you. For this is my blood, the blood of the covenant, shed for many for the forgiveness of sins. Whenever you drink it, do this as a memorial of me.

'For every time you eat this bread and drink the cup, you proclaim the death of the Lord, until he comes. And where two or three have met together in my name, I am there among them.'

Happened in about AD *29 in the spring, probably after 6 p.m. on
   the Thursday of Passover week*
From writings between AD *50 and 95*

A weekly meeting of Jewish families and other groups was common
and a formal meal was usually shared. During the meal the senior   *Last Supper*
man would take some bread and thank God for life and health, and
at the end he would do the same with a cup of wine. The origins of
this particular thanking ritual were probably Jewish. They would   *take*
remind themselves above all of the great escape from Egypt
(readings 14 and 15), and their customary methods of 'giving
thanks' had evolved during the distant corn-growing days of Canaan
(readings 19 to 41), and the nomadic stock-breeding days before
that (readings 6 to 9).

There were variations of this ritual for special occasions like the
Passover. It is not certain however what precisely this 'Last Supper'
of Jesus was in Jewish terms. No matter. Overnight it took on a
new significance among his followers. It became their 'Eucharist',   *Eucharist*
their own thanking ritual with a host of new meanings.

From before the Middle Ages there have been frightful arguments
between churches about what exactly the bread and wine becomes
during a Eucharist. Some have claimed that it becomes the very
body and blood of Jesus, others that it remains purely a symbol.   *symbol*
Some have talked of a 'sacrifice', others of a 'memorial'. Business   *sacrifice*
and politics have confused the issues and some of the results have   *memorial*
been horrendous. Yet they have all been talking about exactly the
same thing: the real presence of their lord. And many people have   *presence*
found that the silences in these various services are the most sacred *silence*
centres of his being, which all can share without schism.

Today the Eucharist (Greek: 'Thankfulness') is called by some 'the   *Eucharist*
Mass' (derived from the original Latin dismissal at the end of the   *Mass*
service), by others 'the Communion' (Latin meaning to 'become one   *Communion*
with' God) and by others simply 'the Lord's Supper'. In the Eastern
churches it has been called 'the Liturgy' (Greek meaning roughly   *Lord's*
'the work of the people') and in the New Testament it was usually   *Supper*
referred to as 'the Breaking of the Bread' (see notes to 139).   *Liturgy*

106 The apostles argue about seniority

*

from Luke 22 and Mark 10: New English Bible

During supper Jesus also said, 'My betrayer is here, his hand with mine on the table.'

At this they began to ask among themselves which of them it could possibly be who was to do this thing. Then a jealous dispute broke out: who among them should rank highest? But he said, 'You know that in the world the recognized rulers lord it over their subjects, and their great men make them feel the weight of authority. That is not the way with you. Among you, whoever wants to be great must be your servant, and whoever wants to be first must be the willing slave of all. For even the Son of Man did not come to be served, but to serve and to surrender his life as a ransom for many.'

Happened between about AD *28 and 29 in the spring after 6 p.m.
on the Thursday of Passover week*
From writings between about AD *50 and 80*

'Ransom' was money paid for the release of a prisoner or a slave. It *ransom*
was a very pregnant word to use here. The writer who recorded it
knew exactly what he was saying: the creator wished to release his
creatures from their wretched, fettered existence and to give them a
new lease of life; he would pay for their freedom with the life of the
man Jesus.

They did not find it difficult to follow this reasoning. Its primitive
thought-form was already clear in their minds. It belonged to the
jargon of sacrifices, and it fitted right into the centre of the famous *sacrifice*
'atonement' formula — see notes to 73. In primitive times men *atonement*
believed it was necessary to sacrifice to their god the most valuable
thing they could manage: such payment would release his favours
among them; besides, he deserved to be given the best. See all
notes to 7.

But the reading opposite showed a new development in their *initiative*
theology (= study of the creator's nature): he made the sacrifice: he *theology*
paid the ransom, he did the giving: the initiative was entirely his (see
notes to 73). They could only be in a position to receive (see notes to
87 on 'children').

For 'betrayer' see reading 103 and its note on 'Judas'.

107   Jesus washes his apostles' feet

***

from John 13 : New English Bible

During supper, Jesus, well aware that the Father had entrusted everything to him, and that he had come from God and was going back to God, rose from table, laid aside his garments, and taking a towel, wrapped it round him. Then he poured water into a basin, and began to wash his disciples' feet and to wipe them with the towel.

When it was Simon Peter's turn, Peter said to him, 'You, Lord, washing my feet?'

Jesus replied, 'You do not understand now what I am doing, but one day you will.'

Peter said, 'I will never let you wash my feet.'

'If I do not wash you,' Jesus replied, 'you are not in fellowship with me.'

After washing their feet and taking his garments again, he sat down. 'Do you understand,' he asked, 'what I have done for you? You call me "Master" and "Lord", and rightly so, for that is what I am. Then if I, your Lord and Master, have washed your feet, you also ought to wash one another's feet. I have set you an example: you are to do as I have done for you. A servant is not greater than his master. Happy are you if you know this and act upon it.'

*Happened in about AD 29 in the spring, probably after 6 p.m. on
the Thursday of Passover week
Written between about AD 90 and 95*

It was customary to remove the shoes when going into a house. It *feet*
was a mark of respect shared by many Middle Eastern peoples.
Moslems do it to this day when entering a mosque because it is a
house of God. It was also customary, on formal occasions anyway,
for guests' feet to be washed and anointed either by a junior
member of the family or, in the wealthier households, by a servant.
Roads were hot and dusty but the powerful ointments of Arabia
were soothing to the feet and merciful to the nostrils.

As he approached his death, Jesus was shown to grow more silent. *silence*
In order for his followers to understand all that he had tried to teach
them he was now acting out his doctrines. Here he dressed and
behaved like a slave. And the word 'Master' here meant slave- *slavery*
master and property-owner. The last example of his doctrine to be
demonstrated in this drama would be, inevitably, his death.

After his death and the subsequent events, his followers called
themselves 'Servants of God'. Gregory the Great used his own vast *serve*
wealth to relieve the sufferings of others and, when he became
Pope in AD 540, signed official documents 'The servant of God's
servants'. A shadow of the theme lingers in England today in the
Latin word 'minister' which means servant. The senior official in the *minister*
land is called 'prime minister'. But in some other administrations the
term has been dropped: it is ironical, for example, that the 'Ministry
of Education' is now a 'Department', so teachers may no longer call *education*
themselves 'slaves'!

108 Judas leaves the supper early

from Mark 14 and John 13 to 15: New English Bible

As they sat at supper, Jesus said, 'I tell you this: one of you will betray me—one who is eating with me.' At this they were dismayed and one by one they said to him, 'Not I, surely?'

One of them, the disciple he loved, was reclining close beside Jesus. So Simon Peter nodded to him and said, 'Ask who it is he means.' That disciple, as he reclined, leaned back close to Jesus and asked, 'Lord, who is it?' Jesus replied, 'It is the man to whom I give this piece of bread when I have dipped it in the dish.' Then, after dipping it in the dish, he took it out and gave it to Judas son of Simon Iscariot.

Jesus said to him, 'Do quickly what you have to do.' No one at the table understood what he meant by this. Some supposed that, as Judas was in charge of the common purse, Jesus was telling him to buy what was needed for the festival, or to make some gift to the poor.

Judas, then, received the bread and went out. It was night.

When Judas had gone out Jesus said, 'Set your troubled hearts at rest. Trust in God always; trust also in me. I am the way; no one comes to the Father except by me.

'My parting gift to you is peace, my own peace, such as the world cannot give. You are my friends—if you do what I command you. This is my commandment: love one another as I have loved you. There is no greater love than this, that a man should lay down his life for his friends.'

Happened in about AD *29 in the spring, after 6 p.m. on the*
  Thursday of Passover week
From writings between about AD *65 and 95*

'Betray' — see reading 103 with its note on 'Judas'.

'The disciple he loved' -- see notes to 122.

Jesus knew his closest friends intimately. He knew exactly how *Judas*
their minds worked. He understood Judas so well that he seemed to *Iscariot*
be almost controlling his will. But that was not his way with *will*
people — see especially reading 90.

The last two paragraphs opposite came from 'The Gospel according *John the*
to Saint John'. It was written between about AD 90 and 95 in *Evangelist*
Ephesus, probably by an old man called John who had heard all the
details from that younger 'disciple whom Jesus loved' (see also *John the*
readings 122, 127 and 133). This unnamed figure who kept *Apostle*
appearing in this fourth Gospel was almost certainly John the
brother of James — see reading 61 and others. So a better title might
have been 'The Gospel of Old John the Evangelist according to the
accounts of Young John the Apostle'. However, there is much
disagreement on this matter.

Whoever the author was, he used material from Mark and Luke,
but, instead of reproducing their short and pithy sayings, he spun
out his yarns with the elaborate patterns of a thoughtful old man.
And, he made no bones about it, he always spoke of Jesus as if he
were the divine son of God. This small sample opposite represents
his style very well.

109 After the supper

**
from Mark 14 : New English Bible

After singing the Passover Hymn, they went out to the Mount of Olives. And Jesus said, 'You will all fall from your faith; for it stands written: "I will strike the shepherd down and the sheep will be scattered." Nevertheless, after I am raised again, I will go on before you into Galilee.' Peter answered, 'Everyone else may fall away but I will not.' Jesus said to him, 'I tell you, tonight before the cock crows you will disown me three times.' But he insisted and repeated, 'Even if I must die with you, I will never disown you.' And they all said the same.

When they reached a place called Gethsemane, he said to his disciples, 'Sit here while I pray.' And he took Peter and James and John with him. Horror and dismay came over him, and he said to them, 'My heart is ready to break with grief; stop here, and stay awake.' Then he went forward a little, threw himself on the ground and prayed that, if it were possible, this hour might pass him by.

Happened in about AD *29 in the spring, towards midnight on the*
   Thursday of Passover week
Written in about AD *65*

The Mount of Olives was a sort of parkland outside the city wall to *Olives*
the east. It was reached by leaving through a gate near the temple,
going down into the Kidron valley and up the other side, a distance
of less than a quarter of a mile. The city's sounds could be heard
from there till the people went to bed and lights were extinguished.
As Jesus was staying with Martha and Mary at Bethany this week *Bethany*
he would have left the city with his friends each evening and come
up this slope to reach the village 3 km (2 miles) away.

A little to the north of this parkland was Gethsemane, a public *Gethse-*
garden on the site of an old olive press. It was right opposite the   *mane*
temple buildings and lay on the main routes to Bethany and Jericho. *olives*
The sight of a detachment of temple guards with torches on some
mission by night coming down from the temple wall and up the
slope would have not have been missed from there (reading 110).

110 Arrest

***

from Luke 22, Matthew 26, John 18 and Mark 14: New English Bible

When he rose from prayer and came to the disciples he found them asleep, worn out by grief. 'Why are you sleeping?' he said. 'Rise and pray that you may be spared the test.' While he was still speaking, Judas, one of the twelve, appeared; with him was a great crowd armed with swords and cudgels, sent by the chief priests and elders of the nation. The place was known to Judas, his betrayer, because Jesus had often met there with his disciples.

Now the traitor had agreed with them upon a signal: 'The one I kiss is your man; seize him and get him safely away.' When he reached the spot, he stepped forward at once and said to Jesus, 'Rabbi,' and kissed him. Then they seized him and held him fast.

Thereupon Simon Peter drew the sword he was wearing and struck the High Priest's servant, cutting off his right ear. (The servant's name was Malchus.) But Jesus said to him, 'Put up your sword. All who take the sword die by the sword.'

At the same time Jesus spoke to the crowd. 'Do you take me for a bandit,' he said, 'that you have come out with swords and cudgels to arrest me? Day after day I sat teaching in the Temple, and you did not lay hands on me.'

Then the disciples all deserted him and ran away. Among those following was a young man with nothing on but a linen cloth. They tried to seize him; but he slipped out of the linen cloth and ran away naked.

Happened in about AD 29 in the spring, probably around midnight
*   on the Thursday of Passover week*
From writings between about AD 50 and 95

The last paragraph is only found in Mark's Gospel. Tradition has it   *Mark*
that the 'young man' was the writer, Mark himself, and this was like
a modest signature: 'I was there.'

Mark was not one of the twelve disciples from the Galilean days.
He lived in Jerusalem and probably only came upon Jesus during
this last week. He was a Jew.

He is thought to have written his Gospel in Rome in about AD 65. He
may have heard about certain writings (known today as 'Q') which   *'Q'*
contained sayings of Jesus, but most of his information is thought
to have come from Peter, who seems to have regarded him as a
son. Papias, a writer in AD 130, recorded that 'Mark became the
interpreter of Peter and he wrote down accurately, but not in order,
as much as he remembered of the sayings and doings of . . . the
Lord'.

111 Trials at night

***
from John 18, Matthew 26, Mark 14 and Luke 22 : New English Bible

The troops with their commander, and the Jewish police, now arrested Jesus and secured him. They took him first to Annas. Annas was the father-in-law of Caiaphas, the High Priest for that year—the same Caiaphas who had advised the Jews that it would be to their interest if one died for the whole people. So Annas questioned Jesus and sent him to Caiaphas.

Jesus was led off under arrest to the house of Caiaphas the High Priest, where the lawyers and elders were assembled. The chief priests and the whole Council tried to find some evidence against Jesus to warrant a death-sentence, but failed to find any. Many gave false statements against him but their statements did not tally.

Finally two men alleged that he had said, 'I can pull down the Temple of God and rebuild it in three days.' At this the High Priest rose and said to him, 'Have you no answer to the charges that these witnesses bring against you?' But Jesus kept silence.

The High Priest then said, 'By the living God I charge you to tell us. Are you the Messiah, the Son of God?'

Jesus said, 'I am.'

Then the High Priest tore his robes and said, 'Need we call further witnesses? We have heard it ourselves from his own lips. You have heard the blasphemy. What is your opinion?' They answered, 'He is guilty, he should die.'

Then they spat in his face and beat him with their fists; and others said, as they struck him, 'Now, Messiah, if you are a prophet, tell us who hit you.'

Happened in about AD *29 in the spring, probably during the night
of Thursday-Friday of Passover week
From writings between about* AD *50 and 95*

The early hours of Friday morning. The private house of the High Priest. Darkness. Many strangers. Sleeplessness. Many opinions. Fear.

It was against Jewish law to conduct trials during the hours of darkness.

law

It was against Jewish law to tell lies in a legal trial — see Rule 9 in the Moses law (reading 17) — 'perjury', in all its forms, possibly the most cancerous crime in any society.

perjury

The witness who picked on 'the temple remark' was, ironically, a 'deaf' person who had misunderstood Jesus' double-think teaching — see reading 98. Or else he was plain malicious.

*deaf
double-think*

Caiaphas was not interested in 'the temple remark': its meaning was too blurred for him to succeed in nailing a death sentence. He needed a clear-cut case of 'blasphemy', an open breach of Rule 3 in the Moses-law. Two words from Jesus gave him exactly what he wanted.

Caiaphas

Unfortunately for Caiaphas and company, the Romans did not allow the Jews to pass a death sentence: all capital offences had to be tried in a Roman court at this time.

Romans

Annas had been High Priest for ten years before Caiaphas and had been deposed by the Roman Procurator of his day. But the Jews seemed to regard him still as having a rightful share in the office.

Annas

112 Peter's cowardice

from John 18 and Luke 22 : New English Bible

Jesus was followed by Simon Peter and another disciple. This disciple, who was acquainted with the High Priest, went with Jesus into the High Priest's courtyard, but Peter halted at the door outside. So the other disciple, the High Priest's acquaintance, went out again and spoke to the woman at the door, and brought Peter in. The maid on duty at the door said to Peter, 'Are you another of this man's disciples?' 'I am not,' he said.

The servants and the police had made a charcoal fire, because it was cold, and were standing round it warming themselves. And Peter too was standing with them sharing the warmth. A little later someone else noticed him and said, 'You also are one of them.' But Peter said to him, 'No, I am not.'

About an hour passed, and another spoke more strongly still: 'Of course this fellow was with him. He must have been; he is a Galilean.' But Peter said, 'Man, I do not know what you are talking about.' At that moment, while he was still speaking, a cock crew; and the Lord turned and looked at Peter. And Peter remembered the Lord's words, 'Tonight, before the cock crows, you will disown me three times.'

Happened in about AD *29 in the spring, during the night of*
   Thursday-Friday of Passover week
From writings between about AD *50 and 95*

The High Priest's house was a kilometre (half a mile) from the   *priests*
temple in the opposite quarter of the city. Being Sadducean, he
would probably have built himself a formal house with a patio, and
perhaps a low upper storey overlooking the yard, and inside its
arched openings this interrogation would have taken place. Below in
the courtyard the detachment of temple police was cold, awaiting
new orders: 2 o'clock? The darkest hour. A few pack-animals in the
shadows, the odd goat, a few chickens perhaps and a cockerel
roosting on a roof top? But all this is conjecture.

'Another disciple?' Was it the apostle John (notes to 108)? Could
Mark have returned? (See notes to 110.) It is not important.

A Galilean talking Aramaic would have a distinctly Northern accent.   *Galilee*

113 The death of Judas

from Mark 15 and Matthew 27: New English Bible

When morning came the chief priests, having made their plan with the elders and lawyers and all the Council, put Jesus in chains; then they led him away and handed him over to the Governor's headquarters.

When Judas the traitor saw that Jesus had been condemned, he was seized with remorse, and returned the thirty silver pieces to the chief priests and elders. 'I have sinned,' he said; 'I have brought an innocent man to his death.' But they said, 'What is that to us? See to that yourself.' So he threw the money down in the temple and left them, and went and hanged himself.

Taking up the money, the chief priests argued: 'This cannot be put into the temple fund; it is blood-money.' So after conferring they used it to buy the Potter's Field, as a burial-place for foreigners. This explains the name 'Blood Acre', by which that field has been known ever since.

Happened in about AD *29 in the spring*
From writings between about AD *50 and 85*

Judas was a hot-headed man. His motives may have been wrongly mixed (see notes to 103) — it will never be known. But it is certain that, whatever crimes he may have committed in his lifetime, none could have been more harmful to him than to imagine that the patient forgiveness of Jesus would be exhausted. He had allowed guilt and remorse to eat out his heart. He had lost touch with the reality of his merciful maker. By killing himself he was trying to punish himself (notes to 3). So the teaching of Jesus had fallen on deaf ears: he had missed the point (see notes to 106).

*Judas
Iscariot*

*punish
kill
self-wound-
ing*

114 Pilate finds no fault in Jesus

***
from John 18 and 19, Luke 23 and Mark 15 : New English Bible

It was now early morning, and the Jews themselves stayed outside the Governor's headquarters to avoid defilement, so that they could eat the Passover meal. So Pilate went out to them and asked, 'What charge do you bring against this man?' 'If he were not a criminal,' they replied, 'we should not have brought him before you.' Pilate said, 'Take him away and try him by your own law.' The Jews answered, 'We are not allowed to put any man to death.'

The chief priests opened the case against him by saying, 'We found this man subverting our nation, opposing the payment of taxes to Caesar, and claiming to be an anointed king.' And they brought many charges against him.

Pilate asked Jesus, 'Are you the King of the Jews?' He replied, 'The words are yours.' Pilate questioned him again: 'Have you nothing to say in your defence? You see how many charges they are bringing against you?' But, to Pilate's astonishment, Jesus made no further reply.

'Do you refuse to speak to me?' said Pilate. 'Surely you know that I have authority to release you, and I have authority to crucify you?' Jesus replied, 'You would have no authority at all over me, if it had not been granted you from above; and therefore the deeper guilt lies with the man who handed me over to you.'

From that moment Pilate tried hard to release him.

Happened in about AD *29 in the spring, probably early in the*
morning of the Friday of Passover week
From writings between about AD *50 and 95*

To the Roman, all Jews were arrogant and stubborn as camels. He *Romans*
would far prefer a tour of duty in some damp and primitive country
like Britain. He had nothing but contempt for these complicated
Jews. He had no interest in their solitary god and their
argumentative babblings about a 'New Age'. They were no better
than a sophisticated type of barbarian, bleating and complaining.
Their ideas about Messiahs and a king were subversive. Jews were
dangerous beasts.

The Roman Governor in Judaea since AD 26 had been Pontius *Pilate*
Pilate. Rome provided him with a large and comfortable palace
called the Antonia. Within this was stationed a strong detachment
of Roman soldiers. The Jews hated their presence. To set foot
inside that pagan place would contaminate them, they believed, and *unclean*
make them unfit to celebrate the Passover properly.

Pilate regarded the charges against Jesus as just one more Jewish
quarrel. In Roman Law their charges were useless because there *law*
was so much disagreement. There was, as far as he was concerned,
no problem. The only thing that puzzled him was the prisoner's brief
and brave remarks. It appealed to his Roman sense of dignity. Was
it possible that he was secretly admiring, of all people, a Jew?

The Antonia was a balanced, classical structure. Such architecture *Antonia*
stood for the open logic of Roman language and law. Jupiter was
supreme. All human authority derived from him. Under his high
heaven, honest men could thrive. That at least was the general idea.

115 From Pilate to Herod

**

from Luke 23 : New English Bible

Pilate then said to the chief priests and the crowd, 'I find no case for this man to answer.' But they insisted, 'His teaching is causing disaffection among the people all through Judaea. It started from Galilee and has spread as far as this city.' When Pilate heard this, he asked if the man was a Galilean, and on learning that he belonged to Herod's jurisdiction he remitted the case to him, for Herod was also in Jerusalem at that time.

When Herod saw Jesus he was greatly pleased; having heard about him, he had long been wanting to see him, and had been hoping to see some miracle performed by him. He questioned him at some length without getting any reply; but the chief priests and lawyers appeared and pressed the case against him vigorously. Then Herod and his troops treated him with contempt and ridicule, and sent him back to Pilate dressed in a gorgeous robe.

That same day Herod and Pilate became friends: till then there had been a standing feud between them.

Happened in about AD *29 in the spring, during the morning of the*
  Friday of Passover week
From writings between about AD *50 and 80*

Herod Antipas — see notes to 101 — seemed to have a puerile thirst   *Herod*
for cruel entertainment. It is not recorded that he actually tried to   *Antipas*
get Jesus to walk across his swimming pool, but that is a fair
comment on his shallow mentality. He felt insulted by the
prisoner's silence. He reacted like a spoilt child — which is probably   *children*
what he still was.

Though he and Pilate had totally different personalities, they now   *Pilate*
shared a common problem. And time was running short.

116 Pilate has Jesus flogged

from John 18 and 19, and Luke 23 : New English Bible

Pilate then went back into his headquarters and summoned Jesus. 'You are king of the Jews, I take it,' he said.

Jesus said, 'Is that your own idea, or have others suggested it to you?'

'What! Am I a Jew?' said Pilate. 'Your own nation and their chief priests have brought you before me. What have you done?'

Jesus replied, 'My kingdom does not belong to this world. If it did, my followers would be fighting to save me from arrest by the Jews. My kingly authority comes from elsewhere.'

'You are a king then?' said Pilate.

Jesus answered, ' "King" is your word. My task is to bear witness to the truth. For this was I born; for this I came into the world, and all who are not deaf to truth listen to my voice.'

Pilate said, 'What is truth?' and with those words went out again to the Jews. 'For my part,' he said, 'I find no case against him. You brought this man before me on a charge of subversion. But, as you see, I have myself examined him in your presence and found nothing in him to support your charges. No more did Herod, for he has referred him back to us. Clearly he has done nothing to deserve death. I therefore propose to let him off with a flogging.'

Pilate now took Jesus and had him flogged.

Happened in about AD *29 in the spring, during the morning of the*
Friday of Passover week
From writings between about AD *50 and 95*

'My kingdom does not belong to this world' — see note to 69 on 'double-think'.

'My kingly authority' — see note to 70 on 'authority'.

' "King" is your word' — see note to 84 on the 'Kingdom'.

'Truth' — see note to 16 on 'justice', 'right' and 'righteous', but of   *true*
course, as this part of the reading comes from St John's Gospel
(notes to 108), the hint was that Jesus himself was the embodiment
of Truth — even though Pilate could not see it. (Or dare not?)

Flogging: the Jews gave thirty-nine stripes with a rod; the Romans
used a bunch of thongs, each with a piece of bone or metal at the   *flogging*
end, so that the flesh was cut and mangled. Giving a flogging was   *Romans*
considered a very unpleasant and unpopular task in the Roman
army. It may have been done here by Syrian recruits. (Each country
occupied by Roman armies was made to produce its own troops
which the Romans trained and officered. The Jews had refused on
religious grounds, so they had to suffer the humiliating presence of
Syrian troops whom they hated — see readings between 32 and 51).

117   Roman soldiers mock Jesus

from Mark 15, Matthew 17 and 27, and John 19 : New English Bible

Then the soldiers took Jesus inside the courtyard (the Governor's head-quarters) and called together the whole company. First they stripped him. They dressed him in purple, and plaiting a crown of thorns they placed it on his head, with a cane in his right hand. Falling on their knees before him, they jeered at him: 'Hail, King of the Jews!' They spat on him, and used the cane to beat him about the head.

Once more Pilate came out and said to the Jews, 'Here he is; I am bringing him out to let you know that I find no case against him.' And Jesus came out wearing the crown of thorns and the purple cloak.

Pilate said, 'Behold the Man!'

Happened in about AD *29 in the spring, during the morning of the
    Friday of Passover week*
From writings between about AD *50 and 95*

An ugly situation. There was the deep scorn in every Roman for the *Romans*
Jews (notes to 114). There were Syrian recruits who had *Syrians*
passionately hated the Southern Jews for as long as they could
remember (reading 38, 47 and 51). And there was this Jew who had
dared to carry on about kings and kingdoms in front of the
Procurator as if he himself were a god-king on earth. Now in the
privacy of these barracks they could express their contempt — what
an opportunity, by Jove!

118 Barabbas

***
from Mark 15, Matthew 27, John 19 and Luke 23 : New English Bible

At the festival season the Governor used to release one prisoner at the people's request. As it happened, the man known as Barabbas was then in custody with the rebels who had committed murder in the rising. When the crowd appeared asking for the usual favour, Pilate replied, 'Do you wish me to release for you the king of the Jews?' For he knew that it was out of spite that they had brought Jesus before him.

While Pilate was sitting in court a message came to him from his wife: 'Have nothing to do with that innocent man; I was much troubled on his account in my dreams last night.'

Meanwhile the chief priests and elders had persuaded the crowd to ask for the release of Barabbas and to have Jesus put to death. So when the Governor asked, 'Which of the two do you wish me to release to you?', they said, 'Barabbas.'

Pilate spoke to them again: 'Then what shall I do with the man you call king of the Jews?' They shouted back, 'Crucify him!' 'Why? What harm has he done?' Pilate asked. They shouted all the louder, 'Crucify him! If you let this man go, you are no friend of Caesar; any man who claims to be a king is defying Caesar.'

Pilate said to the Jews, 'Here is your king.' They shouted, 'Away with him! Away with him! Crucify him!' Their shouts prevailed and Pilate decided that they should have their way.

Happened in about AD *29 in the spring, probably during the morning of the Friday of Passover week*
From writings between about AD *50 and 95*

'King of the Jews' — a soldiers' joke. There he was dressed up in the clown-king clothes the soldiers had found, their contempt for all Jews heaped upon this one man (see reading 117).

kings

Possibly Pilate thought that this Jesus, of all the Jews he knew, was ironically the only one he'd care to call a king. There will always be unanswered questions.

Pilate

The crowd was not a typical Jerusalem crowd. It was a very mixed holiday-minded crowd looking for amusement, the most enjoyable form of which was to see Rome defied.

A riot in Jerusalem just now would be disastrous. For Pilate it would be the end of his career and possibly his life.

riots

There had been a riot in the city recently. One of the rioters had been Barabbas. Some versions named him 'Jesus Barabbas' and, if that was his real name, it may have caused a convenient confusion in that multi-linguistic crowd which the Jewish leaders took advantage of.

Barabbas

'Jesus' was a fairly common name. It was the Greek form of the Hebrew name 'Joshua' (reading 19) meaning, 'Yahweh saves.'

Jesus

119   Jesus is led away

***

from Matthew 27, John 19 and Mark 15 : New English Bible

Jesus was now taken in charge and, carrying his own cross, went out to the Place of the Skull, as it is called (or, in the Jews' language, 'Golgotha').

A man called Simon, from Cyrene, the father of Alexander and Rufus, was passing by on his way in from the country, and they pressed him into service to carry his cross.

Pilate wrote an inscription to be fastened on the cross; it read, 'Jesus of Nazareth King of the Jews.' This inscription was read by many Jews, because the place where Jesus was crucified was not far from the city, and the inscription was in Hebrew, Latin and Greek. Then the Jewish chief priests said to Pilate, 'You should not write "King of the Jews"; write, "He claimed to be king of the Jews".' Pilate replied, 'What I have written, I have written.' Pilate could see that nothing was to be gained, and a riot was starting; so he took water and washed his hands in full view of the people, saying, 'My hands are clean of this man's blood; see to that yourselves.' And with one voice the people cried, 'His blood be on us and on our children.'

He then released Barabbas to them.

Happened in about AD *29 in the spring, probably towards the end of*
the morning of the Friday of Passover week
From writings between about AD *50 and 95*

Crucifixion was not rare. It had been an Oriental form of execution *crucify*
originally, first recorded among the Phoenicians, adopted by the
Romans and by now a normal penalty for violent criminals. One
record says that over a thousand victims were crucified on a single
occasion. On another, they ran out of wood.

Those convicted were taken outside the city. Each, according to
Roman policy, carried the cross piece of the gallows with his name *cross*
and crime written on ot. The Latin word for it meant both 'a
pitchfork' and 'a two-pronged yoke' used to link cattle or slaves in
their work. More than once Jesus had told his followers to take up
their yoke-cross and follow him.

Simon of Cyrene, a North African, selected from the crowd no *Simon of*
doubt for his size and strength. Jesus by now must have been weak *Cyrene*
with tiredness.

Golgotha was possibly a communal burial ground for the poorer *Golgotha*
citizens (reading 72). Or it may have been a rubbish pit and if so, a
convenient place for the execution of foreigners or criminals with no
family who would bury them. The fierce sun and the insects would
cope swiftly with whatever the vultures and wild dogs did not take.

The shape of the hill outside that part of Jerusalem is said to be
roughly skull-shaped. The Latin word for skull produced the other *skull*
name, 'Calvary'. *Calvary*

120 Crucifixion

***
from Luke 23, Matthew 27, and Mark 15 : New English Bible

And when they reached the place called 'The Skull', they crucified him there, and the criminals with him, one on his right and the other on his left. Jesus said, 'Father, forgive them; they do not know what they are doing.'

They divided his clothes among them by casting lots and then sat down there to keep watch.

The people stood looking on. The passers-by hurled abuse at him: they wagged their heads and cried, 'You would pull the Temple down, would you, and build it in three days? Come down from the cross and save yourself, if you are indeed the Son of God.'

So too the chief priests and the doctors of the law jested with one another: 'He saved others,' they said, 'but he cannot save himself. Let the Messiah, the king of Israel, come down from the cross. If we see that, we shall believe.' And, 'Did he trust in God? Let God rescue him if he wants him—for he said he was God's Son!'

The soldiers joined in the mockery and came forward offering him sour wine. 'If you are the king of the Jews,' they said, 'save yourself.'

Happened in about AD *29 in the spring, probably from about midday*
    of the Friday of Passover week
From writings between about AD *50 and 85*

Jesus is reported to have said seven things during his crucifixion. *'seven*
These readings include only four of them. The three which have *words'*
been omitted appear to have been direct quotations from the
Psalms (22:1, 69:21, 31:5).

The Roman soldiers who did the nailing were used to stark matters. *Romans*
They had their orders. They were away from home among a tricky *soldiers*
people. They were not in the habit of questioning why. They were *crucify*
not paid to make moral judgements. They were like automatons.
But this so-called king forgave them.

The Jewish people who mocked him were disappointed people.
They had been expecting so much from their Messiah: a handsome, *Messiah*
David-like king, dynamic and politically invulnerable, martial and
measuring out divine punishment upon all the enemies of the
People.

121 A penitent thief

from Mark 15 and Luke 23 : New English Bible

Even those who were crucified with him taunted him. One of the criminals who hung there with him taunted him: 'Are not you the Messiah? Save yourself, and us.' But the other answered sharply, 'Have you no fear of God? You are under the same sentence as he. For us it is plain justice; we are paying the price for our misdeeds. But this man has done nothing wrong.'

And he said, 'Jesus, remember me when you come to your throne.' He answered, 'I tell you this: today you shall be with me in Paradise.'

Happened in about AD *29 in the spring, between 12 noon and 3 p.m.*
on the Friday of Passover week
From writings between about AD *50 and 80*

The man who talked about Jesus enthroned probably had the popular Belshazzar fixation — see notes to 83. The word 'Paradise' was probably Persian in origin and meant a sort of 'Garden of Eden' (reading 2), a place of bliss. *Paradise*

But, apart from these words used by the writers, the important fact of this event was the man's 'penitence'. A dynamic change came in him at the last moment. A good illustration of 'penitence' was the parable of the Prodigal Son (reading 85). *repent*

122 The death of Jesus

***
from John 19 and Luke 23 : New English Bible

But meanwhile near the cross where Jesus hung stood his mother, with her sister, Mary wife of Cleopas, and Mary of Magdala. Jesus saw his mother, with the disciple whom he loved standing beside her. He said to her, 'Mother, there is your son,' and to the disciple, 'There is your mother.' And from that moment the disciple took her into his home.

By now it was about midday and there came a darkness over the whole land, which lasted until three in the afternoon; the sun was in eclipse. Then Jesus gave a loud cry and said, 'It is accomplished!' He bowed his head and breathed out his life.

The centurion saw it all and gave praise to God. He said, 'Beyond all doubt this man was innocent.'

Happened in about AD *29 in the spring, probably up to 3 p.m. on the
     Friday of Passover week*
From writings between about AD *50 and 95*

The 'disciple whom he loved' was probably John the brother of
James. This seems to have been the first time any disciples
appeared since the arrest. And now it was only the women and this
one man who dared to come close. (See notes to 25 on 'women'
and 'lament'.)

The last cry, 'It is accomplished!' was one of victory. He had at last
reached the goal of his life. He had successfully demonstrated the
crux of all his teachings. Anyone who had missed this, had missed
the lot!

As well as the eclipse, one writer reports an earthquake and various
other unusual and supernatural effects. Whatever objections there
may be to these statements, it remains true to say that those who
wrote them down firmly believed that Jesus was God-on-Earth and
these dramatic thought-forms were among the accepted concepts
of their generation (see notes to 83).

*John the
    Apostle
women*

*death
cross*

elements

apocalypse

123 The approaching Sabbath

***

from John 19 and Mark 15 : New English Bible

Because it was the eve of Passover, the Jews were anxious that the bodies should not remain on the cross for the coming Sabbath, since that Sabbath was a day of great solemnity; so they requested Pilate to have the legs broken and the bodies taken down. The soldiers accordingly came to the first of his fellow-victims and to the second, and broke their legs; but when they came to Jesus they found that he was already dead, so they did not break his legs. But one of the soldiers stabbed his side with a lance, and at once there was a flow of blood and water. (This is vouched for by an eyewitness whose evidence is to be trusted. He knows that he speaks the truth, so that you too may believe.)

After that Pilate was approached by Joseph of Arimathaea (a disciple of Jesus, but a secret disciple for fear of the Jews), who asked to be allowed to remove the body of Jesus. He was joined by Nicodemus (the man who had first visited Jesus by night), who brought with him a mixture of myrrh and aloes, more than half a hundredweight.

Pilate was surprised to hear that he was already dead; so he sent for the centurion and asked if it was long since he died. And when he heard the centurion's report, he gave Joseph leave to take the dead body.

Happened in about AD *29 in the spring, probably between 3 and 6*
p.m. on the Friday of Passover week
From writings between about AD *65 and 95*

The Sabbath, in Jewish timing, started at 6 p.m. on the Friday and   *Sabbath*
ended at 6 p.m. the following day (see notes to 104). The Sabbath
of Passover week was of course particularly sacred. It was
considered a crime and shameful for a Jew to be doing anything   *work*
that could be remotely described as work. There were only three
hours in hand now before this solemn festival began.

Joseph of Arimathaea, a rich Judaean Jew, a respected member of   *Joseph of*
the Sanhedrin, was described as a 'good and just man'. Nicodemus   *Arimathaea*
was a Jewish lawyer, a Pharisee and also a member of the   *Nicodemus*
Sanhedrin. Two top politicians.

Centurions were Roman officers in charge of about a hundred   *centurions*
soldiers. They rose to office from the ranks. They were selected if
they were 'steadfast men with the gift of sober leadership, their
courage deep rather than superficial, not hasty in battle, but if hard
pressed always ready to stand firm and to die in defence of their
post'.

This centurion would take a detachment of his men large enough to   *crucify*
execute the task efficiently. Apart from the bloody business itself,
he had to keep the crowds at bay and see that no rescue attempts
were made. When all those convicted were safely dead he would
report to the Governor and release the bodies. He was permitted 'to
hasten death', should he for any reason find it necessary.

124 Burial

***

from John 19, Matthew 27 and Luke 23 : New English Bible

Joseph of Arimathaea and Nicodemus took the body of Jesus and wrapped it, with the spices, in strips of linen cloth according to Jewish burial customs, and laid it in Jospeh's own unused tomb, which he had cut out of the rock. Then he rolled a large stone against the entrance, and went away.

The women who had accompanied him from Galilee followed. They took note of the tomb and observed how the body was laid. Then they returned home. And on the Sabbath, they rested in obedience to the commandment.

Happened in about AD *29 in the spring, probably between 3 and 6
p.m. on the Friday of Passover week*
From writings between about AD *50 and 95.*

Rich men had tombs specially carved out of rocks in hillsides for *tombs*
themselves and their families. Burial was usually on the day of death *burial*
because of the heat. The body was washed and anointed with
sweet-smelling perfumes and then wrapped in special grave clothes.
There is no record of actual religious services being used at the
funeral of Jews but it is certain that there was much wailing and
lamenting, and sometimes professional mourners were hired. The
body was carried on a bier and simply laid on a shelf in the tomb.
(Poor people, that is most people, were buried in the
ground — sometimes in common graves.) A heavy stone was often
rolled across the mouth of these cave tombs to keep out thieves and
other scavengers like jackals.

In time, when the body had crumbled, they would put the remains *bones*
into a small carved stone box called an ossuary. One such ossuary *relics*
found this century had the inscription 'Jeshua ben Joseph' ('ben'
meant 'son of') but its locality discounted it from being that of
Jesus. Besides, 'Jesus' and 'Joseph' were common names.

125 The tomb is guarded

from Matthew 27: New English Bible

Next day, the morning after that Friday, the chief priests and the Pharisees came in a body to Pilate. 'Your Excellency,' they said, 'we recall how that impostor said while he was still alive, "I am to rise after three days". So will you give orders for the grave to be made secure until the third day? Otherwise his disciples may come, steal the body, and then tell the people that he has been raised from the dead; and the final deception will be worse than the first.'

'You may have your guard,' said Pilate; 'go and make it secure as best you can.' So they went and made the grave secure; they sealed the stone, and left the guard in charge.

Happened in about AD *29 in the spring, between 3 and 6 p.m. on the Friday of Passover week*
From writings between about AD *50 and 85*

The Pharisees themselves believed in a form of 'resurrection' (see notes to 53 and 54). Pilate, clearly, believed nothing of the sort and saw no further danger: death, for him, was the final solution.

resurrection
Pilate
death

The guard may have been the temple police or, since the Sadducees had no use for resurrection theories, these Pharisees may have had to provide their own men.

Matthew's Gospel was the only one in the New Testament to record this incident. But a fragment of writing found in about 1890 and dating back to not later than AD 190 appears to elaborate it. (It is known as 'The Gospel of Peter'.) Here is part of it: 'Pilate gave them Petronius, the centurion, with soldiers, to watch the tomb . . . . And when they . . . had rolled a great stone . . . against the door of the tomb . . . and . . . spread seven wax seals on it and pitched a tent, they kept watch.'

'Peter's Gospel'

This document is thought to have been largely legendary, and its Syrian author fiercely anti-Jew. There is a whole host of such documents in existence outside what theologians call 'the New Testament Canon', tremendously interesting but of variable usefulness. The final contents of the New Testament Canon were more or less agreed upon by about AD 150.

New Testament Canon

126 The empty tomb

***

from Mark 16, Luke 24 and Matthew 28 : New English Bible

When the Sabbath was over, Mary of Magdala, Mary the mother of James, and Salome bought aromatic oils intending to go and anoint him; and very early on the Sunday morning, just after sunrise, they came to the tomb, bringing the spices they had prepared.

They were wondering among themselves who would roll away the stone for them from the entrance of the tomb, when they looked up and saw that the stone, huge as it was, had been rolled back already. They went into the tomb where they saw a youth sitting on the right hand side, wearing a white robe; they were terrified and stood with eyes cast down. But he said to them, 'Fear nothing; you are looking for Jesus of Nazareth, who was crucified. He has been raised from the dead.'

Then they went out and ran away from the tomb, beside themselves with terror. They said nothing to anybody, for they were afraid.

Happened in about AD *29 in the spring, probably at dawn on the*
   Sunday after the Passover Sabbath
From writings between about AD *50 and 85*

No one can say what had actually happened here. There have been   *Jesus*
many guesses and complicated theories. The fact remains that
those who wrote these accounts about Jesus considered it
necessary to record that the tomb was now empty.

That is all.

It looks as if Nicodemus and Joseph of Arimathaea had not had   *burial*
enough time to give the body a proper burial.

The Jewish Sabbath had ended on the Saturday at 6 p.m. By then   *Sabbath*
the evening was closing in, hungry beggars were bolder, and
darkness would give liberty to wild animals and evil spirits. It was
not time for women to leave the city, let alone to visit tombs. There   *women*
was only time for them to buy the oils and to prepare them at home.

After the Jewish Sabbath came 'the first day of the week', the day
which much of the pagan world had hallowed for the sun—symbol   *sun*
of fertility, new life and hope—'Sunday'. Each weekday in the   *Sunday*
pagan world had an astrological significance like this.

The 'youth . . . wearing a white robe' can be safely regarded as an
angel, but see notes to 20 on 'angels'.   *angel*

127 Peter and John at the tomb

***
from Luke 23 and 24, and John 20 : New English Bible

Then the women recalled Jesus' words and, returning from the tomb, they reported this to the Eleven and all the others. So Peter and the other set out and made their way to the tomb. They were running side by side, but the other disciple outran Peter and reached the tomb first. He peered in and saw the linen wrappings lying there, but did not enter.

Then Simon Peter came up, following him, and he went into the tomb. He saw the linen wrappings lying, and the napkin which had been over his head, not lying with the wrappings but lying in a place by itself. Then the disciple who had reached the tomb first went in too, and he saw and believed; until then they had not understood the scriptures, which showed that he must rise from the dead.

Happened in about AD *29 in the spring, probably early in the morning of the Sunday after Passover week*
From writings between about AD *50 and 95*

The 'Eleven' must have had a secret meeting place in the city, possibly the home of someone like Mark's mother — which is mentioned later as a house where they met to pray.   *Mark*

'The other' disciple was almost certainly John the brother of James.

If it is true that Jesus was raised from the dead, Fate could not have chosen a more receptive weekday in which to propagate the concept of 'Resurrection'. In fact, the whole sequence of events was cradled in popular symbolism. For example, on the Friday (the day of Venus, goddess of love), Jesus (the god-man-king) had died (surrendered his personal sovereignty) and had been buried (entered the womb of mother earth); on the Saturday (the day of Saturn, god of agriculture, growth and plenty) Jesus lay dead (subject to the regenerative forces of nature); and on the Sunday (day consecrated to the sun outside the Jewish world, sun being the symbol of life and hope) he was raised from the tomb alive (reborn like any natural seed under the sun).   *Resurrec-tion symbol myth*

Nor could Fate have chosen a better time of year: Springtime had been universally held as the season of 'Resurrection' since time immemorial. This is the very point at which the Christian religion was born. It was not so 'odd of God to choose the Jews' — no other culture could have provided a more experienced midwife with her special Passover qualifications. In fact, had every detail of the Jesus affair been invented, such were the thought-forms and appetites of the age that it could not have failed to take root.   *Christian*

Seeds recently discovered by archaeologists in north Japan were reckoned, by radiocarbon dating, to be over 20 000 years old. When they were put into a damp polythene bag they sprouted after a couple of days and finally grew about a foot high. If they had been found in, say, 1066, no one would have been any the wiser. It is only in this age of the scientific revelation that it has been possible to demonstrate so dynamically such fundamental formulae as 'resurrection'.   *revelation*

Resurrection is the only miracle in which all Christian creeds have demanded belief.   *miracles*

128 Mary Magdalene at the tomb

***
from John 20 : New English Bible

So the disciples went home again; but Mary stood at the tomb outside, weeping. As she wept, she peered into the tomb. 'They have taken my Lord away, and I do not know where they have laid him.' With these words she turned round and saw Jesus standing there, but did not recognise him.

Jesus said to her, 'Why are you weeping? Who is it you are looking for?'

Thinking it was the gardener, she said, 'If it is you, sir, who removed him, tell me where you have laid him, and I will take him away.' Jesus said, 'Mary!' She turned to him and said, 'Rabbuni!' (which is Hebrew for 'My Master'). Jesus said, 'Touch me no more, but go to my brothers, and tell them that I am going to ascend to my Father and your Father.'

Mary of Magdala went to the disciples with her news: 'I have seen the Lord!' she said, and gave them his message.

Happened in about AD *29 in the spring, probably early on the*
  Sunday morning after Passover week
Written between about AD *90 and 95*

Mary of Magdala had witnessed the death of Jesus. Her mind was   *Mary*
conditioned to the fact. When therefore her eyes sent that urgent   *Magdalene*
message to the brain, 'We see Jesus,' the brain coped with the
shock by putting the information into the compartment marked, 'It   *senses*
is someone with a similar appearance.' And even when the ears
whispered, 'We hear the voice of Jesus,' the information was not
dislodged. But when the most intimate and familiar word of all was
breathed, no part of her could resist any more. There was no
mistaking her name on the lips of the one she loved. Then she had   *name*
to touch him — her other senses had to be called in to give evidence.   *touch*

And alongside this simple human account there is the neat mind of   *myth*
the myth-maker at work. 'Rabbuni' is very formal and respectful,   *Rabbuni*
and it is used elsewhere to address God himself. 'Master', here, is   *Master*
another respectful word for teacher, or perhaps even 'master-mind'.
'Ascend' meant literally to go up bodily to heaven, as if going up   *ascension*
stairs. This mythological embroidery is the work of a writer who
believed that Jesus was the Christ. There was no deceit in his work.
The technique was an accepted conceit of his time.

And there was more to the technique than at first meets the eye. It
taught. In this case it said that the natural physical senses of the   *reality*
body could help to make contact with God, but there came a time
when these were not enough; a further step had to be made
beyond the range of the senses if people wanted, IN REALITY, to
'touch' God.   *touch*

129 The tomb guards are bribed

from Matthew 28 : New English Bible

The women had started on their way when some of the guard went into the city and reported to the chief priests everything that had happened. After meeting with the elders and conferring together, the chief priests offered the soldiers a substantial bribe and told them to say, 'His disciples came by night and stole the body while we were asleep.'

They added, 'If this should reach the Governor's ears, we will put matters right with him and see that you do not suffer.'

So they took the money and did as they were told. This story became widely known.

'The Gospel according to Saint Peter' (notes to 125) claimed that
Petronius, the centurion, with his soldiers had left the tomb, full of
fearful tales, and that Pilate had been persuaded to order him to say
nothing, because the result would be 'to fall into the hands of the
people of the Jews and be stoned'.

*'Peter's
Gospel'*

All these accounts (readings 126-34) have been very intriguing for
the busy historian but he has often found that, in turning aside and
contemplating the silence of the empty tomb, he has been given a
more eloquent insight.

history

*contem-
plation*

130 On the road to Emmaus

***
from Luke 24 : New English Bible

That same day two of them were on their way to a village called Emmaus, which lay about seven miles from Jerusalem, and they were talking together about all these happenings. As they talked Jesus himself came up and walked along with them; but something held their eyes from seeing who it was. He asked them, 'What is it you are debating as you walk?' They halted, their faces full of gloom and one, called Cleopas, answered, 'Have you been staying by yourself in Jerusalem, that you do not know what has happened there in the last few days?'

'What do you mean?' he said. They replied, 'All this about Jesus of Nazareth, how our chief priests handed him over to be sentenced to death, and crucified him. But we had been hoping that he was the man to liberate Israel. What is more, this is the third day since it happened, and now some women of our company have astounded us; they went early to the tomb, but failed to find his body, and returned with a story that he was alive. Some of our people went to the tomb and found things just as the women had said; but him they did not see.'

'How dull you are!' he answered. Then he began with Moses and all the prophets, and explained to them the passages which referred to himself in every part of the scriptures.

By this time they had reached the village to which they were going, and they pressed him: 'Stay with us, for the day is almost over.' So he went in to stay with them. And when he had sat down with them at table, he took bread and said the blessing; he broke the bread and offered it to them. Then their eyes were opened, and they recognized him; and he vanished from their sight.

Without a moment's delay they returned to Jerusalem. There they found the Eleven and told how he had been recognized by them at the breaking of the bread.

Cleopas: possibly the husband of the Mary who stood with the other *Cleopas*
two Marys at the Crucifixion (reading 122) and the father of the
apostle James (readings 64 and 134), for 'Alphaeus' may have been
the Aramaic form of the name. Tradition has it that the other man
was Luke. But all this is uncertain and fairly unimportant.

It was clear to the two men that this stranger was some sort of
rabbi. It was normal custom for the senior man present to preside at
a meal, and no one was more senior among the Jews than a man
who knew all about the scriptures.

This strange meeting was similar to that of Mary of Magdala
(reading 128). They saw him and heard him and had prolonged *senses*
cerebral intercourse with him, yet they were ignorant of his real
presence until that familiar moment — the characteristic hands, the *presence*
gracious voice — when he suddenly crystallized for them.

Perhaps the shock was so great that when they 'came to', he had
left.

'The breaking of the bread' — see reading 139.

131 In Jerusalem

**

from John 20 and Luke 24 : New English Bible

Later that Sunday evening, when the disciples were together behind locked doors, for fear of the Jews, Jesus came and stood among them. 'Peace be with you!' he said. Startled and frightened, they thought they were seeing a ghost. But he said, 'Why are you so perturbed? Why do questionings arise in your mind? Look at my hands and feet. It is I myself. Touch me and see; no ghost has flesh and bones as you can see that I have.' After saying this he showed them his hands and feet. They were still unconvinced, still wondering, for it seemed too good to be true. So he asked them 'Have you anything to eat?' They offered him a piece of fish they had cooked, which he took and ate before their eyes.

And he said to them, 'This is what I meant by saying, while I was still with you, that everything written about me in the law of Moses and in the prophets and psalms was bound to be fulfilled.' Then he opened their minds to understand the scriptures. 'This,' he said, 'is what is written: that the Messiah is to suffer death and to rise from the dead on the third day.'

So when the disciples saw the Lord, they were filled with joy. Jesus then said, 'As the Father sent me, so I send you. Receive the Holy Spirit! If you forgive any man's sins, they stand forgiven; if you pronounce them unforgiven, unforgiven they remain.' Then he led them out as far as Bethany, and blessed them with uplifted hands; and in the act of blessing he parted from them.

In a very large number of ghost stories there have been the following *ghosts*
common factors: the ghosts have appeared at dusk or at night,
moved regardless of locked doors, frequented old houses or houses
in which those who have seen them were unfamiliar, been seen by
people who had been feeling insecure or anxious even beforehand,
indulged in monologue rather than dialogue, and tended to say
prophetic things and, more often, enigmatic things. And most
common of all, they have been identified with people who were
dead.

On the other hand, they have not been touchable or felt hungry or
gone for two mile walks with their witnesses, and, most common of
all, they have not often appeared to more than one person at a time.
So if the reading opposite is to be taken seriously, a ghost debate
will be a fairly fruitless one.

The question which keeps forcing itself forward from the pages of
the Bible is the question of meaning. There have been so many gaps *Bible*
to bridge. Take the reading opposite for example. The language *meaning*
spoken was Aramaic, the thought-forms were strongly Hebrew, the
eventual language of the writing was a type of Greek which is no
longer spoken, the translation opposite is modern English, it is read
by people whose minds are furnished with European thought-forms
of very recent vintage, and who are surrounded by experts in all
disguises wishing to tell them what ought to be thought!

So what is the meaning of meaning? If the human mind is in fact
privy to the creator's mind it should, according to most religions,
broadcast profound and utter silence!

'Holy Spirit' — see notes to 9, 59 and 135 on the 'Spirit of God'.

'Forgive' — see the famous atonement formula in notes to 73.

132 Doubtful Thomas

from John 20 : New English Bible

One of the Twelve, Thomas, that is 'the Twin', was not with the rest when Jesus came. So the disciples told him, 'We have seen the Lord.' He said, 'Unless I see the mark of the nails on his hands, unless I put my finger into the place where the nails were, and my hand into his side, I will not believe it.'

A week later his disciples were again in the room, and Thomas was with them. Although the doors were locked, Jesus came and stood among them, saying, 'Peace be with you!' Then he said to Thomas, 'Reach your finger here; see my hands; reach your hand here and put it into my side; be unbelieving no longer, but believe.'

Thomas said, 'My Lord and my God!'

Jesus said, 'Because you have seen me you have found faith. Happy are they who never saw me and yet have found faith.'

Probably happened in about AD *29*
Written between about AD *90 and 95*

Doubting Thomas? Normal Thomas, in great need from time to time of physical reassurance.

doubt
Thomas

'Peace be with you', the customary Jewish greeting and farewell (see the end of notes to 11) became an early Christian greeting. And in the Eucharist it was one of the oldest known parts of the ceremony which has survived today in various forms. At first it was accompanied by an actual 'kiss of peace' but this has now been modified and in many places altogether abandoned.

peace

Eucharist

touch
kiss

The meaning of 'belief' is close to that of 'love'.

'Faith' — see notes to 81.

133   By the Sea of Galilee

**
from John 21 : New English Bible

Some time later, Jesus showed himself to his disciples once again, by the Sea of Tiberias; and in this way. Simon Peter and Thomas 'the Twin' were together with Nathanael of Cana-in-Galilee. The sons of Zebedee and two other disciples were there also. Simon Peter said, 'I am going out fishing.' 'We will go with you,' said the others. So they got into the boat, but that night they caught nothing.

Morning came and there stood Jesus on the beach, but the disciples did not know that it was Jesus. Then the disciple whom Jesus loved said to Peter, 'It is the Lord!' When Simon Peter heard that, he wrapped his coat about him and plunged into the sea. The rest of them came in the boat, for they were not far from land, only about a hundred yards.

When they came ashore, they saw a charcoal fire there, with fish laid on it, and some bread. Jesus said, 'Come and have breakfast.' None of the disciples dared to ask, 'Who are you?' They knew it was the Lord.

Jesus now took the bread and gave it to them; and the fish in the same way.

Probably happened about AD *29*
Written between about AD *90 and 95*

The Romans called the lake at Galilee the Sea of Tiberias.

There are reflections here of several earlier patterns: fruitless efforts at fishing (reading 62); Simon Peter's spontaneous love of Jesus *Peter* (readings 61, 80, 107, 109 and 110); the meal of bread and fish (reading 78).

The most surprising thing about this reading is that it was written by 'John the Evangelist' (notes to 108) who was accustomed to serving *John the* substantial meditations on things like 'the bread of life'; instead, *Evangelist* here is this peaceful scene of morning coolness, and one short *peace* sentence from Jesus: 'Come and have breakfast'! *breakfast*

134   The last time they see him

***

from Matthew 28 and Acts 1 : New English Bible

The eleven disciples made their way to Galilee, to the mountain where Jesus had told them to meet him. When they saw him, they fell prostrate before him, though some were doubtful. Jesus then came up and spoke to them. He said, 'Full authority in heaven and on earth has been committed to me. Go forth therefore and make all nations my disciples; baptise men everywhere in the name of the Father and the Son and the Holy Spirit, and teach them to observe all that I have commanded you. And, be assured, I am with you always, to the end of time.'

When he had said this, as they watched, he was lifted up, and a cloud removed him from their sight. Then they returned to Jerusalem.

Entering the city they went to the room upstairs where they were lodging: Peter and John and James and Andrew, Philip and Thomas, Bartholomew and Matthew, James son of Alphaeus and Simon the Zealot, and Judas son of James. All these were constantly at prayer together, and with them a group of women, including Mary the mother of Jesus, and his brothers.

The followers of Jesus after his death developed this formula called 'The Trinity'. They said that, among the many ways people could experience God, these were the main ones: God in heaven and history as father of the universe, God on earth as Jesus, and God secretly among them as teacher and helper. There has been much argument about the details and a few have rejected the formula altogether. The first paragraph of this reading, which is taken from Matthew's Gospel, is the earliest embryo of the formula but the word 'Trinity' was not used until AD 180. To this day in the vast majority of Christian churches the two essentials of a valid baptism are water and naming with this Trinity formula. Nothing else.

Trinity

baptism

Whether Jesus actually delivered that parting speech is another matter. Matthew's Gospel was the work of a Jew writing to Jews about their long-expected Messiah, and there were many loose ends to tie up, very many thought-forms in need of a focal point.

Matthew

The other two paragraphs opposite come from the second volume of Luke's Gospel called 'The Acts of the Apostles'. It covered many happenings among the earliest Christians during the thirty years which followed this Ascension (readings 135-50). Luke was a gentile by birth, probably a native of Antioch, a physician and well educated. He was writing to a high-ranking gentile official in an attempt to make this new religion acceptable to him. For Luke 'ascension' was the inevitable end of 'incarnation'. The idea of 'incarnation' was already familiar to people all over the world. Incarnation meant 'the coming of a god into human flesh'. In Greece it had been a national sport. In Rome it was fashionable among emperors, while in India it had been known among cotton-bleachers and carpenters' sons. Luke presented his incarnation story with a clear beginning and end — see notes to 56 on 'Luke'.

Luke
'Acts'

Ascension

incarnation

'Clouds' — see notes to 33.

From a plain historical point of view however this 'Ascension' probably simply indicated the last time his followers could remember one of these weird appearances.

Ascension

135 The Pentecost happening

***
from Acts 2 : New English Bible

While the Day of Pentecost was running its course they were all together in one place, when suddenly there came a noise like that of a strong driving wind, which filled the whole house where they were sitting. And there appeared tongues like flames of fire, among them. And they were all filled with the Holy Spirit and began to talk.

At this sound the crowd gathered, all bewildered because each one heard the apostles talking in his own language. They were amazed and exclaimed, 'How is it that we hear each of us in his own native language? Parthians, Medes, Elamites; inhabitants of Mesopotamia, of Judaea and Cappadocia, of Pontus and Asia, of Phrygia and Pamphylia, of Egypt and the districts of Libya around Cyrene; visitors from Rome, both Jews and proselytes, Cretans and Arabs; we hear them telling in our own tongues the great things God has done.'

And they were all perplexed, saying, 'What can this mean?' Others said contemptuously, 'They have been drinking!' But Peter stood up with the Eleven, and addressed them: 'Fellow Jews, give me a hearing. These men are not drunk, as you imagine; for it is only nine in the morning. No, this is what the prophet spoke of. Men of Israel, I speak of Jesus of Nazareth, a man God made known to you through miracles and signs. You used heathen men to crucify and kill him but God raised him to life again. Let all Israel then accept that God has made this Jesus both Lord and Messiah.'

In these and many other words he pleaded with them. Then those who accepted his words were baptised, and some three thousand were added to their number that day.

Happened sometime between about AD *29 and 36 in the early summer*
Written in about AD *85*

A difficult reading: several layers of meaning and mixed symbolism.

The typical phenomena of a poltergeist. 'Poltergeist' – is a German word meaning 'noisy ghost'. The very building seemed to be affected, there was 'wind', 'fire', people jabbering, and the onlookers were perplexed. The scene resembles a black revivalist meeting in the Southern States of America or elsewhere.

ghosts

elements
happenings

To the Jew, 'spirit' and 'wind' referred to the same thing: the source of life in the universe. And 'ghost' was, in their minds, more or less the same thing as 'spirit'.

wind

Spirit of God

'Fire' indicated the same divine presence, and in cultures beyond Judaism it had long been a symbol of super-human energy giving light, life and purity (see notes to 152 and 160 on 'Mithras').

fire

'Babbling' recalled the Babel legend (reading 5). It represented the chaos of international politics when the heavenly Father's authority was disregarded. The legend was familiar all over the Roman Empire wherever the Persians had left their mark.

babble

language

Jews however were looking for a time when swords would be beaten into ploughshares (reading 37 – a favourite text in the founding of the United Nations in 1945). So this babbling event was a remedy to Babel – the power of the Spirit brought, they said, understanding and peace among all nations. That is how the early Christians saw it.

'Pentecost': second festival of the Jewish year, fifty days after 'Passover', traditional cutting of the first wheat, and thanksgiving. Jerusalem, again, full of foreigners.

Pentecost

The closest followers of Jesus were still meeting secretly (readings 131, 132 and 134) and with a growing sense of anticipation. They were thinking over his teaching about 'coming in clouds of glory' (reading 100) – was the kingdom already present in any way or was it still to come? Uncertainty.

second
coming
Kingdom

Putting all these things aside, the most valuable part of this reading from the viewpoint of plain history undoubtedly is Peter's speech. It is a summary, as genuine as can be found anywhere, of the earliest Christian preaching – that is between AD 30 and 60.

preaching

This event was later celebrated as the second most important festival after Easter. In England the festival eventually became known as 'Whitsun', possibly because the newly baptized were dressed in white robes.

Whitsun
baptism

136 Peter and John find they can heal

from Acts 3 and 4 : New English Bible

One day at three in the afternoon, the hour of prayer, Peter and John were on their way up to the temple. Now a man who had been a cripple from birth used to be carried there and laid every day by the gate of the temple called 'Beautiful Gate', to beg from people as they went in. When he saw Peter and John on their way into the temple he asked for charity. But Peter fixed his eyes on him, as John did also, and said, 'Look at us.' Expecting a gift from them, the man was all attention. And Peter said, 'I have no silver or gold; but what I have I give you: in the name of Jesus Christ of Nazareth, walk.' Then he grasped him by the right hand and pulled him up; and at once his feet and ankles grew strong; he sprang up, stood on his feet, and started to walk. He entered the temple with them, leaping and praising God as he went. Everyone saw him walking and praising God, and when they recognized him as the man who used to sit begging at Beautiful Gate, they were filled with wonder and amazement at what happened to him.

The chief priests came upon them, together with the Controller of the Temple and the Sadducees, exasperated at their teaching and proclaiming the resurrection of Jesus. They brought the apostles before the court and began the examination. 'By what power,' they asked, 'or by what name have such men as you done this?' Then Peter, filled with the Holy Spirit, answered, 'Rulers of the people and elders, if the question put to us today is about help given to a sick man, and we are asked by what means he was cured, here is the answer, for all of you and for all the people of Israel: it was by the name of Jesus Christ of Nazareth, whom you crucified, whom God raised from the dead; it is by his name that this man stands here before you fit and well.'

Happened some time between AD *29 and 36*
Written in about AD *85*

For the appearance of the temple see notes to 58. The Beautiful Gate was the main entrance to the eastern courtyard. | *Beautiful Gate*

Jesus was now being called 'the Christ' (reading 55). Suddenly the 'name of Jesus Christ' had gained great power—see 'names' in notes to 137. | *the Christ*

The cripple asked for 'charity' in the modern sense of hard cash, not in the original sense of love described in notes to 67 and 102. | *charity*

The Sadducees being against all the oriental notions of an afterlife now came into increasing conflict with this new Jewish sect which maintained that Jesus was the Christ. And, like the earlier bureaucrats (reading 73), they seemed to have no interest in healing the cripple, no interest in the gifts of real 'charity' (notes to 102). | *Sadducees*

137 Courage, prayer, community, growth

***
from Acts 4 to 6 : New English Bible

Now as the Chief Priests observed the boldness of Peter and John, and noted that they were untrained laymen, they ordered them to refrain from all public speaking and teaching in the name of Jesus. But Peter and John said to them in reply: 'Is it right in God's eyes for us to obey you rather than God? Judge for yourselves. We cannot possibly give up speaking of things we have seen and heard.' The court repeated the caution and discharged them. They could not see how they were to punish them, because the people were all giving glory to God for what had happened.

As soon as they were discharged they went back to their friends and told them everything that the chief priests and elders had said. When they heard it, they raised their voices as one man and called upon God: 'Sovereign Lord, maker of heaven and earth and sea and of everything in them, stretch out thy hand to heal and cause signs and wonders to be done through the name of thy holy servant Jesus.'

They used to meet by common consent in Solomon's Cloister, no one from outside their number venturing to join with them. But people in general spoke highly of them, and more than that, numbers of men and women were added to their ranks as believers in the Lord. In the end the sick were actually carried out into the streets and laid there on beds and stretchers, so that even the shadow of Peter might fall on one or another as he passed by; and the people from the towns round Jerusalem flocked in, bringing those who were ill or harassed by unclean spirits, and all of them were cured.

Many of those who had heard the message became believers. The number of men now reached about five thousand. The word of God now spread more and more widely, the number of disciples in Jerusalem went on increasing rapidly and very many of the priests adhered to the Faith.

Happened some time between AD *29 and 36*
Written in about AD *85*

The vital significance of names has already been referred to in notes *names*
to 6, 95, and 128. It is always cropping up. The Jewish leaders
would not have found these untutored Galileans so irritating if they
hadn't kept saying 'In the name of Jesus.'

'Jesus' was not an uncommon name. It was Greek for the Hebrew *Jesus*
name 'Joshua' which meant, 'Yahweh saves.' In Greek capitals it
was ' **IHΣOYΣ** '. Some Roman translators took to a shortened
version ' **IHΣ** ' out of respect for the person it stood for. (This was
an old Jewish habit — see note to 6 on 'Jahweh' [JHVH]). In the
Latin alphabet however, these three Greek letters got confused and
became 'I H S' which produced a common motif in Christian
designs — and is still used today. From the Middle Ages, Dominican
friars among others used the letters on a medal for the newly
baptized and taught that it stood for *Jesum habemus socium,* that
is, 'Jesus we-have as-our-companion.' And there were several other
interpretations.

The actual stuff of the preaching of this first generation of Christians *preaching*
was quite uncomplicated: 'the long-expected 'Messiah' of the Jews
has come; it is Jesus, who went about doing good, was killed and
raised from death; he will come again with 'power' and 'glory', so
get ready while there is time!' Peter's speech in reading 135 is a
good example. The only tricky point was, and always has been, the
'coming again'. Some have treated the sayings of Jesus (like
reading 100) as clear prophecy. The early Christians certainly did.
Most expected him to return during their lifetime. There was a great
weight of Jewish teaching about a military and political Messiah.
And if 'Acts' (readings 135 to 150) was in fact written after the
destruction of Jerusalem in AD 70 it would be natural to cling all the
closer to that point of view.

But others have treated the sayings of Jesus — especially his
teaching about 'the Kingdom of Heaven' — as a present and active *Kingdom*
reality: 'the kingdom is within you' meant, they have said, that the
reign of God was already established within the hearts of those who
served his purposes. (See all notes to 84.)

Future or present? The tension still exists in the minds of Christians. *second*
Yet it is often a wholesome and regenerative tension. *coming*

138 Gamaliel's advice

from Acts 5 : New English Bible

Then the High Priest and his colleagues, the Sadducean party as it then was, were goaded into action by jealousy. They summoned the 'Sanhedrin', that is, the full senate of the Israelite nation, and they proceeded to arrest the apostles, and put them in official custody, but without using force for fear of being stoned by the people.

So they brought them and stood them before the Council; and the High Priest began his examination. 'We expressly ordered you,' he said, 'to desist from teaching in that name; and what has happened? You have filled Jerusalem with your teaching, and you are trying to make us responsible for that man's death.' Peter replied for himself and the apostles: 'We must obey God rather than men.'

This touched them on the raw, and they wanted to put them to death. But a member of the Council rose to his feet, a Pharisee called Gamaliel, a teacher of the law held in high regard by all the people. He moved that the men be put outside for a while. Then he said, 'Men of Israel, be cautious in deciding what to do with these men. Leave them alone. For if this idea of theirs or its execution is of human origin, it will collapse; but if it is from God, you will never be able to put them down, and you risk finding yourselves at war with God.'

They took his advice. They sent for the apostles and had them flogged; they then ordered them to give up speaking in the name of Jesus, and discharged them. So the apostles went out from the Council rejoicing that they had been found worthy to suffer indignity for the sake of the Name. And every day they went steadily on with their teaching in the temple and in private houses, telling the good news that the Messiah was Jesus.

The 'disciples' now have become 'apostles', no longer 'learners' but *disciples*
'missionaries' and 'ambassadors for their Lord Jesus'. They were *apostles*
irritatingly bold in Jerusalem these rough Northerners and, among
the common people, even more irritatingly successful: the whole
conception of a 'Messiah' now came into focus for them (notes to *Messiah*
55). But the irritated bureaucrats (the Sadducees) feared that riots
and revolution would follow and all would be destroyed. Their fears *Sadducees*
were natural enough — the idle rabble in the city would seize any
excuse for a bit of rioting.

The Pharisees being the champions of the Belshazzar theory (notes *Pharisees*
to 83) now found they had less to quarrel with, in fact, as in the *Belshazzar*
reading opposite (and see reading 145) they found themselves from
time to time siding with the apostles of Jesus of Nazareth. A most
extraordinary *volte-face*!

Gamaliel, a great Jewish rabbi, descendant of a famous liberal *Gamaliel*
rabbi. His family taught tolerance to Jew and gentile alike. Some
have doubted whether so fiery a character as St Paul (notes to 144)
could ever have been taught by him! See, for example, Paul's
intolerance in reading 146.

For Jewish flogging see notes to 116.

139 The seven organizers

from Acts 2 and 6 : New English Bible

They met constantly to hear the apostles teach, and to share the common life, to break bread, and to pray. A sense of awe was everywhere, and many marvels and signs were brought about through the apostles. All whose faith had drawn them together held everything in common: they would sell their property and possessions and make a general distribution as the need of each required. With one mind they kept up their daily attendance at the temple, and, breaking bread in private houses, shared their meals with unaffected joy, as they praised God and enjoyed the favour of the whole people. And day by day the Lord added to their number those whom he was saving.

During this period, when disciples were growing in number, there was disagreement between those of them who spoke Greek and those who spoke the language of the Jews. The former party complained that their widows were being overlooked in the daily distribution. So the Twelve called the whole body of disciples together and said, 'It would be a grave mistake for us to neglect the word of God in order to wait at table. Therefore, friends, look out seven men of good reputation from your number, men full of the Spirit and of wisdom, and we will appoint them to deal with these matters, while we devote ourselves to prayer and to the ministry of the Word.' This proposal proved acceptable to the whole body. They elected Stephen, a man full of faith and of the Holy Spirit, Philip, Prochorus, Nicanor, Timon, Parmenas, and Nicolas of Antioch, a former convert of Judaism. These they presented to the apostles, who prayed and laid their hands on them.

Happened somewhere between AD *29 and 36*
Written about AD *85*

Commune-ism — communism pure and simple.   *Communism*

But the community at Jerusalem was also sustained by various
other things. There was a tremendous sense of excitement
stemming from a refined version of 'the Belshazzar theory' (notes to   *Belshazzar*
83). Now it was focused on the person of Jesus. There was the
familiar rhythm of Jewish synagogue-type worship (notes to 60).
And there was this 'Breaking of Bread' developing.

'Breaking of Bread' — see all notes to 105. In readings 78, 105, 130,   *break*
133, 150 and 151, a pattern can be seen:

    He took bread,
    He gave thanks,
    He broke it,
    He gave it to them.

The symbolism of this central action was profound and   *symbol*
tremendously potent from whatever aspect it was viewed — as a
thanksgiving, a commemoration, a sacrifice, a communion or a
mystery. See an example of interpretation in one of Paul's
letters — reading 151.

This ritual meal was eaten in private houses behind locked doors. It
took on the name 'eucharist', that was 'gratitude'. It seemed to   *Eucharist*
bring them peace of mind, joy in their togetherness, and a very
powerful confidence in the future. It was like a domestic synagogue
to them (notes to 60), and wherever they met secretly like this was
called their 'church' which simply meant 'meeting'. (Their enemies   *church*
became very suspicious — see notes to 156.)

140 The death of Stephen

***
from Acts 6 to 8 : New English Bible

Stephen, who was full of grace and power, began to work great miracles and
signs among the people. But some members of the synagogue came forward
and argued with Stephen, but could not hold their own against the inspired
wisdom with which he spoke. They then put up men who alleged that they
had heard him make blasphemous statements against Moses and against
God. They stirred up the people and the elders and doctors of the law, set
upon him and seized him, and brought him before the Council. They
produced false witnesses who said, 'This man is for ever saying things
against this holy place and against the Law. For we have heard him say that
Jesus of Nazareth will destroy this place and alter the customs handed down
to us by Moses.' And all who were sitting in the Council fixed their eyes on
him, and his face appeared to them like the face of an angel.

Then the High Priest asked, 'Is this so?' And he said, 'My brothers, you
always fight against the Holy Spirit. Like fathers, like sons. Was there ever
a prophet whom your fathers did not persecute? They killed those who
foretold the coming of the Righteous One; and now you have betrayed him
and murdered him, you who received the Law as God's angels gave it to you,
and yet have not kept it. How stubborn you are, heathen still at heart and
deaf to the truth!'

This touched them on the raw and they ground their teeth with fury. Then
they made one rush at him and, flinging him out of the city, set about
stoning him. The witnesses laid their coats at the feet of a young man named
Saul. So they stoned Stephen, and as they did so, he called out, 'Lord Jesus,
receive my Spirit.' Then he fell on his knees and cried aloud, 'Lord, do not
hold this sin against them,' and with that he died. And Saul was among
those who approved of his murder.

Happened somewhere between AD *29 and 36*
Written about AD *85*

All the early preachers were called 'martyrs', a Greek word meaning *martyrs*
'witness', that is one who sees and knows. But after the death of
this 'martyr' Stephen, the word referred only to those witnesses
who were punished or killed. And from this point, persecutions
spread and raged scattering abroad the small groups of Christians
which had developed. The blood of the martyrs caused the spread
of these Christian groups, therefore, and their remains were
reverently collected and kept as trophies. In these early days they *second*
died believing firmly that they would rise again out of their graves at *coming*
'the second coming' of Jesus.

Martyrs were soon considered first among the 'saints' and from now *saints*
on communities began to celebrate the death of these their most
heroic members with a feast. The Feast of Saint Stephen for
example eventually settled on 26 December.

Stephen was probably a Jew of Greek descent and language. He *Stephen*
was made a 'deacon' in the Christian community. The manner of his
death as it was described here was strangely similar to that of
Jesus — his fearlessness, the fury and blind injustice of the Jewish
leaders, his words of forgiveness and of trust.

Judging was usually done at the gate of a Jewish city — in public. At *law*
least two witnesses had to be present. If their evidence was found to
be true, and if it led to a sentence of death by stoning, they had to *perjury*
cast the first stones; if they were found to give false evidence, they
themselves were stoned. *stoning*

Stoning was the customary Jewish punishment of capital offences.
'Capital offences' ranged from murder to a son's rebellion against
his parents. (See the Moses law, Rules 5 and 6.) The offender was
taken outside the city wall where the whole population pelted him
till he was not only dead but also buried by the stones.

The shadowy figure of the 'young man named Saul' came to light *Paul*
later, reading 144.

141 Persecution, growth, baptisms in Samaria

***
from Acts 8 : New English Bible

This was the beginning of a time of violent persecution for the church in Jerusalem; and all except the apostles were scattered over the country districts of Judaea and Samaria. Stephen was given burial by certain devout men, who made a great lamentation for him. Saul, meanwhile, was harrying the church; he entered house after house, seizing men and women, and sending them to prison.

As for those who had been scattered, they went through the country preaching the Word. Philip came down to a city in Samaria and began proclaiming the Messiah to them. The crowds, to a man, listened eagerly to what Philip said, when they heard him and saw the miracles that he performed. For in many cases of possession the unclean spirits came out with a great outcry; and there was great joy in that city.

A man named Simon had been in the city for some time, and had swept the Samaritans off their feet with his magical arts, claiming to be someone great. All of them, high and low, listened eagerly to him. They listened because they had for so long been carried away by his magic. But when they came to believe Philip with his good news about the kingdom of God and the name of Jesus Christ, they were baptised, men and women alike. Even Simon himself believed, and was baptised, and thereupon was constantly in Philip's company. He was carried away when he saw the powerful signs and miracles that were taking place.

Happened in about AD *36*
Written in about AD *85*

The blood of the martyrs forced new life and growth into the young community — exactly as they had always believed the blood of any sacrificial animal had done in more primitive times; outside the so-called pure Judaism centred in Jerusalem, even as far as the so-called mongrel outcasts of Samaria.

blood martyrs

'Philip' here was the deacon mentioned in reading 139, not the same person as 'Philip the Apostle' in readings 61 and 64. Little is known of him except that he had four daughters, probably settled in Caesarea and knew Paul. He is known as 'Philip the Evangelist', that is 'giver of good news'.

Philip the Evangelist

'The Word' — of vital importance, meaning everything between God himself, source of reality, spirit, will, soul, life, laws, commands, breath, voice, reason, vision, light, understanding, power, salvation, and Jesus himself. Not an easy expression to define briefly! On the one hand it had a very physical meaning — see reading 44; on the other, it was plain philosophy — see reading 160.

Logos

142 Samarian confirmations

from Acts 8 : New English Bible

The apostles in Jerusalem now heard that Samaria had accepted the word of God. They sent off Peter and John, who went down there and prayed for the converts, asking that they might receive the Holy Spirit. For until then the Spirit had not come upon any of them. They had been baptized into the name of the Lord Jesus, that and nothing more. So Peter and John laid their hands on them and they received the Holy Spirit.

When Simon saw that the Spirit was bestowed through the laying on of the apostles' hands, he offered them money and said, 'Give me the same power too, so that when I lay my hands on anyone, he will receive the Holy Spirit.' 'You and your money,' said Peter sternly, 'may you come to a bad end, for thinking God's gift is for sale! You have no part nor lot in this, for you are dishonest with God. Repent of this wickedness and pray the Lord to forgive you for imagining such a thing. I can see that you are doomed to taste the bitter fruit and wear the fetters of sin.' Simon answered, 'Pray to the Lord for me yourselves and ask that some of the things you have spoken of may fall upon me.'

And so, after giving their testimony and speaking the word of the Lord, they took the road back to Jerusalem, bringing the good news to many Samaritan villages on the way.

Happened in about AD *36*
Written about AD *85*

This was 'Simon the Sorcerer', a weird enthusiast who seemed to shadow Simon Peter wherever he went. He followed the apostle, according to one tradition, as far as Rome. His crime of trying to buy spiritual power with money has been called 'simony' to this day.

Simon the Sorcerer

This incident in Samaria indicated the growth of a formal structure. Questions arose all the time as this new faith mushroomed. Baptism, the first apostles claimed, had to be done properly (see notes to 134 on 'Trinity' and 'Baptism'). This unusual confirmation of baptism at Samaria has been the cause of much dispute about membership, and different churches have spent hundreds of years arguing exhaustingly about it.

baptism
confirmation

This Samaritan enthusiasm about the new so-called Christian faith marked a significant step outwards. People of Samaria seldom had any use for matters to do with Jerusalem: see reading 83, notes to 82 and, of course, readings 32, 38 and 47.

Samaria

143 The first gentile Christians

***

from Acts 10 : New English Bible

Peter was lodging at Joppa with a tanner whose house was by the sea. One day about noon, Peter went on the roof to pray. He grew hungry and wanted something to eat. While they were getting it ready, he fell into a trance. He saw a rift in the sky, and a thing that looked like a great sheet of sail cloth slung by the four corners and being lowered to the ground. In it he saw creatures of every kind, whatever walks or crawls or flies. Then there was a voice which said to him, 'Up, Peter, kill and eat.' But Peter said, 'No, Lord, no: I have never eaten anything profane or unclean.' The voice came again a second time: 'It is not for you to call profane what God counts clean.' This happened three times; and then the thing was taken up again into the sky.

While Peter was still puzzling over the meaning of the vision, messengers arrived from a Centurion in Caesarea, a religious man whose whole family joined in the worship of god. 'We are from the Centurion Cornelius,' they said. 'He told us to ask you to his house so as to hear all that you have to say.' So Peter gave them a night's lodging and next day he set out with them, accompanied by some members of the congregation at Joppa.

When he arrived at Caesarea, he found Cornelius and a large gathering in his house. He began: 'I now see how true it is that God has no favourites, but that in every nation the man who does what is right is acceptable to him. You know about Jesus of Nazareth. He went about doing good and healing. He was put to death but God raised him to life and commanded us to proclaim him to people.'

Peter was still speaking when the Holy Spirit came upon all who were listening to the message. The believers who had come with Peter, men of Jewish birth, were astonished that the gift of the Holy Spirit should have been poured out even on Gentiles.

Then Peter ordered them to be baptized in the name of Jesus Christ. After that they asked him to stay on with them.

Happened in about AD *37*
Written about AD *85*

Another vital step, like readings 140, 141 and 142, towards the spread of the gospel of Jesus beyond the boundaries of plain Judaism. Samaritans were half-caste but this Cornelius was pure 'gentile' — that is non-Jew and, traditionally, beyond the pale of Yahweh's concern. (See also note to 50 on 'gentile'.) *gentile*

There was nothing magical about this trance. It was a straight-forward day-dream on an empty stomach, vivid and memorable. *visions* Obviously Peter had been mentally conjuring with the pros and cons of gentile interest in the gospel of Jesus. Dreams are safety-valves *dreams* for anxieties like these — and also indicators; the Jews would say 'instructions'.

Jewish food was basically whatever could be wrested from the land. *food* There were certain 'unclean' meats however which were forbidden *unclean* by the Law, for example: any sea creatures without scales and fins, certain birds such as ospreys, kites, buzzards and seagulls; all insects except locusts; bats and various other mammals like camels, hares and pigs. And even with regard to the 'clean' meats they had to be properly slaughtered and the blood drained off; they could not be eaten if found already dead or killed by another animal — though it was permissible to sell these to foreigners!

There were complicated reasons for these taboos. Pigs, for *pigs* instance, had been sacred among Syrians, their hated neighbours, and were consequently 'unclean' for themselves (see notes to 20). Yet this is an oversimplification, for the Jews also felt the need to wash after touching sacred things — they washed after reading the scriptures. So Jewish 'untouchability' was strict, but difficult to define exactly.

'Congregation' simply means people flocking together like sheep. *congregation* Note the familiar pattern of Peter's speech. (See readings 135 and 137.)

144 Saul of Tarsus

***
from Acts 9 : New English Bible

Meanwhile Saul was still breathing murderous threats against the disciples of the Lord. He went to the High Priest and applied for letters to the synagogues at Damascus authorizing him to arrest anyone he found, men or women, who followed the new way, and bring them to Jerusalem.

While he was still on the road and nearing Damascus, suddenly he fell to the ground. Light flashed all around him and he heard a voice saying, 'Saul, Saul, why do you persecute me?' 'Tell me, Lord,' he said, 'who you are.' The voice answered, 'I am Jesus, whom you are persecuting. But get up and go into the city, and you will be told what you have to do.' Meanwhile the men who were travelling with him stood speechless; they could see no one. Saul got up from the ground, but when he opened his eyes he could not see; so they led him by the hand and brought him into Damascus. He was blind for three days, and took no food or drink.

There was a disciple in Damascus named Ananias. He entered the house, laid his hands on him and said, 'Saul, my brother, the Lord Jesus, who appeared to you on your way here, has sent me to you so that you may recover your sight, and be filled with the Holy Spirit.' And immediately it seemed that scales fell from his eyes, and he regained his sight. Thereupon he was baptized, and afterwards he took food and his strength returned. He stayed some time with the disciples in Damascus.

Happened between about AD *35 and 38*
Written about AD *85*

Sunstroke? Hallucinations? It happened in the desert where such *visions* things do happen to this day. What actually happened matters not: *dreams* this man became the most powerful human personality in the history of the Christian religion — apart from its founder of course.

Paul was a native of Tarsus, a commercial town with a university. Tarsus had a mixed population of Greeks and Orientals with some dispersed Jews, and had become famous as the meeting-place of Mark Antony with Cleopatra in 38 BC. Paul, who was born about the *Paul* same time as Jesus, was the son of a Jew of the tribe of Benjamin, and inherited from his father the great advantage of Roman citizenship with its special privileges. His parents gave him a strictly Pharisaic upbringing — the 'Puritans' of the Jewish world. He was small in height and a tent maker by trade. His Jewish name was 'Saul' and his gentile name 'Paul'; later he was referred to as 'the Apostle of the Gentiles'. He was the best educated of all the writers about the Jesus event in the Bible, for he was experienced in Jewish and Roman law, with a thorough knowledge of Jewish scriptures and had spent some time in Jerusalem at the feet of the famous liberal-minded rabbi, Gamaliel (see reading 138).

He clearly considered he could best serve his god by rooting out this new contamination which claimed that a blasphemous Galilean carpenter's son was the Christ. But in about AD 35, as he later said, 'I was arrested by Christ Jesus.'

He subsequently spent three years in Arabia and, after a brief visit to Peter in Jerusalem, there were ten more hidden years back in Cilicia. Then after visits to the churches in Antioch and Jerusalem, he set out upon extensive missionary journeys all over the Roman Empire. For about ten years he travelled and preached, claiming to be a 'man of Christ', collecting small groups of like-minded people (that is 'churches') and writing them long letters (or epistles — see notes to 157). Possibly he died during the persecutions of Nero (see notes to *Nero* 156) sometime between AD 64 and 67.

145 Arguments about circumcision

*

from Acts 15 : New English Bible

Now certain persons who had come down from Judaea began to teach the brotherhood that those who were not circumcised in accordance with Mosaic practice could not be saved. That brought them into fierce dissension and controversy with Paul and Barnabas. And so it was arranged that these two and some others from Antioch should go up to Jerusalem to see the apostles and elders about this question.

When they reached Jerusalem they were welcomed by the church and the apostles and elders, and reported all that God had helped them to do. Then some of the Pharisaic party who had become believers came forward and said, 'They must be circumcised and told to keep the Law of Moses.'

The apostles and elders held a meeting to look into this matter; and, after long debate, Peter rose and addressed them. 'My friends,' he said, 'in the early days, as you yourselves know, God made his choice among you and ordained that from my lips the Gentiles should hear and believe the message of the Gospel. And God, who can read men's minds, showed his approval of them by giving the Holy Spirit to them, as he did to us. He made no difference between them and us; for he purified their hearts by faith. Then why do you now provoke God by laying on the shoulders of these converts a yoke which neither we nor our fathers were able to bear? No, we believe that it is by the grace of the Lord Jesus that we are saved, and so are they.'

At that the whole company fell silent and listened to Barnabas and Paul as they told of all the signs and miracles that God had worked among the Gentiles through them. When they had finished speaking, James summed up: 'My friends,' he said, 'listen to me. We should impose no irksome restrictions on those of the Gentiles who are turning to God, but instruct them by letter to refrain from doing to others what they would not like done to themselves.'

Happened between about AD *49 and 50*
Written about AD *85*

Circumcision is a very sensitive business. It has been practised by Jews and Moslems, among Australian aboriginal tribes, in Africa and many other parts of the world. Up to the time of this reading every Jew religiously circumcised each of his baby boys eight days after birth, that is, he cut off the foreskin of the child's penis. It had become, since the early days of the Moses law, the distinctive physical mark of a genuine Jew. Later, as at the time of this reading, anyone of whatever age who wished to become a Jew (a 'proselyte') had to submit himself to this ordeal. By modern utilitarian standards, its only value seems to have been hygiene. But in those days it was everything. Hence the arguments. And one of the rudest things a Jew could say to an enemy was to call him 'uncircumcised'. It was as insulting as 'bastard' is today. *circumcision*

The new Christian community quickly dispensed with the custom and said it was more important to cut the mark of membership into the heart (see also reading 41, paragraph 3). Membership was not *heart* brought about by the extravagant efforts of man, they said, but by 'the grace of the Lord Jesus' — see notes to 27 and 56 on 'grace'. *grace*

The 'James' opposite was one of the brothers of Jesus (see note to 74 on 'family'). He was known as 'the first Bishop of Jerusalem' *Jesus'* from a very early date. *family*

James of
A 'bishop' was an elder member of the community who was *Jerusalem* appointed to supervise its running and preside over its meetings.

'Barnabas' — see notes to 146. *bishop*

146 Paul and Barnabas quarrel

*

from Acts 15 and 16: New English Bible

After a while Paul said to Barnabas, 'Ought we not to go back now to see how our brothers are faring in the various towns where we proclaimed the word of the Lord?' Barnabas wanted to take John Mark with them; but Paul judged that the man who had deserted them in Pamphylia and had not gone on to share in their work was not the man to take with them now. The dispute was so sharp that they parted company. Barnabas took Mark with him and sailed for Cyprus, while Paul chose Silas and travelled through Syria and Cilicia bringing new strength to the congregations.

As they made their way from town to town they handed on the decisions taken by the apostles and elders in Jerusalem and enjoined their observance. And so, day by day, the congregations grew stronger in faith and increased in numbers.

Happened between about AD *49 and 50*
Written in about AD *85*

Paul went on several missionary journeys which took him to cities in
Lebanon, Cyprus, Syria, Turkey, Greece and Italy. He started in
Jerusalem and Antioch and ended in Rome. His adventures were
recorded by his friend, Luke, who was sometimes with him.
(Recorded in 'The Acts of the Apostles'.)   *Luke*

Paul

No detailed records are known which refer to the operations of other
missionaries like Paul.   *mission*

'John Mark' was the Mark described in notes to 110. He was   *Mark*
thought to have become the first Bishop of Alexandria.

'Barnabas' was his cousin, a Jewish Levite of Cyprus, who became   *Barnabas*
one of the earliest Jerusalem Christians. After Paul's sudden
conversion (reading 144) it was Barnabas who had befriended him
and introduced him to the Christians at Jerusalem who were at first,
naturally enough, suspicious. After this quarrel with Paul, there was
mention of him continuing as a missionary in parts of Turkey,
Greece and possibly Italy. He almost certainly was the founder of
the Christian church in Cyprus. He was probably martyred in Cyprus
in AD 61.

147   The jailer at Philippi

from Acts 16 and 17: New English Bible

So we sailed from Troas to Neapolis, and from there to Philippi, a city of the first rank in that district of Macedonia, and a Roman colony. Here we stayed for some days.

Following his usual practice Paul went to show that the Messiah had to suffer and rise from the dead. But they seized Paul and Silas and dragged them to the city authorities in the main square. After giving them a severe beating they flung them into prison and ordered the jailer to keep them under close guard.

About midnight Paul and Silas, at their prayers, were singing praises to God, and the other prisoners were listening, when suddenly there was such a violent earthquake that the foundations of the jail were shaken; all the doors burst open and all the prisoners found their fetters unfastened. The jailer woke up to see the prison doors wide open, and assuming that the prisoners had escaped, drew his sword intending to kill himself. But Paul shouted, 'Do yourself no harm; we are all here.' The jailer called for lights, rushed in and threw himself down before Paul and Silas, trembling with fear. He then escorted them out and said, 'Masters, what must I do to be saved?' They said, 'Put your trust in the Lord Jesus, and you will be saved, you and your household.' Then they spoke the word of the Lord to him and to everyone in his house. At that late hour of the night he took them and washed their wounds; and immediately afterwards he and his whole family were baptized. He brought them into his house, set out a meal, and rejoiced with his whole household in his new-found faith in God.

When daylight came the magistrates sent their officers with instructions to release the men. On leaving the prison, they went to Lydia's house, where they met their fellow-Christians, and spoke words of encouragement to them; then they departed.

Happened between about AD *49 and 52*
Written in about AD *85*

Philippi, the Greek town in Macedonia, under Roman jurisdiction, was named after Philip of Macedon, the father of Alexander the Great (notes to 51). Luke, the writer, was with Paul here. Little is known of Silas. He was possibly a Greek; he is said to have died somewhere in Macedonia. *Philippi*

Luke

Lydia was a gentile businesswoman, a dealer in purple dyes and purple clothes in Philippi. She was probably quite wealthy because purple dye was in great demand in Roman society as a symbol of authority and distinction. Every male Roman citizen in public wore a toga with a purple hem — Paul would have had one (notes to 144). High-ranking officials and soldiers, as well as their women, wore clothes dyed entirely purple. It was obtained from mixing the red and blue juices from certain molluscs. Every ordinary soldier had a reddish cloak dyed from these. *Lydia*

robes

purple

toga

The jailer seemed more afraid of Paul than of the earthquake, believing he was a holy man with power over the natural elements — an ancient superstition (see notes to 17 and 78). *elements*

This was an emotional conversion. There was little preaching or intellectual persuasion (as in readings 148 and 149). Instead there was this spontaneous faith in the personality of Paul which was quickly rewarded with baptism. However, the man may have spent some of his off-duty hours listening to Paul's preaching before the arrest. *convert*

148 Paul at Athens

from Acts 17: New English Bible

Now while Paul was waiting for them at Athens he was exasperated to see how the city was full of idols. So he argued in the synagogue with the Jews and gentile worshippers, and also in the city square every day with casual passers-by. And some of the Epicurean and Stoic philosophers joined issue with him. Some said, 'What can this charlatan be trying to say?' others, 'He would appear to be a propagandist for foreign deities'—this because he was preaching about Jesus and Resurrection. Now the Athenians in general and foreigners there had not time for anything but talking or hearing about the latest novelty.

Then Paul stood up before the Court of Areopagus and said: 'Men of Athens, I see that in everything that concerns religion you are uncommonly scrupulous. For as I was going round looking at the objects of your worship, I noticed among other things an altar bearing the inscription "To an Unknown God." What you worship but do not know—this is what I now proclaim.

'The God who created the world and everything in it, and who is Lord of heaven and earth, does not live in shrines made by men. It is not because he lacks anything that he accepts service at men's hands, for he is himself the universal giver of life and breath and all else. He created every race of men of one stock, to inhabit the whole earth's surface. He fixed the ordered seasons and the limits of their territory. They were to seek God, and, it might be, touch and find him; though indeed he is not far from each one of us, for in him we live and move, in him we exist. He will have the world judged, and justly judged, by a man of his choosing; of this he has given assurance to all by raising him from the dead.'

When they heard about the raising of the dead, some scoffed; and others said, 'We will hear you on this subject some other time.' And so Paul left the assembly. However, some men joined him and became believers.

Happened between about AD *49 and 52*
Written in about AD *85*

Athens, the capital of Greece, the homeland of Zeus, the lord of the *Athens*
heavens (notes to 51). Her people had never been inclined to think *Zeus*
in terms of an afterlife, yet they were connoisseurs of all religions
from Spain to Persia. Since the empire, the Stoic philosophy had *Stoics*
flourished. (Ben Sira (notes to 52) had for example been influenced
by it.) It was a form of enlightened materialism: God was everywhere (pantheism) and the laws of nature were supreme; good men *pantheism*
were wise men and addressed themselves to duty, hard work, *good*
learning, the control of passions and an indifference to pain and
pleasure. This was receptive and fertile ground for the Christian *Christian*
ideas which Paul was sowing.

The Epicurean philosophy, which was as old, was a form of refined *Epicurean*
hedonism: truth could only be perceived through the senses; all *hedonism*
matter consisted of various arrangements of a limited number of *atomism*
particles (atomism) and the stuff of the universe possibly contained
gods but they did not affect human affairs: man should seek *senses*
happiness through sensual pleasures but with sensitiveness and
prudence. Paul knew about all this when he talked (in this reading) *touch*
of seeking God and perhaps touching and finding him, and so on.

There is a small spur jutting out from the western end of the
Acropolis in Athens called Mars Hill. A small council called 'The
Court of Areopagus', had met here from very early times. They had
formerly been judicial but now they were religious or philosophical
and mildly political.

A 'charlatan' was a quack, an ignorant pretender of knowledge or
skill, a hypocrite. But Paul was, on the contrary, quite the opposite!

Note the beginning of the third paragraph of this reading and
compare it, for example, with the end of the third paragraph in
reading 33: a great leap forward in theology! They had discovered *theology*
that there was NOTHING they could give the creator which he hadn't
got already: they could ONLY receive from him. The beginnings of
this idea were back in stories like Job (reading 49). *Job*

149 Diana of the Ephesians

from Acts 19 and 20 : New English Bible

Now about that time, the Christian movement gave rise to a serious disturbance. There was a man named Demetrius, a silversmith who made silver shrines of Diana and provided a great deal of employment for the craftsmen. He called a meeting of these men and the workers in allied trades, and addressed them. 'Men,' he said, 'you know that our high standard of living depends on this industry. And you see and hear how this fellow Paul with his propaganda has perverted crowds of people, not only at Ephesus but also in practically the whole of the province of Asia. He is telling them that gods made by human hands are not gods at all. There is danger for us here; it is not only that our line of business will be discredited, but also that the sanctuary of the great goddess Diana will cease to command respect; and then it will not be long before she who is worshipped by all Asia and the civilised world is brought down from her divine pre-eminence.'

When they heard this they were roused to fury and shouted, 'Great is Diana of the Ephesians!' The whole city was in confusion; they seized Paul's travelling-companions, the Macedonians Gaius and Aristarchus, and made a concerted rush with them into the theatre. Paul wanted to appear before the assembly but the other Christians would not let him. Even some of the dignitaries of the province, who were friendly towards him, went and urged him not to venture into the theatre. Meanwhile some were shouting one thing, some another; for about two hours they kept on shouting.

The town clerk, however, quieted the crowd. 'Men of Ephesus,' he said, 'we run the risk of being charged with riot for this day's work. There is no justification for it, and if the issue is raised we shall be unable to give any explanation of this uproar.' With that he dismissed the assembly.

When the disturbance had ceased, Paul sent for the disciples and, after encouraging them, said good-bye and set out on his journey to Macedonia.

Diana was the Roman name for Artemis, the Greek goddess of woodlands, animal fecundity, hunting, pregnant women, childbirth and motherhood — in that order her legendary image had emerged from antiquity. It was not by modern standards a pretty image: the statues found of her are multi-breasted female figures hung about with symbols of exuberant fecundity. Doubtless her craftsmen carved their statues and souvenirs with as much devotion as any modern ecclesiastical furnisher. No wonder they did not welcome Paul's diversions — before long there would be mass unemployment and perhaps even a local slump. Such a catastrophe was unthinkable, for the temple of Artemis at Ephesus was one of the seven wonders of the world — the tourist trade was enormous (they were called 'pilgrims') — and besides, it contained the original statue of the goddess which had been cast down from heaven (everyone knew that). *Diana Artemis trees*

work

This sort of situation in Ephesus was to be repeated all over the Roman world wherever Christianity took itself. After the times of the Bible a great Christian sport developed among intellectuals, namely, heresy-hunting. Long explanations were written to show how pre-Christian religions had been misguided. Any similarities between Christianity as it was developing and those religions it sought to replace (see notes to 148) were said to be the work of the Devil, that 'Father of Lies'. One such collection of writings dating from before AD 50 to after AD 200 was later put down to a single heresy-hunter, 'Saint Hippolytus', who, according to conflicting traditions, had been commemorated as a bishop, a writer, a soldier, a doctor and a martyr. The chief bête-noir of this (possibly non-existent) champion was said to be the fertility worship of the goddess Artemis. A strange coincidence. According to the Greek cult of Artemis, one of her former lovers who had been killed was also named 'Hippolytus'. And another coincidence: 'Saint Hippolytus' was given his feast day on 13 August, which had previously been the date of the annual festival of the goddess Artemis. *Christianity*

heresy

Devil

Hippolytus

But such pagan cultures contained at the very least a germ of true religion and, in spite of being so badly treated, their unashamed descendants have survived throughout Europe: mid-summer beauty contests and pageants, sheep shearing, tossing the pitchfork, harvest festivals, devil-beating, holly and ivy, 'Betsy', mummers, Britannia Coconut dancing, May Day celebrations, Whitsun games, Morris dancing, cheese rolling and round to the midsummer galas again — with perhaps a shy Diana emerging from her shadowy groves and smiling on the scene. *pagan*

trees

150 Shipwreck

from Acts 27 and 28 : New English Bible

When it was decided that we should sail for Italy, Paul and some other prisoners were handed over to a centurion named Julius, of the Augustan Cohort. By now much time had been lost and it was risky to go on with the voyage, but we embarked in a ship and put to sea.

For days on end there was no sign of either sun or stars, a great storm was raging, and our last hopes of coming through alive began to fade. The fourteenth night came and we were still drifting in the Sea of Adria. In the middle of the night the sailors felt that land was getting nearer. Shortly before daybreak, Paul urged them to take some food. He took bread, gave thanks to God in front of all, broke it, and began eating. Then they plucked up courage and took food themselves. There were on board two hundred and seventy-six of us in all. When they had eaten as much as they wanted, they lightened the ship by dumping the corn in the sea.

When day broke, they could not recognize the land, but noticed a bay with a sandy beach on which they planned, if possible, to run the ship ashore. So they slipped the anchors and let them go; at the same time they loosened the lashings of the steering paddles, set the foresail to the wind, and let her drive to the beach. But they found themselves caught between cross currents, and the ship ran aground so that the bow stuck fast and remained immovable while the stern was being pounded to pieces by the breakers.

The soldiers thought they had better kill the prisoners for fear that they should swim away and escape; but the centurion wanted to bring Paul safely through, and prevented them from carrying out their plan. He gave orders that those who could swim should jump overboard first and get to land; the rest were to follow, some on planks, some on parts of the ship. And thus it was that all came safely to land.

The island was Malta and the rough islanders treated us with uncommon kindness.

After many exciting adventures Paul was arrested in Jerusalem, *Paul*
taken under heavy escort to Caesarea, tried before the Roman
procurator and given such shoddy treatment that he took advantage
of his Roman citizenship and appealed to be tried properly at the
imperial court in Rome. 'I appeal to Caesar.' *emperor*

He sailed with Luke. For 'centurion', see notes to 123. It was the
wrong time of the year for sailing—the treacherous autumn
equinox.

After Malta, he eventually reached Rome where, awaiting trial for
two years, he was allowed to stay under house arrest. He wrote
many letters to the churches he had established—see readings 152 *letters*
and 154.

In AD 61 he was released, travelled probably to Spain among other
places, and after imprisonment in Rome is thought to have been
beheaded somewhere between AD 64 and 67. But there is some
disagreement about this.

151 From a letter—the 'Body of the Christ'

from 1 Corinthians 10 and 11 : Letters to Young Churches

The lesson we must learn, my brothers, is at all costs to avoid worshipping a false god. I am speaking to you as intelligent men: think over what I am saying.

When we break the Bread, do we not actually share in the Body of Christ? The very fact that we all share one bread makes us all one Body. Look at the Jews of our own day. Isn't there a fellowship between all those who eat?

The Lord Jesus, in the same night that he was betrayed, took bread, and when he had given thanks he broke it and said, 'Take, eat, this is my body which is being broken for you. Do this in remembrance of me.' This can only mean that whenever you eat this bread, you are proclaiming that the Lord has died for you.

So a man should thoroughly examine himself, and only then should he eat the bread—or drink of the cup. He that eats or drinks carelessly is blind to the presence of the Lord's Body.

Part of a letter written by Paul to Christians in Corinth in about AD *56*

It is thought that Paul had founded the church in Corinth in about AD *Corinth*
50. Corinth was a very important seaport, a garrison town and a
strategic road junction. It had a cosmopolitan population. It was a
byword for carnal perversions, many of them stemming from
twisted variations on the worship of Venus (the Roman name for *Venus*
Aphrodite — see notes to 20). Venus was the goddess of beauty and
love, and the worship of her involved of course a plethora of venery
activities; they were tremendously attractive and stimulating,
naturally enough, but the venereal diseases and miseries which *VD*
naturally followed were not so appetizing.

Whilst at Ephesus, Paul heard rumours about the Christian
community at Corinth. He wrote several letters, parts of them very
severe, trying to clear up their thinking about 'the Christ' in that
confusing context. Here is one extract. Another is in reading 157.

The meditation in this reading was simple: just as people could not
get nourishment from bread unless it was broken and shared, so the *break*
body of Jesus would have been useless unless it had been 'broken' *cross*
on the cross and the 'life' released (see notes to 139). *life*

Compare this conception with the primitive Tammuz-Baal-Adonis
cypher (notes to 20 and 26).

There was at one time rumour in Rome that the Christians in
their secret meals were indulging in cannibalism and other *cannibalism*
'abominations'! (See notes to 156, and note to 139 on 'eucharist'.)

152 From a letter—the example of Jesus

**

from Philippians 2 : Letters to Young Churches

Let Christ himself be your example as to what your attitude should be. For he stripped himself of all privilege, and having become man, he humbled himself by living a life of obedience—even to the extent of dying (and the death he died was the death of a common criminal).

That is why God has now lifted him so high, and has given him the Name beyond all names, so that at the Name of Jesus every knee shall bow. And that is why, in the end, every tongue shall confess that Jesus Christ is the Lord, to the glory of God the Father.

So then, my dearest friends, do all you have to do without grumbling or arguing, so that you may be God's children, sincere and shining like lights in a dark place.

Paul was prouder of this church at Philippi than of any other. *Philippi*
Remember part of his visit in reading 147.

In the extract from his letter opposite, there was the 'Suffering *suffer*
Servant' cypher of Isaiah — see reading 46. For 'humbling' and
'exalting' see notes 89. And see again the significance of 'kneeling'
in notes to 81, and of 'names' in notes 6.

It was clear now that, in the minds of people like Paul, Jesus was *Jesus*
more than a god, he was 'THE LORD OF HEAVEN', 'Yahweh' — or
perhaps, for the Philippians, the name 'Zeus' would be in mind, *Zeus*
(notes to 51).

Roman soldiers stationed at Philippi would probably be loyal to the
Persian sun-god, Mithras; it was a popular faith in the Roman army. *Mithras*
So Paul's picture of a shining cross of glory would have appealed to
them as well (see notes to 160).

153 From a letter—only criticize yourself

**

from Romans 14 : Letters to Young Churches

The truth is that we neither live nor die as self-contained units. At every turn, life links us to God. In life or death we are in the hands of God. Christ lived and died that he might be the Lord in both life and death.

It is to God alone that we have to answer for our actions. Why, then, criticize your brother's actions? Why try to make him look small?

Let us therefore stop turning critical eyes on one another. If we must be critical, let us be critical of our own conduct. Your personal convictions are a matter between yourself and God. So let us concentrate on the things which make for harmony, and on the growth of one another's character.

Part of a letter written in about AD *57 by Paul to Christians in Rome*

Practical advice to a community living at close quarters. It echoes the teaching about criticism in readings 69 and 91.

It is not known who founded the church in Rome. Perhaps it was *Rome* the infiltration of Christian travellers and traders. Most of its members were gentiles but the atmosphere there seems to have been very similar to the communistic community in Jerusalem, (reading 139). There has been a fond tradition that Simon Peter *Peter* founded it and reference is made of course to Bible passages like reading 80, paragraph 4.

'The hands of God' — a favourite motif: see especially reading 45. It *hands* was a magnificent concept, echoed this present century by Pierre Teilhard de Chardin: '. . . and I encounter and kiss your two marvellous hands — the one which holds us so firmly that it is merged, in us, with the sources of life; and the other whose embrace is so wide that, at its slightest pressure, all the springs of the universe respond harmoniously together.'

And hands were not thought of only in this philosophical sort of *initiative* way, but also as the actual limbs of the divine initiative (see the *healing* atonement formula in notes to 73) — they handled forgiveness, *forgive* healing and blessing: readings 44, 61, 81, 150, 131 (end), 137, 139 *bless* and 142; they conveyed the love of the creator. *love*

154   From a letter—the 'new life of the Christ'

*

from Colossians 3 : Letters to Young Churches

If you are then 'risen' with Christ, reach out for the highest gifts of heaven, where your Master reigns in power. Give your heart to heavenly things, not to the passing things of earth. For, as far as this world is concerned, you are already dead, and your life is a hidden one in Christ.

In so far, then, as you have to live upon this earth, have nothing to do with dirty-mindedness and the lust for other people's goods. Put all these things behind you: no more evil temper, no more evil thoughts or words about others. And don't tell each other lies any more. For you have begun life as a new man, who is out to learn what he ought to be, according to the plan of God.

In this new man of God's design, there is no distinction between Jew or Gentile, foreigner or savage, slave or free man: Christ is all that matters, for Christ lives in them all.

Part of a letter from Paul to Christians in Colossae written in about AD *62*

The church in Colossae was probably founded by a Christian from Ephesus taught by Paul. It was a city of great antiquity. A philosophy called Gnosticism (*gnosis* was knowledge) seems to have been popular there. This was rather a shapeless theosophy based on 'the virtue of knowledge', and spiced with obscure mythologies drawn from a variety of other religions.

Gnostics

knowledge

The young church in Colossae looked as if it was about to be swallowed and lost in this situation where 'everyone had a right to his own opinion'. Paul set out, therefore, to clarify 'the Christ'.

Colossae

opinions
the Christ

Astrology was another popular philosophy at Colossae. It held that people's lives were entirely predestined by the planets. Paul also set out to free people from that. Predestination conflicted with the Christian idea of free will (notes to 90). Unfortunately, astrology has been so thoroughly pilloried that little attention is now given to its scientific value.

astrology

predestina-
tion

The reading opposite shows one of the central processes of Christians: if they wanted to share the 'life of the Christ' (see notes to 76 on 'life') they had to put to death all their selfishnesses, they had to 'die daily' — as he said in another letter.

death

Death, scientifically speaking, is change; it is simply a disintegration of the physical organism and a redistribution of its elements in the earth and atmosphere which in time renders them useful in other forms of life. The formulas of the scientific revelation substantiate this principle: 'matter is indestructible', 'energy is conserved and transmitted without loss' — nothing is wasted. If this is the pattern of physical things on the planet, other dimensions of existence are not likely to be dissimilar. So those who fear death, fear change; they are unfamiliar with it in everyday life.

revelation

155 From letters—the nature of the Church

*

from Romans 12 and Ephesians 2 : Letters to Young Churches

With eyes wide open to the mercies of God, I beg you, my brothers, as an act of intelligent worship, to give him your bodies, as a living sacrifice. Don't let the world around you squeeze you into its own mould, but let God remould your minds from within so that you may prove in practice that the Plan of God for you is good and moves towards true maturity.

As your spiritual teacher I give this piece of advice to each one of you. Try to have a sane estimate of your capabilities. For, just as you have many members in one physical body and those members differ in their functions, so we (though many in number) compose one Body in Christ and are all members of one another.

You are no longer outsiders but fellow-citizens with every other Christian—you belong now to the household of God, the actual foundation stone being Jesus Christ himself. In him, each separate piece of building, properly fitting into its neighbour, grows together into a temple consecrated to God.

You are all part of this building in which God himself lives by his Spirit.

The temple had accommodated 'Yahweh' (reading 30). Now each *third temple*
of them was to accommodate the Christ (reading 160). The pattern *the Christ*
of thought had been transferred, it was not new: he had abandoned
his temple and would now live in the hearts of his faithful people *heart*
(reading 41).

They were also to think of their little community as an organic body
fit to house the Spirit of Yahweh.

Furthermore, there was the beginning of thinking in terms of a
world-wide Church made up of these cellular communities. *church*

156   From a letter—real Christian behaviour

from Romans 12 : Letters to Young Churches

Let us have no imitation Christian love. Let us have a genuine break with evil and a real devotion to good. Let us have real warm affection for one another as between brothers, and a willingness to let the other man have the credit. Let us not allow slackness to spoil our work; let us keep the fires of the spirit burning as we do our work for God.

Base your happiness on your hope in Christ. When trials come, endure them patiently: steadfastly maintain the habit of prayer. Give freely, never grudging a meal or a bed to those who need them.

Share the happiness of those who are happy, and the sorrow of those who are sad. Live in harmony with each other. Don't become snobbish but take a real interest in ordinary people. Don't become set in your own opinions.

As for those who try to make your life a misery, bless them. Don't curse, bless. Don't pay back a bad turn by a bad turn, to ANYONE; live at peace with everyone. Never take vengeance into your own hands, my dear friends: stand back and let God punish—IF HE WILL. For these are God's words:

> 'If thine enemy hunger, feed him;
> If he thirst, give him to drink.'

Therefore, take the offensive—overpower evil by good!

Part of a letter written by Paul to Roman Christians in about AD *57*

The clouds were gathering in Rome. Nero had become emperor in AD 54. There was much feeling against the Christians. Tacitus, a Roman historian, wrote this account of the fury that broke upon them in the summer of AD 64 when the city caught fire:

Rome
Nero

'All the emperor's largesse . . . did not suffice to . . . banish the belief that the fire had been ordered. And so, to get rid of this rumour, Nero set up as the culprits and punished with the utmost refinement of curelty, a class hated for their abominations who were commonly called Christians. [See the end of notes to 151.] Christus, from whom their name is derived, was executed at the hands of the procurator Pontius Pilate in the reign of Tiberius. Checked for a moment, this pernicious supersitition again broke out, not only in Judaea, the source of the evil, but even in Rome, that receptacle of everything that is sordid and degrading from every quarter of the globe, which there finds a following. Accordingly, arrest was first made of those who confessed; then, on their evidence, an immense multitude was convicted, not so much on the charge of arson as because of hatred of the human race. Besides being put to death they were made to serve as objects of amusement; they were clad in the hides of beasts and torn to death by dogs; others were crucified, others set on fire to illuminate the night when daylight failed. Nero had thrown open his grounds for the display, and was putting on a show in the circus, where he . . . drove about in his chariot. All this gave rise to a feeling of pity . . . for it was felt that they were being destroyed not for the public good but to gratify the cruelty of an individual.'

Christian

martyrs

157 From a letter—Christian love

***

from 1 Corinthians 13 : Letters to Young Churches

If I speak with the eloquence of angels, but have no love, I become no more than blaring brass or crashing cymbal.

If I have the gift of foretelling the future, and hold in my mind not only all human knowledge but the very secrets of God, and if I also have that absolute faith which can move mountains, but have no love, I amount to nothing at all.

If I dispose of all that I possess, but have no love, I achieve precisely nothing.

This love of which I speak is slow to lose patience—it looks for a way of being constructive. It is not possessive. It is neither anxious to impress, nor does it cherish inflated ideas of its own importance.

Love has good manners and does not pursue selfish advantage. It is not touchy. It does not compile statistics of evil, or gloat over the wickedness of other people.

Love knows no limit to its endurance, no end to its trust, no fading of its hope: it can outlast anything. It is, in fact, the one thing that still stands when all else has fallen.

Paul wrote most of his letters after the age of fifty. They were nearly all intended to meet the particular needs of his readers in a particular situation. Yet, as the reading opposite shows, they also had a universal value.

Paul letters

Paul, with boundless energy and determination, strove to make himself 'all things to all men' (as he put it) for the sake of his 'Lord Jesus Christ'. In that name, he exposed himself to all kinds of danger and led a life of constant self-denial. In the reading opposite Paul has unconsciously drawn his own portrait.

name

The 'Four Evangelists', Matthew, Mark, Luke and John, gave a more human picture of Jesus. They used the plain name 'Jesus' slightly more often than the various titles like 'The Lord Jesus' and 'Jesus the Christ'. And they were dealing more with 'history'. Paul, on the other hand, was interpreting 'Jesus'. It is almost certain that he never met the man Jesus himself, but he did have more than one life-like vision of him. Paul made no bones about it: his lord and master was 'Jesus the Christ', risen, glorious, triumphant, powerful, supreme and everlasting! In his writings, the ratio of splendid titles to the plain name 'Jesus' was eleven to one.

the Christ

It is through the creative mind of this little man that all the roots of Christian thinking have passed. Yet he himself admitted that his knowledge was only partial; it was, he said, like trying to see through a glass darkly — there were puzzling reflections.

knowledge

The 'love' here was not that erotic, physical love needed for breeding. Nor was it that close affection of children for their parents, needed for rearing. It was between the two, the natural love of friendship.

love

See also notes 151 about Corinth, the city of Venus.

158 A dream about war in heaven

From Revelation 12 : New English Bible

Then appeared a great portent in heaven: a great red dragon with seven heads and horns, and with his tail he swept down a third of the stars in the sky and flung them to the earth. The dragon stood in front of God and his throne.

Then war broke out in heaven. Michael and his angels waged war upon the dragon. The dragon and his angels fought, but they had not the strength to win, and no foothold was left them in heaven. So the great dragon was thrown down (that serpent of old that led the whole world astray, whose name is Satan)—thrown down to the earth, and his angels with him.

Then I heard a voice in heaven proclaiming aloud: 'This is the hour of victory of our God, the hour of his sovereignty and power, when his Christ comes to his rightful rule! For the Devil is overthrown.

'Rejoice then, you heavens and you that dwell in them! But woe to you earth and sea, for the Devil has come down to you in great fury!'

When the dragon found that he had been thrown down to the earth, he grew furious and went off to wage war on those who maintain their testimony to Jesus.

Part of a letter to fortify his fellows written in Patmos, probably by a Jewish Christian, in about AD *95*

This is probably the work of a Jew who had grown up in an age which thrived upon visions of supernatural solutions (notes to 83), who had himself probably received an intimate knowledge about Jesus of Nazareth and had been baptized a Christian, had seen the total destruction of his beloved Jerusalem and the awful persecutions in Rome (notes to 156) and elsewhere, and now as living on an island (Patmos), well on in years, waiting for the divine justice to descend upon the world! He had not been the first to think in terms of such a final solution — see the first paragraph of reading 83.

apocalypse
Patmos

'The Revelation of Saint John the Divine' was the title of his book. 'The Divine' meant 'the theologian' or 'one who studies the nature of the creator'. But it is unlikely that this John was either the Apostle (notes to 108) or the Evangelist (notes to 108). He was probably simply an old man, a poet with very apocalyptic symbols in his mind (notes to 54).

Revelation
John the
* Divine*
divine
theology

Roughly speaking the meaning of the reading opposite was this: 'The battle against the Devil is not determined on earth. It has already been settled in heaven. The Christ has gone up and the Devil has come down. On earth, every time a person does a Christ-like thing the Devil's downfall is confirmed. But, beware! The Devil is out to trip up all the supporters of the Christ.'

the Christ
Devil

159 Dream about a new Jerusalem

from Revelation 21 : New English Bible

Then I saw the holy city, new Jerusalem coming down out of heaven. I heard a loud voice proclaiming: 'Now at last God has his dwelling among men! For the old order has passed away!'

Then he who sat on the throne said to me, 'Write this down.' And he said, 'Behold, I am making all things new! For I am the Alpha and the Omega, the beginning and the end.'

So in the Spirit he showed me the holy city of Jerusalem coming down out of the heaven. The streets of the city were of pure gold, like translucent glass. I saw no temple in the city; for its temple was the sovereign Lord God. It had a great high wall, and on the gates were inscribed the names of the twelve tribes of Israel, each gate being made from a single pearl.

The foundations of the city wall were adorned with jewels of every kind: emerald, chrysolite, beryl, topaz, turquoise and amethyst. The wall had twelve foundation stones, and on them were the names of the twelve apostles.

And the city had no need of sun or moon, for the glory of God gave it light. By its light shall the nations walk. The gates of the city shall never be shut but nothing unclean shall enter, nor anyone whose ways are false.

Part of a letter to encourage his fellows, written in Patmos, probably by a Jewish Christian in about AD *95*

This is more apocalypse from the old man, 'John the Divine' — see notes to 158. Whoever talks of the thing he loves is a poet, and he must be allowed to do it. For it is his bridge and it may be useful only to himself. But it is his bridge.

poetry

This was his heavenly Jerusalem (for there was now no longer one on earth), it was his return to the Garden of Eden (reading 2), his vision of peace (notes to 50), his source of eternal life (notes to 76, 84, and 90). It was only a dream, maybe, but 'We are such stuff as dreams are made on, and our little lives are rounded with a sleep.'

visions

160 Incarnation

from John 1 : Authorized Version

In the beginning was the Word, and the Word was with God, and the Word was God. The same was in the beginning with God. All things were made by him; and without him was not any thing made that was made.

In him was life; and the life was the light of men. And the light shineth in darkness; and the darkness comprehended it not.

That was the true Light, which lighteth every man that cometh into the world. He was in the world and the world was made by him, and the world knew him not.

He came unto his own and his own received him not. But as many as received him, to them gave he power to become the sons of God, even to them that believe on his name: which were born not of blood, nor of the will of the flesh, nor of the will of man, but of God.

A brief vision, probably written by a Christian leader in Ephesus between AD *90 and 95*

Somewhere since the beginning, man's mind had dawned — raised between sun and earth. Naturally for him the sun became the earliest of all his gods. And mysterious fire became the symbol of that superhuman energy which gave him life and light and purity.

man
mind
sun
fire
light

In a temple of Mithras at this time, sun and light were the heart of the god. The religion of Mithras had spread from India and Persia in the East carried by Roman merchants and soldiers and slaves right across the new empire even as far west as an island which they called Britannia. (Its temples can be seen today in London and Colchester.) It was strangely similar to the earliest forms of Christianity: the 'Logos' was the 'Word of God' which created and preserved, and it was the spirit of light and life which descended to the earth and, wherever it was given access, released 'eternity'.

Mithras

Logos
life

A religious philosophy which also prevailed at this time was the Gnostic faith. At its centre was a picture of warfare between angels of light and devils of darkness, between truth and lies, between knowledge and ignorance. The reading opposite was part of an attempt to knit together such popular beliefs as these, and to claim that the world had been waiting for the Jesus event all along.

philosophy
Gnostic

Jesus

Perhaps it retains its freshness today because it appears to focus the light of the scientific revelation. This is amazing. The writer could hardly have known, for instance, that as the velocity of matter increases towards the speed of light, it approaches a point of transmutation when it becomes light; or, that matter and time and light are after all elastic in their relationship. He could not have known that modern minds would be furnished with nuclear patterns and many other apparently new thought-forms.

revelation

This reading is used by Christians to this day at Christmas time. Since time immemorial there had been a primitive feast in mid-winter to celebrate the birth of the unconquered sun. From Stonehenge across to archaeological sites in the eastern Mediterranean sun symbols have been found — gold discs with fourfold sunbeams were very common. And under the dome of St Peter's in Rome a Christian mosaic has been excavated depicting the Christ as a sun god driving a chariot, with flying cloak and rayed nimbus behind his head. So it seems the Christians' Jesus soon became their 'Sun of Righteousness', born in mid-winter, plunging forth in glory, commanding the long nights to decrease. And so for example, the Swedish St Lucia with her crown of candles, the shining German Christmas Tree, and the Yule logs and fiery puddings of England all retain their ancient symbolism. For their deepest origins are very much older than Christianity.

nativity
sun

Index

Index

Index

Index

Index

Index

Index

Index

Index

Index

Index

Index

Index

Index

Map 1

covering about 2000 to 900 BC *(readings 1 to 32)*

HITTITES

CILICIA

Harar

R.

The Great Sea

Byblos

ARAM

CANAAN

ARABIA

SHUR SIN

GOSHEN MIDIAN

Memphis

Ezion-Geber

LOWER EGYPT

Marah? SINAI

R. Nile

UPPER EGYPT Thebes

Red Sea

0	100	200	300	400	miles
0	200	400	600	km

Sheba (see map 5)

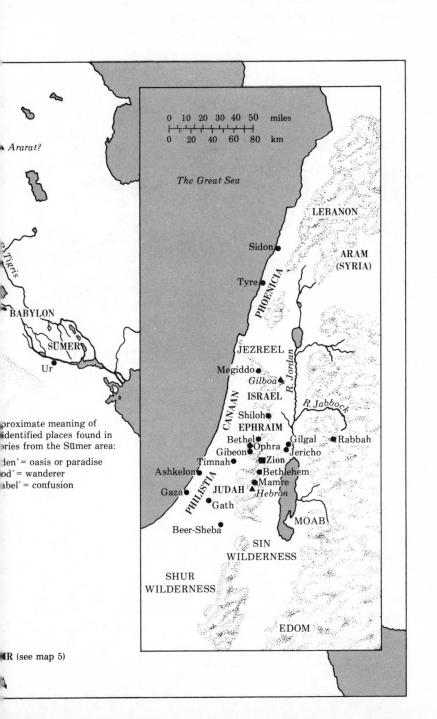

Ararat?

R. Tigris

BABYLON

SUMER

Ur

proximate meaning of
identified places found in
ories from the Sūmer area:

len' = oasis or paradise
od' = wanderer
abel' = confusion

0 10 20 30 40 50   miles
0   20   40   60   80   km

The Great Sea

LEBANON

ARAM
(SYRIA)

Sidon

Tyre

PHOENICIA

JEZREEL

R. Jordan

Megiddo

Gilboa

ISRAEL

R. Jabbock

Shiloh

EPHRAIM

Bethel   Gilgal   Rabbah

Gibeon Ophra   Jericho

Timnah   Zion

Ashkelon   Bethlehem

Gaza   *Mamre*

PHILISTIA JUDAH *Hebron*

Gath

MOAB

Beer-Sheba

SIN
WILDERNESS

SHUR
WILDERNESS

EDOM

R (see map 5)

Map 2

covering about 900 BC *to* AD *10 (readings 33 to 58)*

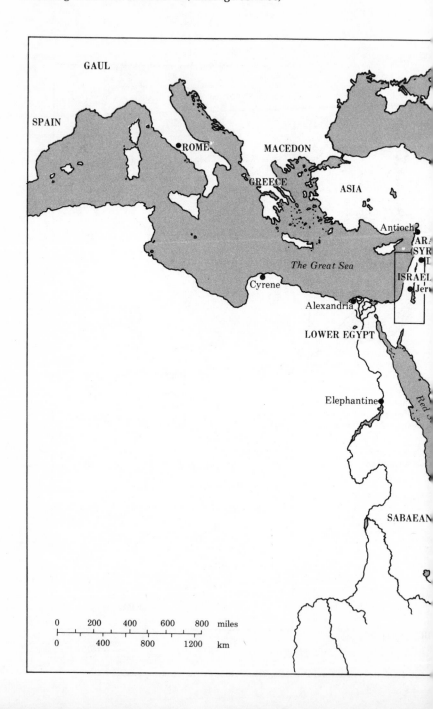

GAUL

SPAIN

●ROME

MACEDON

GREECE

ASIA

Antioch●

ARA
(SYR
L

ISRAEL
●Jer

The Great Sea

Cyrene●

Alexandria●

LOWER EGYPT

Elephantine●

Red S

SABAEAN

| 0 | 200 | 400 | 600 | 800 | miles |
| 0 | 400 | 800 | 1200 | | km |

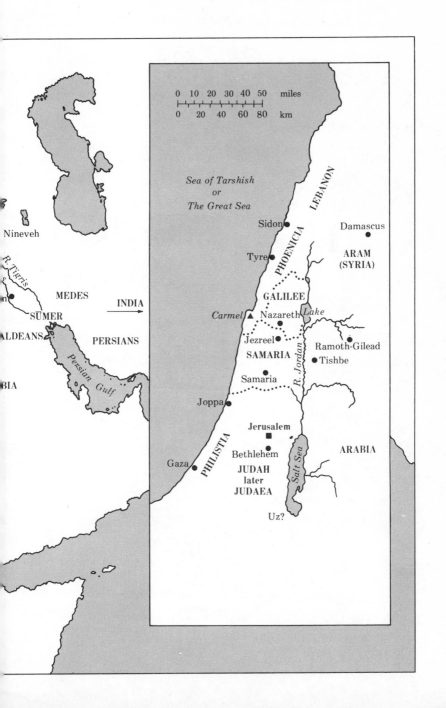

Map 3

covering about AD *25 to 30 (readings 59 to 125)*

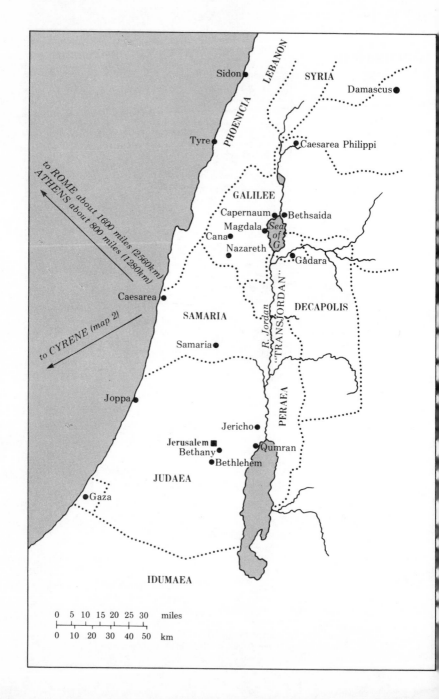

Map 4

covering about AD *20 to 70 (readings 94 to 150)*

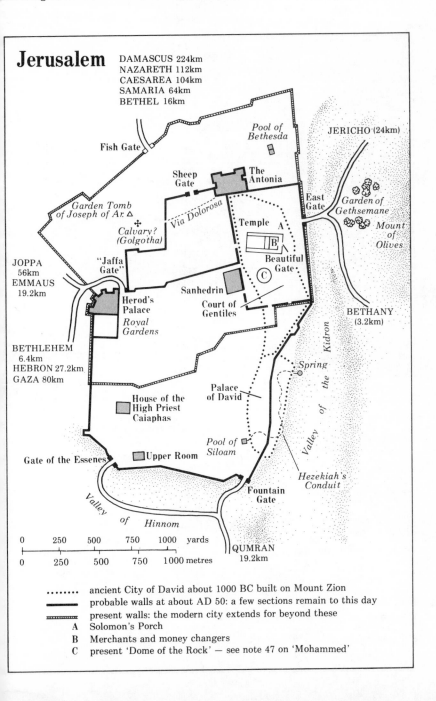

Jerusalem

DAMASCUS 224km
NAZARETH 112km
CAESAREA 104km
SAMARIA 64km
BETHEL 16km

JERICHO (24km)

Pool of
Bethesda

Fish Gate

Sheep
Gate

The
Antonia

East
Gate

Garden of
Gethsemane

Garden Tomb
of Joseph of Ar.

Via Dolorosa

Temple   A

Mount
of
Olives

Calvary?
(Golgotha)

B

JOPPA
56km
EMMAUS
19.2km

"Jaffa
Gate"

Beautiful
Gate

C

Sanhedrin

Court of
Gentiles

BETHANY
(3.2km)

Herod's
Palace

Royal
Gardens

BETHLEHEM
6.4km
HEBRON 27.2km
GAZA 80km

Spring

Palace
of David

House of the
High Priest
Caiaphas

Valley   of   the   Kidron

Pool of
Siloam

Gate of the Essenes

Upper Room

Hezekiah's
Conduit

Fountain
Gate

Valley   of   Hinnom

| 0 | 250 | 500 | 750 | 1000 | yards |
| 0 | 250 | 500 | 750 | 1000 | metres |

QUMRAN
19.2km

.... ancient City of David about 1000 BC built on Mount Zion
───── probable walls at about AD 50: a few sections remain to this day
▭▭▭▭ present walls: the modern city extends for beyond these
A   Solomon's Porch
B   Merchants and money changers
C   present 'Dome of the Rock' — see note 47 on 'Mohammed'

Map 5

covering about AD *29 onwards (readings 126 to 160)*

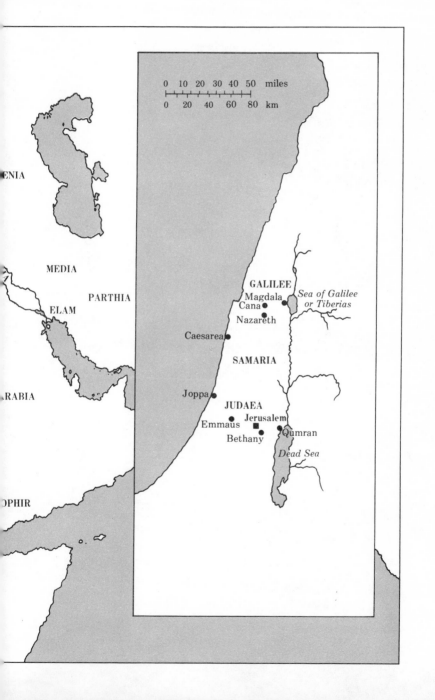